GOOD HOUSEKEEPING

E A T I N G   F O R   A

HEALTHY BABY

In Association with Birthright

GOOD HOUSEKEEPING

EATING FOR A

HEALTHY BABY

In Association with Birthright

EBURY PRESS LONDON

PUBLISHED BY EBURY PRESS
an imprint of Century Hutchinson Ltd
20 Vauxhall Bridge Road
London SW1V 2SA

British Library Cataloguing in Publication Data
Good Housekeeping eating for a healthy baby.
  1. Pregnant women. Health. 2. Pregnant women. Food –
Recipes
  I. Birthright   II. Series
613'.04244

ISBN 0-85223-772-3

EDITORS Barbara Croxford, Helen Southall,
and Sally Crawford
DESIGN Peter Bridgewater Design
PHOTOGRAPHY Tim Hill
STYLIST Zöe Hill
ILLUSTRATOR Annie Ellis

COVER PHOTOGRAPH: Lamb Chops with Mint (page 82);
Open Sandwiches (page 50); Cauliflower Broccoli and
Pepper Salad (page 135); French Fruit Tart (page 141)

Typeset by Textype Typesetters, Cambridge
Printed and bound in Italy by New Interlitho, S.p.a., Milan

Contents

Introduction

While you are pregnant, eating is particularly important because what you eat goes towards making a new life, that of your baby. Fortunately, nature has arranged things so that if you eat a healthy balanced diet, from a wide range of foods, your body will absorb the nutrients it needs in just the right amounts, not only to make a healthy baby, but to keep you in perfect health, too. This goes for the vital first three months of pregnancy when the fetus is forming, and for the last six months during which time it grows to become a strong, healthy and beautiful baby, ready to be born with the best possible start in life.

Scientific evidence suggests that nature has introduced many safeguards to protect the developing baby, even from nutritional deprivation. If food is scarce, the mother may suffer but the baby will not only survive, but, in most cases, actually do quite well. Never-the-less, when there is no shortage of food – indeed, where there is so much choice – it makes sense to make those choices wisely so that you eat well enough, not only for the baby, but so that your own health is protected or even enhanced. The introductory section of this book, and the recipes that follow, will help you to do just that. As well as your own nutritional needs and those of your developing baby, the book discusses other health aspects such as your weight, how to assess the risks of fetal abnormality, whether or not to drink alcohol, how to deal with nausea, food cravings and constipation, and all the other aspects of pregnancy that may concern you.

As well as giving you a range of healthy food ideas that will take you confidently through the nine months, the recipes include nutritional breakdowns listing the amounts of essential nutrients that each one contains. This nutritional analysis will enable you, not only to enjoy putting together interesting daily menus, but also to monitor your intake of essential nutrients throughout your pregnancy.

PRE-CONCEPTUAL NUTRITION

Ideally, good nutrition (for you and your partner) should start at least six months before you plan to conceive. During that time you should make sure you are eating a balanced diet, chosen from a wide range of good foods. You should also be aware of any foods that, if taken to excess, can block the absorption of essential nutrients or impair your body's ability to repair the damaging effects of smoking, alcohol or a previously poor diet.

How true is it that alcohol intake can put the early fetus at risk? What is the reported link between the absence of some micronutrients (vitamins and minerals) and the incidence of spina bifida? Is there an increased risk of complications if you start pregnancy when you are already overweight? These important issues are discussed first so that any fears you may have are dealt with. Whether this is your first baby or you have already been through the experience of pregnancy, the advice given here can make your current pregnancy your best ever.

ALCOHOL AND RISK TO THE EARLY FETUS

Alcohol has long been recognised as having an influence upon early fetal development. Indeed, anxiety about its effect has been expressed since the time of the ancient Greeks when bridal couples were forbidden by law from drinking wine on the wedding-night because of the risk of a defective child being conceived. An attempt to describe the specific effect of alcohol upon the developing baby was first made in 1968 following a study of 127 babies born to mothers who either drank excessively themselves or whose husbands did. The babies observed showed problems that included defects of the heart, lips and palate, hands and eyes, and eventually the term 'fetal alcohol syndrome' (FAS) was coined to describe these phenomena. This is not to say that all mothers (or their partners) who drink excessively go on to have a physically abnormal child. The most that can be said is that people who are consistently heavy drinkers impair their overall general health. Even so, there is still the problem of defining how much alcohol an individual has to consume, and how often, for there to be a real risk to the baby. The important thing is that women who happen to have had a 'good night out' before realising they have conceived should not spend the rest of their pregnancy worrying that they might have caused their baby to be malformed. At present, cases of fetal alcohol syndrome are rare in this country among heavy drinkers and no increase in congenital anomalies has yet been proven at all in moderate drinkers. In cities like Liverpool and Glasgow, however, where alcohol consumption is comparatively high, there are reported cases of FAS.

MICRONUTRIENTS AND SPINA BIFIDA

The possible relationship between a poor diet and spina bifida (more accurately known as neural tube defect or NTD) is also widely known and it has been suggested that taking large doses of vitamins will help prevent the condition. The problem with taking vitamin supplements in pill form concerns timing. The baby's spine is fully formed by five to six weeks so spina bifida and similar problems, if they are going to occur, will have occurred virtually by the time the mother has begun to wonder if she is pregnant or not. Hare-lip and cleft palate will also have occurred by seven weeks and the formation of the heart will be virtually complete by seven to eight weeks. For all practical purposes all major organ formation is complete by 10 weeks. We know, therefore, that to prevent NTD, any agent (be it vitamins or some as yet unknown factor), would have to be present and exerting its influence before six weeks of pregnancy.

Even with the availability of modern pregnancy tests, a period must still be missed to alert you to the fact that conception may have taken place. On this basis, therefore, pregnancy will rarely be confirmed before any malformation has occurred. Thus; to protect you from the risk of having a spina bifida baby it is pointless taking multivitamin preparations after pregnancy has been diagnosed; to be effective they must be taken from the time conception is being attempted, yet another reason for taking care of pre-conceptual health. It is actually more difficult to cover your pre-conceptual needs through supplements than it is through diet itself. With supplements, a woman may have to go on taking quite large daily doses of vitamins until she has conceived – something that may take longer to achieve than some couples anticipate.

Should a woman go on taking these supplements if she has failed to conceive in three months, six months, a year, two years – and so on? Commonsense dictates that there must be a limit but no-one can say what that limit should be. Women who stop their supplements after six months may conceive in month seven; will any 'benefit' still be present? No-one knows. There is every indication to suggest that all essential nutrients can be obtained from a sensible, well-balanced diet – in other words if your pre-conceptual daily diet is good you should not require additional supplements. Your overall general health will be kept at a high standard and the needs of your early fetus catered for whenever conception happens to occur.

THE IDEAL STARTING WEIGHT FOR PREGNANCY

If you begin your interest in diet before you conceive, you can measure your height and aim to achieve a starting weight that is as close to the 'ideal' as possible. If you look at Table 2, right, you will be able to work out the 'ideal' weight (referred to as body mass) you should be for your age and height. As an example of how to use the table, a woman whose height is 152 cm (column 1) should weigh between 51 and 54 kg (columns 2 to 4), depending on her age. When you have established your weight accurately, you may be surprised to learn that you are already somewhat overweight! If this is the case, now is the time for some prudent dieting – or at least for trying to ensure that while you attempt to conceive you do not put on further weight. Occasionally, some women find that their starting weight turns out to be *less* than ideal, an indication that their bodies' nutrient stores may be somewhat depleted. If so, attempt to gain some weight before conceiving by using the high energy meals suggested in the recipes.

In general, tall, heavy women tend to have larger babies than small, thin women so it would be unrealistic to expect there to be a 'British Standard' baby for the whole population. As far as your health is concerned, the main problem of being overweight is not the effect on the baby's birthweight but the possible complications that can occur during the pregnancy. Raised blood pressure is more common in obese women and they also tend to have prolonged and difficult labours. In addition, if obese mothers need to have a forceps delivery or caesarean section then complications such as deep venous thrombosis, haemorrhage and infection occur more frequently. The major purpose of weight control before and during pregnancy, therefore, is not so much an attempt to reduce infant birthweight as to reduce the incidence of maternal complications.

THE DEVELOPING BABY'S NEEDS

Traditionally, the length of a pregnancy is timed from the first day of the last menstrual period (LMP) but, of course, a woman is not actually pregnant from that day. An egg usually matures (at ovulation) about 2 weeks after the first day of the period, so when a doctor says that a woman is '10 weeks pregnant' she is actually only eight weeks in the biological sense of how long a fetus has been inside her womb. However, for simplicity, the stage of pregnancy will be given in here weeks from LMP.

During pregnancy we eat in order to supply the body with the raw materials to build a baby. The demands of the baby change throughout the nine months of pregnancy. Between conception and the end of the third month, the mass (weight) of the fetus will increase two million-fold! This remarkable rate of growth can be illustrated another way: if the baby continued to grow at the same rate between months four and nine it would weigh four million tons at birth. Thus, day by day and even hour by hour during the first three months, the baby is growing and developing at a rapid rate. Thereafter it increases in weight, continuing to grow until it has achieved its ideal birthweight. Table 2, overleaf, illustrates this.

It is also important to understand that, for all practical purposes, the baby is fully formed during the first 10 weeks of pregnancy. It is during this early phase that vitamins, minerals and essential nutrients may play their most vital roles. The actual amounts required are small (the fetus still weighs only 16 g at this stage) but the whole range of nutrients will be needed. During the second phase, from months four to six, the baby grows in length and its organs improve their functional ability in readiness for maintaining the baby as an independent individual from the moment of birth. During this phase the baby's weight will increase to about 1000 g but it will still not be a major drain on the resources of a reasonably nourished mother. So up to six months you can both supply the needs of your baby and build up your own nutrient stores.

During the final three months, the baby will increase in weight and lay down the fat stores that will see it through the first weeks of life. It is during this phase that the baby makes maximum demands on your nutrient stores so your daily diet must be sufficient both in energy and nutritional content. If your baby's nutritional demands are not met at this stage, growth may be somewhat retarded and the baby may not achieve its optimum birthweight. Having said this, however, the majority of low birthweight babies are born to mothers who have eaten sufficiently during pregnancy so it is difficult to blame food intake entirely. In cases of low birthweight, it seems possible that the supply of nutrients available from the mother, no matter how abundant, may not be transferred to the baby. In other words, for reasons we do not yet understand, nutrient transfer across the placenta from mother to baby may not work properly.

In principle, then, all mothers should enter pregnancy in a well-nourished state, with their nutrient

TABLE 2

development at 12 weeks:	major organs like spinal cord and heart formed; weight about 16 g (½ oz)
development at 26 weeks:	fetus grows in length; organs increase functional ability; baby reaches point in its maturity where it is almost capable of independent survival; weight about 1 kg (2 lb)
development at 32-40 weeks:	baby increases in weight; fat stores laid down

stores well filled, and should continue to eat a well-balanced diet throughout the pregnancy.

NOURISHING THE GROWING BABY

The baby has no need to use its digestive system while developing in the womb because the mother does the eating and digesting for both and then presents everything in a 'predigested' state. She therefore eats complex carbohydrates (from grains, pulses, vegetables, fruits and seeds) but breaks these down to simple sugars before absorbing them into her bloodstream for transport to the placenta where they can cross to her baby. When fats are eaten, they are digested to their component 'fatty acids' and they, too, cross the placenta to supply the growing baby. Proteins are broken down through digestion to their simpler 'building blocks', amino acids, and cross by the same route.

ALCOHOL DURING PREGNANCY

Alcohol, too, crosses the placenta. Is it harmful? Very heavy alcohol intake during pregnancy *may* be harmful to the baby but the possible association with the effects of cigarette smoking, age and so on must also be borne in mind. Drinking to a moderate degree is probably not a cause for concern. Commonsense, however, dictates that alcohol consumption during pregnancy should be kept to a minimum for the same reasons that it should in the non-pregnant. However, it would be quite wrong to advise all pregnant women never to drink alcohol at all; a glass of wine on a special occasion will do no harm. What matters is not that you drink or what you drink but how much and how frequently you drink.

Because of the differences in alcoholic strength between various drinks, alcohol intake can most conveniently be measured in terms of 'units' of alcohol. A single unit can be made up of a half pint of beer or cider, a 60 ml glass of wine or a single measure of spirits. If one to two of these units are taken every day this adds up to about 100 grams of alcohol per week and this is regarded as the dividing line. Any pregnant woman taking more than 100 g (14 units) per week would be regarded as a heavy drinker and between

TABLE 1

'Ideal' weight (average body mass for height without shoes or clothing)

Height (without shoes)	20-24 years	25-29 years	30-39 years	40-49 years	50-59 years	60-69 years
	kg					
142 cm	44.5	46.7	48.5	50.3	52.2	53.1
143 cm	45.0	47.3	48.9	50.9	52.6	53.5
144 cm	45.7	48.0	49.5	51.6	53.1	54.0
145 cm	46.3	48.5	49.9	52.2	53.5	54.4
146 cm	47.4	49.0	50.3	52.8	54.4	55.3
147 cm	48.5	49.4	50.8	53.5	55.3	56.2
148 cm	48.8	49.7	51.2	53.8	55.6	56.6
149 cm	49.1	50.0	51.7	54.1	55.9	57.1
150 cm	49.4	50.3	52.2	54.4	56.2	57.6
151 cm	50.3	51.4	52.8	55.2	57.1	58.2
152 cm	51.3	52.6	53.5	56.2	58.1	59.0
153 cm	51.7	52.8	53.8	56.5	58.3	59.3
154 cm	52.4	53.2	54.4	56.8	58.6	59.8
155 cm	53.1	53.5	54.9	57.2	59.0	60.3
156 cm	53.8	54.3	55.6	57.9	59.7	61.1
157 cm	54.9	55.3	56.7	59.0	60.8	62.1
158 cm	55.2	55.6	57.0	59.2	61.2	62.4
159 cm	55.7	56.2	57.5	59.8	61.9	63.0
160 cm	56.2	56.7	58.1	60.3	62.6	63.5
161 cm	56.8	57.4	58.6	60.9	63.1	64.2
162 cm	57.3	58.1	59.1	61.4	63.7	64.9
163 cm	57.6	58.5	59.4	61.7	64.0	65.3
164 cm	58.4	59.0	60.2	62.7	64.7	66.1
165 cm	59.0	59.4	60.8	63.5	65.3	66.7
166 cm	59.6	60.1	61.4	64.1	66.1	67.5
167 cm	60.3	60.8	62.1	64.9	67.0	68.4
168 cm	60.8	61.2	62.6	65.3	67.6	68.9
169 cm	61.8	62.2	63.6	66.0	68.6	69.7
170 cm	62.6	63.0	64.4	66.7	69.4	70.3
171 cm	63.3	63.9	65.1	67.4	69.8	70.7
172 cm	64.2	65.0	66.0	68.3	70.4	71.3
173 cm	64.9	65.8	66.7	68.9	70.8	71.7
174 cm	65.5	66.2	67.4	69.6	71.4	72.1
175 cm	66.2	66.7	68.0	70.3	72.1	72.6
176 cm	67.0	67.5	68.8	70.8	72.6	73.1
177 cm	68.1	68.5	69.9	71.5	73.4	73.8
178 cm	68.9	69.4	70.8	72.1	73.9	74.4

50-100 g (7-14 units) a moderate drinker. Of course some people drink considerably more and this is where frequency of drinking should be taken into account. There seems little doubt that drinking more than 80 g (11 units) per day is drinking to excess and this is associated with the birth of abnormal babies. This is extremely difficult to 'prove' scientifically, however, because women who drink heavily are likely to report their alcohol consumption to be lower than is actually the case. There may also be other associated factors which could affect the baby, such as the age of the mother, whether she smokes, how many previous babies she has had, her social circumstances and whether she is a drug abuser. Many women, however, even heavy drinkers, modify their drinking habits when they become aware they are pregnant.

MEDICINES DURING PREGNANCY

It has already been said that the vital time to protect yourself and your growing baby from the effects of alcohol is before the fetus has formed its spine, spinal cord and major organs such as the heart – all of which are complete by 10 weeks. Nothing you eat or drink after this time will result in the baby having major physical malformations. The same applies to tablets and medicines which you may be advised to take by your doctor – none will cause a major structural defect in the baby after 10 to 12 weeks. If drugs or other potentially harmful agents are taken later in the pregnancy, the growth of the baby may be affected, or its ability to function physically or mentally may be impaired, but even major drug abuse could not cause, for example, spina bifida at 26 weeks of pregnancy because spinal formation is completed much earlier. Equally, nothing taken after 10 to 12 weeks can prevent a major structural problem because it will already have occurred.

Since the effect of taking the drug thalidomide during pregnancy became known, much needless anxiety has been generated over the taking of medicines by pregnant women. Naturally it is wise to avoid taking any medication unless there is an obvious benefit to be gained by taking it. In the case of nausea, for example, most women can control the situation without drugs. However, infections of the kidney or bladder

are common during pregnancy and some mothers develop other infections such as chest problems. Medical help to cure these is available and is safe. Such medically prescribed drugs should be used, therefore, where appropriate, and failure to do so could disadvantage the baby to a greater degree than the pharmaceutical preparations themselves.

The major fear, of course, of every pregnant woman is that she will have an abnormal baby, and unfortunately about one in 40 women does have an abnormal child. As discussed above, however, the baby is virtually complete in its physical formation *before* any medications are likely to be required, something that should reassure the most anxious mother. It should also be remembered that the incidence of abnormal babies being born to the general non-drug-taking population is the same as for those who take drugs. This means that if 80 mothers took one vitamin pill each day, two might give birth to an abnormal baby. Over the same period, two out of a group of 80 mothers who did not take pills might also deliver abnormal babies but because no pills had been taken they would accept this as an 'Act of God'; the pill takers would always wonder if it was the pills. Thus it is not sufficient for people to say 'I took so-and-so drug and had an abnormal baby' because that could be coincidence. It must also be shown that women taking a particular drug had more abnormal babies than would have occurred by chance anyway.

COPING WITH NAUSEA AND VOMITING

Feelings of nausea or actual vomiting are relatively common during pregnancy, particularly during the early stages when it is often known as 'morning sickness'. This is an unfortunate title because, as many women know to their cost, it can be 'afternoon sickness', 'evening sickness' or, indeed, 'all day sickness'. Feelings of nausea are more common than the actual act of vomiting but unpleasant nonetheless. Both conditions may be exacerbated by the smell of cooking food and many husbands 'share' the problems of early pregnancy when they have to eat endless salad-dishes which are relatively odourless to prepare! In the majority of cases these feelings of nausea reduce by 10 to 12 weeks and are often resolved completely by about 16 weeks. However, in a few women feelings of nausea and occasional vomiting may persist throughout their pregnancy.

WILL NAUSEA OR VOMITING HARM YOUR BABY?

For all practical purposes the answer is no but, as with almost everything in life, there are exceptions. If vomiting is so prolonged and severe that virtually no food or fluids are being kept down by the mother then it is possible she will become dehydrated and generally unwell. In the past, women have even died from this condition (known as *hyperemesis gravidarum*) but this degree of severity is very rare and can now be treated successfully so that no harm comes to mother or baby. It should be emphasised again that some degree of nausea and vomiting is relatively common during perfectly normal, healthy pregnancies and, while un-pleasant to experience, causes no problem to the developing baby.

ARE THERE ANY OTHER CAUSES FOR NAUSEA AND VOMITING?

The most likely cause is an infection of the bladder or kidneys. Indeed, if a previously well woman suddenly develops nausea and vomiting during the second half of pregnancy, a urinary tract infection can be suspected and must be investigated, so all such symptoms should be reported to your doctor. Another very rare compli-cation of pregnancy occurs when the baby fails to form (a condition called *hydatidiform mole* or *vesicular mole*) and mothers with this condition often experience intractable vomiting. However, this condition is rare and mentioned only for completeness.

WHAT NON-MEDICAL REMEDIES CAN YOU TRY?

Women who experience nausea first thing in the morning can be helped if they eat a small amount of something bland before getting out of bed. A cup of tea, milk or similar drink with a plain biscuit or piece of toast, sitting up in bed, followed by a 5 to 10 minute 'lie-in', can often help. When the time to get up can no longer be put off, sit up in bed and slowly swing your legs to the floor; remain seated on the side of the bed for a couple of minutes then stand up slowly. Any sudden change in posture – particularly from lying flat

to upright – can cause slight 'lightheadedness' and the start of feelings of nausea. In addition, the feelings of hunger associated with not having eaten all night can also promote nausea. By paying attention to both these matters, feelings of nausea can be lessened.

The feeling of hunger itself may also bring on feelings of sickness so get into the habit of eating small, frequent snacks of easily digested foods rather than sticking to the usual 'meal-times'. As the smell of cooking can also promote nausea, warn your family that their support will be needed while you switch to cooking bland but nutritious meals that require the minimum of 'hot oil' cooking. Grilling causes less smell than frying but even this may be too much for some women. If frying is inescapable (and mothers with growing children will know that chips, for example, seem to be vital to their mental as well as physical health), then open the kitchen windows as wide as possible while cooking and eat something you like beforehand so that your own feelings of hunger do not worsen the situation.

Something like a piece of fresh celery with some cheese and half a glass of milk will make a nutritious, appetising and odourless little snack that will satisfy you before you tackle the rigours of cooking a meal for the rest of the family. Keep salad vegetables like celery in the fridge so that they stay crisp and crunchy: you will find this adds to their appeal. Fizzy drinks may also upset the stomach so switch to plain water or unsweetened fruit juices and avoid drinks that are heavily sweetened or made up of very acidic fruits.

ARE MEDICINES FOR SICKNESS SAFE TO TAKE?

The answer is yes – if the symptoms mean that your food and fluid intake is being interfered with. The drugs that are given for sickness simply dampen down the nausea control centre in the brain and, under medical supervision, are perfectly safe to take. Without appropriate medicines, prolonged and persistent vomiting could require hospital care where fluids would be given directly into a vein. The risks associ-ated with any particular medical preparation, there-fore, even if there were any, are no greater than the risks to the baby from nausea and vomiting of such severity that hospital admission becomes necessary.

Occasionally nausea or vomiting can follow an

attack of 'heartburn'; in such circumstances your doctor may prescribe an antacid. This will neutralise some of the acid in the stomach thereby preventing the heartburn and any sickness. Such medicines are safe to take because they are not absorbed into the bloodstream. Of course, it is preferable for the feelings of sickness to be controlled by diet and attention to the various points already mentioned, but if sickness does persist you would be wise to take any medicine that is prescribed by your doctor.

COPING WITH FOOD CRAVINGS

The need to eat certain foods and avoid others is common during pregnancy. Fried or fatty foods, for example, may be deliberately avoided because they begin to cause indigestion and heartburn. On the other hand, you may develop a liking for highly flavoured foods like pickles and kippers. You may even develop mild aversions to foods and drinks you have previously enjoyed. At the other end of the spectrum, marked 'cravings' may emerge, especially for fresh fruits, and you may feel the need to eat these in amounts that far exceed your previous consumption.

It is difficult to obtain information about the more unusual food cravings (called 'pica') – for soap or coal, for example – because women may feel embarrassed about desires which they imagine to be unnatural and therefore conceal these urges.

In 1957, the BBC invited women to write in about cravings after a radio broadcast about the subject. They received 514 letters reporting 991 cravings; of these 261 were for fruit, 105 for vegetables, 187 for other foods (usually pickles or raw cereals) but 88 were for 'non-foods': coal (35), soap (17), disinfectant (15) and toothpaste (14). This is not to suggest that 88 out of every 514 pregnant women experience pica – such individual surveys usually provide a distorted picture because of an inbuilt bias – only those with the problem bother to write in. However, it suggests pica may be more common than believed because some of the correspondents acknowledged that they took great pains not to be found out, presumably because they felt guilty about a habit they thought to be 'odd'.

A report in 1935 suggested that any increased desire for well-salted and spiced foods during pregnancy arose because the mother experienced a dulling or blunting of the sense of taste for all flavours, be they salty, sweet, sour or bitter. The desire to eat kippers, pickled onions or strong curries may be to 'restore' taste appreciation to its usual level.

If food cravings are experienced and you are worried about them then they should be discussed with your doctor who will usually be able to offer reassurance that all is well. If your need is for fresh fruit or vegetables then benefits will be experienced in terms of vitamin intake; even if pica occurs, it will rarely cause problems if not indulged to excess because the substances eaten are rarely toxic. Exceptions might be carbon- and clay-containing substances: coal, cinders, charcoal or kaolin, for example. These things are not toxic in themselves but they have the ability to absorb such things as vitamins and minerals thereby preventing their proper absorption by the mother's body. It is unlikely you could ever eat sufficient carbon or clay to cause a vitamin or mineral deficiency but if you do happen to fancy large amounts of coal or clay, you should discuss this, in confidence, with your doctor.

WEIGHT GAIN AND PREGNANCY

DOES PREGNANCY MEAN EATING FOR TWO?

In the sense of having to eat appreciably more, as though the baby had its own specific appetite requirement equivalent to a second adult, the answer is no. Expectant mothers should resist this argument (usually put forward by future grandmothers!) because excessive weight gain can cause problems.

Many women become aware of an increase in their appetite, particularly during the early weeks of pregnancy; some also experience an increased sense of thirst. Dietary studies during which pregnant women are allowed to eat 'to appetite' (that is, until they are satisfied), but the food is weighed before being eaten, reveal that more food is usually consumed even when the mothers are not aware of any change in their appetite. This might arise because the wish for large, formal meals decreases but an increased number of snacks are eaten.

All expectant mothers will gain some weight and the question to consider is how much of this is inevitable and how much is desirable?

HOW MUCH WEIGHT GAIN IS 'NORMAL'?

It is obvious that everything to do with the growth of the baby is 'extra' in terms of weight gain. However, there are other extras which should not be forgotten. The maternal breasts, for example, increase in size, so does the uterus (womb) and the amount of blood circulating in the mother and in the fetus and placenta.

The placenta is a vital part of the process of growing a baby and in fact weighs about one-sixth of the weight of the newborn baby. There are, of course, wide variations amongst different mothers but in general a full term baby will weigh about 3.2 kg (7 lb), the placenta about 450 g (1 lb) and the water around the baby about 900 g (2 lb). So the inevitable part of pregnancy weight gain is about 4.5 kg (10 lb). However, you must add on essential stores of fat and water so you should expect a total weight gain of 10 to 12 kg (22 to 26 lb). As has been said above, you may, according to your particular circumstances, gain a little more or a little less. However, a weight gain of more than 12 kg or less than 4.5 kg is unusual although it is not necessarily harmful either to you or your baby.

In order to check your weight it is not necessary to weigh yourself daily. Don't be fanatical. Over the last six months of pregnancy the average weight gain is around 2 kg per month but this weight gain is not necessarily smooth at the steady rate of 500 g (half a kilogram) per week. On some occasions you may appear to have gained more weight than usual. Have you? The time you weigh yourself is highly significant. Weighing yourself after a full meal or when bowel or bladder is full can add 2 to 2½ kg to the reading. Wait a couple of days and weigh yourself again.

Rapid weight gain, particularly towards the end of pregnancy, is not due to an increase in body tissues such as fat – the usual explanation for non-pregnant people who put on weight. Some mothers may gain 1 to 2 kg in a single week and true fat stores can not be accumulated at that pace. On the other hand 1 litre of water weighs 1 kg and expectant mothers are able to retain water to a marked degree. This is not harmful in itself though 'puffy ankles' may be one obvious feature. The same phenomenon, reversed, may also explain a sudden marked decrease in weight through water loss. Again, this is no cause for concern particularly in warmer weather in those mothers who do not have other problems.

DOES THE AMOUNT OF FOOD YOU EAT ACTUALLY HAVE AN EFFECT ON THE EVENTUAL SIZE OF YOUR BABY?

In an average society, with access to the usual range of foods, the important question is usually whether eating too small or too large a quantity can directly affect the growth and wellbeing of the growing baby. A mother who has delivered a large baby previously, may wonder whether reducing her food intake during a subsequent pregnancy would help to prevent the baby from growing to the same degree, thereby making labour and delivery easier. Conversely, a mother who has given birth to a very small baby in the past might wonder if an increased food intake during her current pregnancy would increase growth in the developing infant.

There are certainly some interesting facts on the relation between maternal weight and birthweight. Mothers who have given birth to a baby which weighs eight pounds (3.6 kg) or more may well feel they have delivered a 'big' baby, but are human babies large compared to those of other animals? It is useful to express baby weight as a percentage of the weight of the mother and, indeed, comparisons must take into account the size of the mother since human babies are obviously bigger than puppies but smaller than baby whales. In the Blue Whale, for example, the baby is only five per cent of its mother's weight; in the rabbit, the total litter weight can come to about 20 per cent of the mother's weight. The 'champion' in this respect is probably the guinea pig whose total litter weight can be as much as 60 per cent of maternal weight.

A human baby of eight pounds (3.6 kg) born to a mother who weighs eight stones (50.8 kg) would be seven per cent of maternal weight and this gives us a useful average. But it is only an average. A comparatively 'large' baby, for example, weighing nine pounds (4 kg) and born to a mother of 10 stones (63.5 kg), would represent six per cent of maternal weight while a 'small' baby of six pounds (2.7 kg) born to a seven stone (44.4 kg) mother is also six per cent of the mother's weight. It could be argued that both mothers had delivered a 'large' baby relative to their own size.

CAN YOU EAT TOO LITTLE?

On average, about 2000 kilocalories per day are needed for the maintenance of normal body function. If this is regarded as the basic minimum for a non-pregnant person then any diet during pregnancy that contains fewer than 2000 kilocalories would have to be regarded as less than optimal. However, this daily need is largely used for maintaining body heat and physical activity so, in theory, if a woman could reduce her daily work activity to a minimum and live in a warm climate then she could perhaps save the extra 200 kilocalories per day usually needed for pregnancy, and still get along on the basic 2000 kilocalories without eating extra food. It is difficult to set up an experiment to prove this point because women living in hot climates have different social and working conditions and are usually not Caucasion. They may also be exposed to infections or other disorders not usually found in Europe or North America. However, it seems that there is little relationship between the amount eaten and the birthweight of the baby. In a survey comparing Scottish women with mothers in Africa (the Gambia), the Scottish mothers consumed a total of 67000 kilocalories of extra energy and their babies weighed, on average, 3.4 kg; the Gambian women had a total of only 1900 kilocalories extra but their babies still weighed 3.0 kg. The energy intake of the Gambian women was only 28 per cent of that of the Scottish women but they produced babies that were only 12 per cent lighter, with a weight difference of only 400 g (just under 1 lb).

DOES A BIG BABY MEAN YOU'VE EATEN TOO MUCH?

No. There are examples of very large babies being born to mothers who have *diabetes mellitus* (sugar diabe-

tes). Women with this disorder tend to have higher concentrations of glucose in their blood and so excess glucose is transported across the placenta to the baby. It is suggested that if the mother's blood glucose is at a high level for most of the pregnancy then the excess sugar sent to the baby is stored as fat, leading to a baby with a higher than average birthweight. The apparent logic of this argument has recently been challenged, however, by the fact that mothers who control their blood glucose levels by careful supervision and monitoring of their insulin doses can still have very large babies.

BALANCING FOOD INTAKE AND ENERGY EXPENDITURE

It has been calculated that in terms of energy consumed, a total of around 56000 additional kilocalories (Calories) are required over the total pregnancy. As pregnancy lasts for 280 days this amounts to an extra 200 kilocalories per day. In other words, if an average of 2400 kilocalories are normally eaten each day then the pregnant woman has to eat only one-twelfth as much again to cover all her pregnancy needs.

WHAT ARE CALORIES?

Many compounds have energy stored within them and this can be released by burning. In the literal sense, coal and wood have been burned for centuries to release their energy as fireside heat. The human body is interesting because it has evolved to work best at an internal temperature of 37°C. This is a great deal warmer than the everyday temperatures in which most people live and the body must therefore 'burn' fuel to keep warm. Indeed the need to maintain body temperature is one of the major reasons for our eating as often as we do – to obtain the fuel for our internal central heating system.

This concept of heat production is used to quantify the amount of energy contained in various foodstuffs and has given rise to the much quoted *Calorie*. This is actually the amount of heat required to raise the temperature of 1 gram of water from 15°C to 16°C, one degree. However, it is such a tiny amount of heat that for most purposes heat is measured in metric units of 1000 Calories (the kilocalorie, called kcal for short). If 1 gram of glucose is burned it releases 4.1 kcal of heat but 1 gram of fat yields 9.3 kcal, more than twice as much. Theoretically, protein releases 5.3 kcal per gram but for rather complicated reasons only yields the same as glucose – about 4.1 kcal per gram. In general terms, the average resting male or female adult requires about 2000 kilocalories per day for the maintenance of body temperature, movement and other basic functions. Those in sedentary occupations will require an additional 500 kilocalories for the extra activity involved in everyday living, while those doing heavy manual work may require as much as an additional 2500 kilocalories. During pregnancy, energy needs go up by about 250 to 350 kilocalories per day.

THE ENERGY LAW

The human body must, like any other machine, obey the laws of physics. One of these laws tells us that energy cannot be created or destroyed when it is converted from one form to another; in practice this tells us that when energy is taken in (that is, when we eat in order to release the energy 'trapped' in food), it must be converted completely, either to heat and activity, or it must be stored. Obviously the most economical way to store energy is as fat because 1 gram of fat stores 9.3 kilocalories of energy, thus making fat a more compact form of storage than, say, carbohydrate where 1 gram stores 4.1 kilocalories. Any increase in food intake above normal day-to-day requirements must therefore be balanced by an equal increase in energy output either as growth, movement (exercise) or as new body activity, such as the growth of a new baby.

> We can express this in the form of a simple equation:
> non-pregnant: energy in = energy out + energy stored
> pregnant: energy in = energy out + energy stored + energy for new baby growth

If food intake is *not* increased much above day-to-day requirements, energy can also be conserved by reducing energy output in the form of movement and general physical activity. As doctors regularly advise all expectant mothers to rest as much as possible, real savings

can be achieved. Indeed, in less developed parts of the world, where food may be scarce, pregnancy needs may have to be met from the usual daily diet plus energy conservation. For women in western societies it is probable that, provided enough rest is taken, the total extra needs of pregnancy could be met by eating an extra 100 kilocalories of food daily rather than the 250 to 350 kilocalories more active mothers require.

Whatever your energy intake in terms of calories you can work out the proportions of each food type needed to add up to this amount in terms of how much protein, carbohydrate and fat you consume. This is because although calorie intake may change up or down, depending on your food intake and energy expenditure, the proportions of each food type will remain more or less the same – in a ratio of 10-15 per cent protein and 25-30 per cent fat balanced by the remaining 50-75 per cent which will be made up of carbohydrate. Whatever proportion of each nutrient you choose, you can make up the balance by choosing more or less from the other two. For example, if you choose to have a fat intake of 10 per cent you can make up the balance – 90 per cent – from protein or carbohydrate. Gram for gram, protein, fat and carbohydrate give different amounts of energy of course: 50 g of fat will supply 465 kcal (50×9.3), while 50 g of protein or carbohydrate will supply 205 kcal (50×4.1).

THE PRINCIPLES OF A HEALTHY PREGNANCY DIET

Food is divided into three basic categories: carbohydrates, fats and proteins. For the first group, **carbohydrates**, many of us would think of the sugar we either put into tea and coffee or into cakes and puddings. If asked to give an example of a starch-containing food most people would think of potatoes. Both of these examples are correct but carbohydrates occur in most foods, from the toast and cornflakes we have at breakfast to the yoghurt we enjoy after dinner. In fact, since carbohydrates occur in all grains, pulses, fruits, milk and vegetables, they make up 50 per cent or more of our energy intake.

Describing all the different **fats** is no easier and if people are asked for examples of fatty foods they might mention 'beef fat', 'bacon fat', 'pork fat' and so on. In other words, fat, to most of us, is the rather greasy substance around our Sunday joints or our breakfast rashers. The reality is in fact quite different because there are as many types of fat as there are types of carbohydrates and, like carbohydrates, fats, too, are vital for our well-being. Substances as apparently different as milk and milk products, nuts and seeds all contain 'fat' in one form or another.

When we try to describe **proteins** things become even more complicated. When most people think of proteins they think of 'meat' or 'eggs'. Meat, poultry, fish and eggs certainly contain protein but it is also present in bread, nuts, milk and many other foods. As long as sufficient essential amino acids (the building blocks of protein) are contained in your daily protein intake it does not matter if the majority of the protein is from an animal source or from vegetables. The important point is that all of us, and especially pregnant women, need to obtain the whole range of nutrients necessary for the daily maintenance of our bodies – or the growth of a baby. Carbohydrates, fats and proteins are just some of the important nutrients we need and it is the job of digestion to make them available to us from the food we eat.

Digestion is basically the breaking down of all types of food into absorbable units. Most minerals (such as iron) and vitamins are absorbed unchanged, but complex foods such as carbohydrates, fats and proteins have to be reduced to their constituent building blocks before the stomach and intestines can absorb them into the bloodstream. This breaking down is achieved in a step-by-step manner by chemicals known as enzymes, some of which work at the start of the digestive process (like those in saliva), some in the stomach (where stomach acid is also produced) and some in the various sections of the intestines. The liver also makes bile (a valuable digestive aid) and this enters the section of the intestines that leads out of the stomach.

YOUR DIETARY 'ESSENTIALS'

Just as the human body can break down foods to their component parts it can build these into new proteins,

new carbohydrates and new fats. In some cases, however, the body cannot manufacture what it needs from the products of digestion and so some nutrients are needed 'ready made' in the diet. These nutrients, because the body cannot make them, are termed 'essential' nutrients and include some amino acids (from proteins), some fatty acids (from fats), vitamins, minerals like calcium, and tiny amounts of some minerals such as iron, zinc and magnesium. If animals are fed a fat-free diet, for example, they will fail to grow, develop various diseases and become infertile. Adding a single essential fatty acid to their diets will allow the animals to grow normally. If the other essential fatty acids are added to their diet, all the disorders caused by the otherwise fat-free diet will disappear. Such studies would not be ethical in humans so it is not possible to state absolutely that these fatty acids – known respectively as linoleic, linolenic and arachidonic acid – are 'essential' in man but it seems probable that they are – especially for growing children.

PROTEINS

Proteins are complex substances rather like buildings that are made up of many individual 'bricks' – the amino acids. Some proteins have a small number of bricks and can be regarded as 'ordinary homes' while others have many bricks and are equivalent to 'palaces'. Despite their size and complicated structure, however, all proteins are composed of the same types of bricks. When we eat dietary protein in the form of meat, eggs, fish and so on, we use our digestive processes to break them down to these bricks which are then absorbed into the bloodstream. From there they are transported to the liver and to the muscles where new, human, proteins of many sorts are created; the protein for new bone, for example, or for new heart muscle. Figure 1 shows this diagrammatically; various amino acids when assembled into a particular pattern may be called beef, but when we break them down into their individual parts by digestion and absorb them, the human body can then reassemble these same amino acids into a different pattern, one we know as, say, human heart muscle. This explains why the actual source of our dietary protein does not matter; a balanced vegetarian diet will be just as nutritious and healthy as one containing animal protein because the same building blocks are made available by digestion. This also explains how a cow which eats grass can create beef. Likewise, the baby developing in your womb has no idea where its amino acids originally come from and uses those that are available from the mother's bloodstream to create its own proteins for growth and development.

FIGURE 1

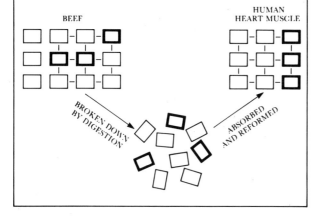

An example of how individual amino acids, joined together in a certain pattern, make a specific protein – say beef. When broken down by digestion to the individual amino acids, they can be absorbed and reassembled in the human body to make a new protein such as heart muscle.

While proteins are the mainstay of the diet in terms of supplying the important building blocks for growth and repair of the body, they are also a source of energy. However, if the diet has little protein in it the body will preferentially use glucose and fat for its energy needs and 'spare' protein for its more vital uses in the creation of tissues for growth or repair. The ability of the human body to store protein is very limited, however, so a regular intake is vital to good health. In the same way, excess protein will not be stored either so the body will break it down for energy.

In humans, health and growth can only be maintained when eight specific amino acids are available in the diet. They are phenylalanine, valine, tryptophan, threonine, lysine, leucine, isoleucine and methionine. These are therefore termed 'essential' amino acids. Broadly speaking these amino acids are widely available from meat, fish and eggs and from balanced vegetable protein (grains and pulses). Other 'non-essential' amino acids can be manufactured by the body from any spare protein 'building blocks'.

PROTEINS AND YOUR BABY

Because of its growth needs, a baby's blood contains even more amino acids than the blood of its mother. What constitutes an 'essential' amino acid to a baby, however, is less easy to define. There is no doubt that the same eight amino acids described above are essential but there is less information about the ability of the human baby to make the non-essential forms for itself while still in the womb. We know that an amino acid called glycine is very important though it is not 'essential' to an adult. It is presumed that the baby too can manufacture glycine from raw materials but we do not know this for certain. So a healthy diet during pregnancy should contain a balanced intake of all the amino acids.

CARBOHYDRATES

Much is made of the 'sins' of eating too much 'sugar' or sugar-containing foods; in fact it is not the act of eating sugar which matters but *how much* sugar. Do not fall into the trap of thinking it is the type of carbohydrate you eat which makes you fat – it is the amount. Remember, once again, that if half of your daily calories are to come from carbohydrates then a daily need for, say, 2600 kilocalories with 50 per cent from carbohydrate means 1300 kilocalories or 325 g (about 12 oz).

This is not much when consumed over a whole day considering that two Weetabix alone contain 67 g! Use the recipes given later in the book to make the carbohydrate part of your diet as varied and interesting as possible. There is nothing wrong with the occasional plate of chips, just don't eat them every day.

There are three basic building blocks (called simple sugars) which make up carbohydrates: glucose, fructose and galactose (in milk). No matter what form our carbohydrate-containing foods are in they will be broken down to simple sugars before we can absorb them; eating simple sugars directly merely saves us the effort of having to digest more complex carbohydrates. A good example would be table-sugar (sucrose) which is composed of glucose and fructose. A single enzyme, sucrase, rapidly converts table-sugar to these two simple sugars which are then quickly and easily absorbed.

Starches on the other hand are complex arrangements of these simple sugars and need several different enzymes to achieve complete breakdown before absorption. The more a diet contains simple sugars (glucose, fructose and galactose) the more easily digested. Many 'convenience' foods, however, contain high amounts of simple sugars so we can unwittingly consume too much. It is possible, for example, to eat a daily diet of perhaps 2500 kilocalories as main meals then eat sweets and cakes, *in addition*. Many drinks, too, have added sugar.

Simple sugars can, however, be of benefit to some women during early pregnancy – if, for example, they feel nauseous. Fizzy drinks should be avoided but if a mother does not feel like eating a particular meal, for example because of 'morning sickness', then a small glass of a Lucozade-like glucose drink (100 ml or 3 fl oz) contains about 20 g of glucose. If this is kept in the refrigerator and allowed to lose its effervescence it will still be palatable to drink and will contain about 80 kilocalories of energy. Foods containing simple sugars may also require little or no cooking, making them easy on the digestion. Milk sugar (lactose) is a combination of galactose and glucose and is broken down by a single enzyme called lactase.

Once absorbed from the intestine, simple sugars are taken into the bloodstream for three major purposes – four during pregnancy. First, they are transplanted to the liver where glucose can be stored in a special form known as *glycogen*. This can be released for energy production at any time by being converted back to glucose. For example, while we are asleep (and therefore not eating), these stores of glycogen will be called upon to keep the glucose in our blood at the correct level. This would also be true if we deliberately fasted for any length of time. The reason why our blood glucose must be maintained is that for all practical purposes glucose is the only fuel our brains can use

so it is vital that sufficient is always available. Secondly, simple sugars are broken down or metabolised to provide the energy the various tissues and organs of our body need to keep us functioning, as well as maintaining our body temperature. Thirdly, they can be converted to other essential compounds. During pregnancy there is a fourth function; to provide the baby with glucose for its own energy and building needs. The third and fourth uses of glucose are a bit more complicated but understanding them will make it a little easier to understand how fat and protein are used by the body. Even though we have called glucose a 'simple' sugar it is made up of other smaller building blocks, carbon, hydrogen and oxygen, which in turn can be reassembled as another substance, say, fat, which in fact is composed of the same three basic elements.

Figure 2 shows how these changes can occur; the 'bricks' of carbon, oxygen and hydrogen, when held together in one formation, make glucose. When broken down to release energy some hydrogens and oxygens

FIGURE 2

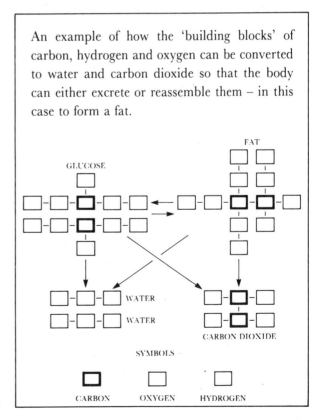

An example of how the 'building blocks' of carbon, hydrogen and oxygen can be converted to water and carbon dioxide so that the body can either excrete or reassemble them – in this case to form a fat.

combine to form water while some carbons combine with oxygen to make carbon dioxide. Another alternative however is that the glucose 'bricks' can be taken up by certain organs of the body and reassembled to form the substance we know as fat. The same diagram also illustrates that fat can be broken down for its energy content and the leftover 'bricks' excreted as water and carbon dioxide. Similarly, fat can be re-formed into glucose. While not shown in the diagram, we could add another 'brick' called nitrogen (obtained from protein) and show that some proteins can be converted to sugars, and some sugars and fats used to make proteins and so on.

CARBOHYDRATES AND YOUR BABY

Glucose from the mother's blood is fed to the baby via the placenta; the baby then has the choice of breaking it down for energy and excreting the water and carbon dioxide, or it can use the carbon, hydrogen and oxygen to create fat or use the same elements in the formation of certain proteins. This remarkable power of the body (adult *or* baby), to start with relatively indigestible substances such as starches and end up by creating a protein is what makes the carbohydrates such an important part of the diet. The body has, however, a limited capacity to store sugars so taking in more than is required causes conversion to fat and storage of the excess not needed for immediate energy needs.

FATS

All of us can conjure up a picture of 'fat' in our food but in reality fats include more than just the butter on our bread or the lard or oil used in cooking. Virtually all foods have some 'fat' content but this is composed of a family of three subgroups, technically known as triglycerides (ordinary fats), phospholipids (which form part of cell membranes) and sterols (an example being cholesterol). Once again the idea of bricks or building blocks can be used to help explain fat structure. There are two main building blocks, fatty acids and glycerol. These building blocks are shown in diagrammatic form in Figure 3. During digestion, beginning in the first part of the intestines, enzymes

from the pancreas separate the fatty acids from the glycerol and these released fatty acids are absorbed into the bloodstream to be taken to the liver. Once again, the production of energy is the principle use to which these fatty acids are put and in fact fats contain about twice as much in energy terms as either proteins or carbohydrates. In one sense, since eating fat is pleasurable, it is unfortunate that fat contains so much concentrated energy because we do not need to eat much of it to provide for the daily energy needs of our body, even during pregnancy.

The next important subgroup of 'fats' are the phospholipids and their importance lies not in energy production but in forming part of the structure of the body. Our bodies are made up of millions of individual cells and phospholipids form part of the outer membranes of these cells. For example, if we imagined ourselves to be made up of millions of cod liver oil capsules, then phospholipids would be represented by the gelatine capsules containing the cod liver oil. As adults, we are constantly repairing ourselves and must

FIGURE 3

An example of a basic fat (triglyceride). The 'frame', called glycerol, is always the same but there are several different 'side groups', the fatty acids. Different types of fats are formed depending upon which fatty acids are present.

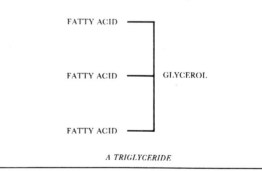

A TRIGLYCERIDE

have some 'fat' in our diet to provide these structural phospholipids if nothing else; a pregnant woman is building a baby so she needs to form thousands of millions of new cells as well as to cater for her own daily needs. So fat in the diet is important.

The final fat subgroup is composed of the sterols of which the most familiar is 'cholesterol', an important compound which is found only in animals. Related substances do occur in plants but humans do not absorb these so our cholesterol comes mainly from egg yolks and animal fats. However, cholesterol is such an important compound that the body actually manufactures it in the liver. It forms part of membranes around cells as well as being an important component in the manufacture of some of our hormones – particularly the type of hormones found in pregnancy. Since the liver will continue to make cholesterol from basic raw materials whatever the dietary intake, a cholesterol-free diet would not lead to a cholesterol-free person. This is just as well in view of its importance to health!

Many people associate cholesterol with ill-health having read of its association with heart disease and atherosclerosis. Both associations are true but this should not blind us to the fact that cholesterol is vital to the efficient functioning of our bodies. About 93 per cent of the total cholesterol in our body is actually inside the cells, only 7 per cent is in our blood. It is only when blood levels rise much above this 7 per cent due to some underlying condition that an individual is at risk of heart problems and other complications.

FATS AND YOUR BABY

Once fats are digested, the fatty acids released are absorbed and cross the placenta to supply the growing baby. The essential fatty acids must be provided for the baby from the mother's diet but the remainder can be made up from raw materials which, together with phospholipids and cholesterol (either from the diet or made by the mother), cater for all the needs of the developing baby. Human babies do have a feature not found in other mammals – large fat stores. About 15 per cent of the weight of a newborn baby is made up of fat. If we consider the energy content of this fat, about 60 per cent of the total calorie content of a human baby is in its fat. This may seem a large reserve but it is probably necessary when we consider how helpless a newborn human baby is in terms of being able to feed itself from the time it is born. Of course the fat formed by the baby does not come only from the fatty acids and cholesterol derived from the mother but also from the conversion of sugars.

IMPORTANT VITAMINS

A great deal of folklore surrounds these compounds, promoted, in some degree, by those pharmaceutical firms which manufacture them. They were first discovered when it was realised that diets which were adequate in calories, carbohydrates, fats, proteins and minerals still failed to maintain health. Vitamins have two major characteristics: first, they cannot be manufactured by the body and, second, while they are necessary for life, health and growth, they do not supply dietary energy.

There are two major groups of vitamins: those which dissolve easily in water and those which are soluble in fat. This difference is important because water-soluble vitamins are easily absorbed, even when people are not in the best of health. However, some dietary fat is necessary to assist the absorption of the fat-soluble vitamins as is the presence of bile from the liver and a particular enzyme from the pancreas called lipase. While diseases of the pancreas are uncommon during pregnancy, liver problems causing jaundice might occur and deficiency of the fat-soluble vitamins then develop even when the dietary content is adequate.

Initially the vitamins were called after the letters of the alphabet but as more were discovered this system had to be modified – particularly when a vitamin previously thought to be a single compound was found to be a group of related compounds. The fat-soluble vitamins are A, D, E and K. There are, however, two forms of vitamin A – A1 and A2. The water-soluble vitamins are thiamin (B1), riboflavin (B2), niacin, pyridoxine (B6), pantothenic acid, biotin, the folates (sometimes known as folic acid), cyanocobalamin (B12) and vitamin C.

IS IT POSSIBLE TO TAKE IN TOO MANY VITAMINS?

In general you cannot 'overdose' on the water-soluble vitamins because the kidney is able to excrete them in the urine. However, it is not so easy for the body to dispose of the fat-soluble forms and toxic effects are possible. Arctic explorers who had eaten the livers of polar bears (which contain high levels of vitamin A) developed toxic symptoms from an overdose of this vitamin. Similarly, side effects can be experienced from taking large doses of vitamin D or vitamin K. Such effects cannot occur from the amounts present in a normal diet or from taking modest amounts of vitamin supplements; however, taking 'megadoses' of vitamins should be avoided because there are no added benefits from taking these excessive amounts.

VITAMINS AND YOUR BABY

Vitamins are vital to life, health and growth. In the adult, growth is confined to the repair of damaged tissues but in the developing fetus and newborn baby it is growth which creates the dominant need for vitamins. It is necessary to keep up a steady dietary supply because both mother and baby only have a limited capacity to store these compounds. While all of the vitamins are necessary, the folates are particularly important. They are mainly found in leafy green vegetables and when there used to be a seasonal variation in the availability of such vegetables deficiencies could occur during the winter months in some countries. However, as folates are well preserved by deep-freezing and vegetables are available all the year round, folate deficiency is unlikely to occur in pregnant women eating an average, balanced western diet. Even if minor degrees of insufficiency do occur, the developing baby will take all it needs from the mother and it is the mother who will suffer the lack by developing a special form of anaemia called megaloblastic anaemia. However, even minor deficiencies can be avoided by simple attention to the daily diet.

ASSESSING YOUR NEEDS FOR FOLIC ACID

A mother who has delivered a baby with spina bifida or some other abnormality will naturally want to do all she can to prevent this happening again. Whether taking extra vitamins before conception will help prevent the problem in a subsequent pregnancy is still not certain. For the reasons described above, taking extra tablets or capsules for months on end while attempting to conceive might be neither sensible nor practicable.

What is very practicable, however, is to pay attention to your diet. The recipes in this book, for example, list essential nutrients, including the folic acid content. Supplements of folic acid, an important water-soluble B vitamin, have been given, under controlled conditions, to women who have had spina bifida babies. Since it is water-soluble some of it will be lost if foods are given prolonged boiling, in large quantities of cooking water. However, a quick glance at Table 3, right, will show you how little you actually have to eat to ensure that you get enough from the diet rather than from supplements. One reasonable portion of cornflakes, for example, (excluding the added milk which also contains folic acid) will provide virtually all the vitamin and iron needs of pregnancy, and two such

TABLE 3

The nutritional composition of 100 g (3½ oz) of a well known brand of cornflakes. The second column shows the extra amount recommended to cover the needs of pregnancy.

100 g cornflakes	Extra amount recommended for pregnancy
355 kcal	200 kcal
5.3 g protein	6 g
6.7 mg iron	4-6 mg
1.0 mg thiamin	0.1-0.4 mg
1.5 mg riboflavin	0.3 mg
250 μg folic acid	50-400
16 μg niacin	2
2.8 μg vitamin D	5
1.7 μg vitamin B12	1

portions would provide for many of the everyday needs (with the exception of protein) as well. Many breakfast cereals contain folic acid, as well as niacin, riboflavin, thiamin, vitamin D and vitamin B$_{12}$. Indeed, as Table 3 shows, 100 g of cornflakes contains 250 micrograms (μg) of folate which is almost as much as the suggested supplement of three tablets and certainly far in excess of the daily amounts needed for normal pregnancy. Remember that cereals are not the only source of folate and the rest of your dietary intake will come mainly from leafy green vegetables. Provided your diet is good and contains fresh fruit and vegetables and sensible amounts of milk and eggs, your daily vitamin needs can be easily achieved.

IMPORTANT MINERALS

Minerals are another dietary essential. The body cannot manufacture them so they must be present in the diet. A number of minerals must be eaten daily to conserve health but it is difficult to imagine diets deficient in most of them since they are contained in such a wide range of foods. Sodium and potassium, for example, are vital minerals but it would be virtually impossible to eat a diet that did not contain these two substances. Calcium, phosphorus, magnesium, zinc, iodine and iron are all necessary to our health but under most conditions women will take in sufficient of these minerals from their daily diet to ensure the development of a healthy baby. The two most commonly needed minerals for pregnancy are calcium and iron and these deserve further discussion.

ASSESSING YOUR NEEDS FOR CALCIUM

Obviously the baby will require extra calcium for its own needs during bone and tooth formation and that is why the recommendations shown in Table 4 suggest more than double the average daily amount should be consumed during the last three months of pregnancy. But if we look at it from another viewpoint it can be shown that the extra calcium intake suggested during pregnancy is actually only 3 per cent of the calcium present in the mother's skeleton. There is more than sufficient to provide for the baby from this 'store' if absolutely necessary. If the baby does have to call upon the mother's calcium reserves this will not cause the mother's teeth to decay faster or the bones of the mother to 'thin'. Care of the teeth and gums, however, is important during pregnancy because higher than usual levels of hormones can have the effect of making the gums slightly elastic which means that gum disease is more likely, especially if mouth hygiene is poor.

As far as the baby is concerned, it is never likely to call upon the calcium in your skeleton because the average diet contains more than enough calcium for its needs. An intake of 250 mg per day during the last 10 weeks of pregnancy will provide all the calcium needed for the baby's bones at birth. The recipes in this book give the calcium content so that you can easily calculate the amount you are consuming; you should also remember that semi-skimmed milk contains the same amount of calcium as whole milk, although energy and fat-soluble vitamin content is lower. It is also important to keep up your supply of vitamin D (contained in whole milk, fish, eggs, butter and margarine, and also manufactured by the action of sunlight on the skin). Vitamin D forms part of the hormone that makes calcium available to the body.

ASSESSING YOUR NEEDS FOR IRON

The major demand for iron in anyone, be they adult, child or developing baby, is to make red blood cells. The reason why blood looks red is because the millions and millions of little blood cells floating in our plasma contain a red, iron-containing pigment known as haemoglobin. The function of haemoglobin is to transport oxygen from our lungs to all the cells of the body – including the cells of the developing baby. This explains why babies can live surrounded by water in the womb: they have no need to breath because the placenta transfers oxygen directly from the mother's blood to that of the baby. The two bloodstreams, that of the baby and that of the mother, flow very closely together in the placenta, indeed so close that the oxygen vital to the baby can cross from the mother without the two bloodstreams actually mingling. Equally, the waste gas, carbon dioxide, can cross from the baby's blood to that of the mother to be transported to her lungs to be breathed out. It is important to realise that mother and baby have separate blood supplies: the blood of the mother does not cross to the baby. The baby makes its own blood cells and it may well be born with a blood group quite different to that of the mother. It is therefore important that there are sufficient blood cells in the mother and the baby to transport the oxygen vital to the well being of both and this requires the presence of iron to form haemoglobin.

During pregnancy is dietary iron enough or should extra iron be taken? The great majority of women living in Europe and the USA have a daily diet that contains more than sufficient iron to cater for the needs of both mother and baby during pregnancy. Why then is there so much emphasis on giving pregnant mothers extra iron as a supplement to the diet more or less from the time pregnancy is diagnosed?

There are actually two major schools of thought. The first holds that pregnant women do not generally need extra iron and it should not be given routinely. This is not to say that some mothers will not develop anaemia (the name given to the condition where there is reduced red cells from lack of iron) but that iron supplements should be reserved for those who need them and not given to everyone. Iron supplements can cause nausea, indigestion, constipation or diarrhoea in many mothers and such side effects are best avoided.

The second school accepts that there is a lot of iron in the food we eat each day but that much of it does not become absorbed. We absorb about 10 per cent or 2 mg of our dietary iron and some people believe this is about all we can manage. During pregnancy the need for iron increases to 6 mg per day but since it is held that only 2 mg can be absorbed, iron insufficiency is bound to occur and relatively large doses of extra iron should be prescribed. Many pills contain 300 mg and some doctors suggest three tablets or capsules to be taken each day. On this basis the total pregnancy iron requirement is being consumed each day!

This second school does agree that the dietary iron can be absorbed more easily by sensible attention to the composition of our meals. For example, iron in meat is more easily absorbed than the iron from some cereals. If citric or ascorbic acid (from fruits), is taken regularly these, too, will increase absorption and this is where fresh fruit or fruit juices in the diet are particularly important. In addition, some vegetables, especially those that contain ascorbic acid, like cauliflower, release iron more easily than others. Unless there are some particular circumstances, then, and a woman fails to follow a sensible diet, her needs for iron will be supplied by her diet and her body will absorb all the iron she and her developing baby needs.

However, if you wish to take extra iron or your doctor recommends it because you have evidence of anaemia, then the preparation – be it tablet or capsule – should be taken on an empty stomach and washed down with orange or grapefruit juice. It should not be taken during or after a meal and particularly not washed down with tea. Unfortunately following this good advice during pregnancy may often cause heartburn or indigestion – a reason why mothers are tempted to take iron preparations after their meals.

TABLE 4
Recommended Daily Amounts of vitamins and minerals (DHSS, 1979)

	Non-pregnant	Pregnant
Calcium (mg)	500	1200*
Iron (mg)	12	13
Vitamin A (μg)	750	750
Thiamin (mg)	0.9	1.0
Riboflavin (mg)	1.3	1.6
Niacin (mg)	15	18
Vitamin C (mg)	30	60
Vitamin D (μg)	–	10
*During last 3 months		

COFFEE AND OUR DIET

Some reports suggest that excessive coffee drinking may increase the number of low birthweight babies or even the risk of fetal malformation. The problem of assessing such reports is similar to that concerned with alcohol consumption, that is, what constitutes 'excessive' coffee-drinking? In the few reports available 'excessive' is defined as more than eight cups per day but the writers of these reports are careful to point out that coffee intake is only one of several possible influencing factors such as the marital and economic status of the mother, her cigarette smoking and so on. Unfortunately, despite the inadequacy of the evidence, the United States Food and Drug Administration have seen fit to advise pregnant women to avoid caffeine-containing foods or to use them sparingly.

Taken at the same time as a meal containing essential vitamins and minerals, coffee may reduce the rate at which the body absorbs these nutrients. So try to enjoy your meals without an accompanying cup of coffee. Having said this, it seems unlikely that the coffee drinking habits of the average pregnant woman has any adverse influence upon her developing child.

TEA AND OUR DIET

Tea drinking during pregnancy has not been studied to the same extent as coffee drinking but the problems of assessing its effect remain the same. Tea does, however, contain chemicals such as tannates and these can reduce the amount of iron, zinc, magnesium and other trace elements absorbed from the diet. In fact, many substances found in food, such as the phosphates and phytate found in flour, as well as the tannates in tea can all help to make essential minerals such as iron insoluble and therefore less easy for the body to absorb. However, whether in normal everyday living and eating this can have any harmful effect upon the baby in the womb seems highly unlikely. For tea drinkers, especially if you drink several cups of tea with meals, as with coffee, try to enjoy your cuppa after your meal.

CIGARETTES AND OUR DIET

In general it can be said that women who smoke may not eat well since smoking does cut down the enjoyment of food. The effect of smoking on depressing the appetite, however, is very difficult to prove. Smoking also seems to inhibit some of the body's enzyme systems and may use up more of the body's limited stores of vitamin C.

The biggest effect on the body is in fact the reduction in the substance most essential to its survival: the oxygen in the air we breathe. One of the products of cigarette smoke is carbon monoxide and some of this gas combines with red blood cells so that they take up less oxygen. This may in turn affect oxygen transfer across the placenta. In fact, if you monitor the fetal heart rate in mothers who smoke you may notice a drop in the baby's heart rate shortly after the mother lights up a cigarette. Mothers who do smoke tend to have babies that are, on average, about 150 g lighter than babies born to non-smoking mothers.

SALT AND OUR DIET

Much has been written about the apparent consequences of eating too much salt and its possible effect on blood pressure. While it may be true that in men and women with high blood pressure or heart disease a reduction in salt intake can be beneficial, this is not the same as saying that the amounts of salt eaten by normal healthy women of child-bearing years is harmful. Of all the things we eat, salt is the substance the body monitors most closely because it is essential for life; to be totally deprived of salt would cause death. The kidneys have sophisticated and complex systems for conserving salt (as sodium); if we eat too much the extra is excreted in the urine, whereas if we eat too little the kidney will conserve it and little will be lost in the urine. There is also some evidence to suggest that high stress levels cause the body to retain salt so it is also important to relax and if you feel under stress to share that feeling with someone who can help, like your doctor, your husband or other member of your family, or a good friend.

Those with diseases of the kidney which may be causing high blood pressure and consequent heart problems do need to take care with dietary intake. But for healthy women and healthy pregnant women, the amount of salt in the average diet is unlikely to be harmful. Indeed, as discussed earlier, pregnant women often experience a 'blunting' of taste perception and may find themselves attracted to robust flavours such as kippers. Many such flavours do rely upon a high salt content and as long as they are not eaten to excess will not cause harm to mother or baby. The salt content of the recipes in this book is given for interest and information and, if you have no particular change in your taste perception, then balancing salty foods with dishes that contain reduced amounts of salt would not be out of place. However, it would be quite wrong to become obsessional about salt intake, wrong to confine yourself to a bland and uninteresting diet and to reduce your salt intake in the belief that this would be of benefit to either you or your baby. Even worse would be to think you might be harming your developing baby in any way because you develop a taste for salty foods and eat a lot of them during the first three months of pregnancy.

PREGNANCY AND EXERCISE

While you attempt to conceive or after you have become pregnant there is no need to cut down on exercise or even an active sporting life if you enjoy it. Indeed, recent work suggests that exercise improves blood flow to the uterus and to the baby. This is not to say that pregnant mums should immediately start training to run the four-minute mile; such strenuous exercise would require more blood flow to the muscles and would be counterproductive. But, contrary to popular belief, moderate exercise such as swimming, brisk walking or gentle jogging, actually tunes up the whole circulation and this includes the circulation to womb, placenta and baby. As far as the energy needs of exercise are concerned, be guided by your appetite – if increased exercise makes you hungry, by all means have a sandwich or a nutritious snack.

HOW TO WORK OUT YOUR DAILY INTAKE OF THE MAJOR NUTRIENTS

Using the nutritional breakdown given in the recipes that follow, you can easily work out the number of kilocalories of each of the major nutrients – protein, fat and carbohydrate – that you consume. Write down the content of the meals you eat on an average week-day. If you are the type of person who has fairly regular eating habits then whatever day of the week you choose will represent your diet as a whole. However, if some days are more active than others, then keep a record of what you eat from Monday to Friday and take the average. Meals on Saturdays and Sundays should also be assessed separately because many people eat more over the weekends than during the week. You can then calculate the grams of carbohydrate, fat and protein contained in your 'average' daily diet. To take an example: an egg contains 6.1 g protein, 5.5 g fat and 0.4 g carbohydrate; 2 small slices of toast (50 g or 2 oz) contain 7.8 g protein, 3.6 g fat and 32.6 g car-

bohydrate. Add these amounts and you get 13.9 g protein, 9.1 g fat and 33 g carbohydrate. Remember that carbohydrates and protein give 4 kilocalories per gram and fat 9 kilocalories per gram. In the case of egg on toast this would be 7.8×4 (35 kcal), 3.6×9 (82 kcal) and 32.6×4 (132 kcal), a total of 269 kcal. Using the figures given in the recipes you can add up the protein, fat and carbohydrate content of other meals. This will allow you to work out the proportion of each nutrient you are consuming on a daily basis – the 'balanced' ratio of 10-15 per cent protein, 25-30 per cent fat and 50-75 per cent carbohydrate – and also your energy intake in kilocalories. Remember that in pregnancy, averaged out over the whole 280 days, you need about 200 kilocalories per day above the average 2400 kilocalories that is reasonable for non-pregnant women with an average daily activity. In reality, you may experience a considerable increase in appetite during the first few months of pregnancy and decrease your intake later. This is perfectly acceptable if the total calories consumed do not become excessive. A way to cope with this increase in appetite is to use the suggested recipes in the book which are high in fibre (which is satisfying) but low in calories. In this way you can keep feelings of hunger at bay without too great an increase in food energy. Alcohol should also be remembered in this context; all alcohols contribute 7 kilocalories per gram so even when taken in moderation they do contribute to your total daily calories.

GETTING THE BALANCE RIGHT

Remember that if at least half of your daily calories are to come from carbohydrates then a daily need for, say, 2600 kilocalories means that 1300 kilocalories should come from carbohydrate, that is 325 g (about 12 oz). As far as fats are concerned, we need only eat about 70 g (2½ oz) of fat per day to remain healthy. As much, or more, has been written about the amount and type of fat in our diet as about any other nutrient. Much emphasis is placed upon the type of fat – whether it is 'saturated' or 'unsaturated' – but rather less on the amount. It is actually easier to remember that we should restrict our daily amount of fat to 70 g (2½ oz) per day as an alternative to trying to remember which foods contain the 'healthy' or unsaturated fats since all fats contain both types. As a broad generalisation, the fats in meat and dairy products tend to contain more of the saturated fats while fish and cereals contain more of the unsaturated variety. As an example, milk fat is predominantly saturated; skimmed milk, however, has a low fat content but the same water-soluble vitamin and protein content. In losing its fat content, however, milk also loses some of its taste as well as some of its energy content. A compromise would be for those who enjoy it to drink whole milk but to cook with semi-skimmed or skimmed milk. Similarly, fish is both tasty and nutritious and makes a good alternative to meat on some occasions because fish oils are predominantly unsaturated. Margarines that are low in saturated fats can be used as an alternative to butter.

Eating fish and drinking skimmed milk, however, will not necessarily be 'better' for the baby, nor will eating meat and butter be worse if the total daily intake is 70 g or less. If you can balance your diet and maintain satisfaction by using 'healthy' fats this will be to your advantage, and it is on this basis that the recipes in this book suggest foods and cooking methods which favour unsaturated fats as much as possible.

It should be emphasised that the weights discussed for carbohydrates, fats and proteins refer to the 'pure' content of a particular nutrient and are nothing to do with the weight of the food. Thus 100 g (3½ oz) of liver contains 19.2 g of protein so 28 g (1 oz) of liver contains only 7 g. For baked beans, 100 g contains 5.1 g so 140 g (5 oz) contains 7 g of protein, the same amount as in 1 oz of liver. When a particular food has a high water content, the protein content is even more 'dilute'. Thus 28 g (1 oz) of bread and 140 g (5 oz) of potatoes both contain the same amount of protein, 2 g.

NUTRITIONAL ANALYSIS OF RECIPES

Each recipe that follows is accompanied by a nutritional analysis that gives you the amount of each nutrient per portion. Where the recipe gives a range of servings, 3-4 portions for example, the smaller portion has been used. The analysis provides you with information on calories (kilojoules), protein, carbohydrate, fat, saturated fat, fibre, added sugar and salt as well as on three nutrients known to be important during pregnancy – calcium, iron and folic acid (a B vitamin).

The recipes have been devised not just with a healthy pregnancy in mind but with healthy eating for all the family. In general, the diet in the UK contains too much fat, saturated fat, salt and sugar and too little fibre. High fat, high sugar foods tend to be low in fibre, vitamins and minerals. Simply by cutting down your fat and sugar intakes while maintaining your calorie intake, you will increase the vitamins and minerals which are essential for a healthy pregnancy for you and your baby.

The recipes have been star rated to show you at a glance how high in a particular nutrient each recipe is. You can thus use the star rating to establish how much protein, fat, saturated fat, fibre, added sugar, salt, calcium, iron or folic acid a recipe contains. For each of the star rated nutrients, to gain 4 stars a recipe must either be low in total fat, saturated fat, salt or low added sugar; or high in protein, fibre, calcium, iron or folic acid.

RECOMMENDED DAILY AMOUNTS OF NUTRIENTS The Department of Health and Social Security have made recommendations for the daily amount of certain nutrients for groups of people according to their age, sex and activity level as well as for pregnancy and lactation. The recommendations (see Table 5, right) are designed to cover the needs of most healthy, pregnant and breast feeding mums. Since they include a margin of safety, the fact that you may be having a little less than the recommended amount does not necessarily mean that you are not having sufficient for your particular individual needs. This is because we all have different rates of absorption and efficiency in using these nutrients. The recommendations are therefore only meant as a general guide and are not designed for individuals. Recommendations for kilocalories do not have a margin of safety added but are averages, and again, there are large variations in individual requirements.

TABLE 5

Recommended Daily Amounts of nutrients for population groups (DHSS, 1979)

	Non-pregnant	Pregnant	Breast Feeding
Kcals	2150	2400	2750
Protein g	54	60	69
Calcium mg	500	1200[1]	1200
Iron mg	12	13	15
Folic acid[2] μg	300	500	400
[1]3rd trimester only i.e. 26 weeks until term			
[2]Folic acid recommendations were withdrawn by the DHSS in 1985 because of insubstantial evidence.			

FAT AND SATURATED FAT The amount of fat used in these recipes has been kept to a minimum without losing the overall flavour of the dish. Analysis of meat dishes for instance, has been done on the basis that visible fat has been trimmed off before cooking; there will be enough integral fat to ensure that the meat will be succulent and well flavoured. Semi-skimmed milk has been used in the recipes to reduce fat, particularly saturated fat. You may of course use skimmed milk if you want to reduce your fat further but do remember it is important to maintain an adequate calorie intake during pregnancy. All the important nutrients, including calcium, are retained in low fat milk; the only nutrients lost, besides fat, are the fat soluble vitamins A and D. Since milk is not one of the more important sources of these two vitamins, using low fat milk should not be a problem. Remember low fat milks are not recommended for young children (under 5 years old). This is because milk is likely to provide a major source of energy in their diet and it would be difficult to provide sufficient calories for their needs using low fat milks. It is generally agreed that semi-skimmed milk may be introduced from the age of 2 years providing the child is eating a wide variety of foods.

Some recipes may have a relatively high fat content but the type of fat or oil used in the recipie will be low in saturated fat. By combining, say, a comparatively high fat meat recipe (none of the recipes are very high in fat) in a meal with a low fat vegetable recipe, the overall result will be a moderate fat intake which is what you should aim for, that is approximately 70 g of fat a day, of which no more than 35 g should be saturated fat.

FIBRE The average UK intake of fibre is about 20 g per day. Experts have recommended that this should be increased to 30 g a day. A high fibre intake is often a good indicator of a high nutrient intake because high fibre foods such as wholegrain cereals and bread, fruit and vegetables are all good sources of vitamins and minerals. Meat and fish contain no fibre so meat and fish recipes are generally low in fibre but when combined in a meal with high fibre vegetable dishes or wholegrain cereals, the overall fibre content of the total meal should be satisfactory. Constipation is often encountered during pregnancy; if you suffer from this problem, try to choose high fibre (4 star rating) recipes whenever possible.

ADDED SUGAR Experts recommend a reduction in added 'refined' sugar from an average of about 130 g per day to 50 g. This means reducing not just sugar added in tea or coffee but also the large proportion of hidden sugars found in many processed foods. Sugar provides kilocalories (about 20 kcals per teaspoon) but no other nutrients. Added sugar analysis includes white and brown sugar but not naturally occurring sugars as, for instance, those in fresh fruit.

SALT While some salt is essential to our diet, in general our palate has become adapted to want more salt in our food than we either need or is good for us. Doctors suggest we should reduce our salt intake from an average 7 to 10 g per day to around 5 g (5000 mg). The recipes have been analysed without including added salt unless a specified amount has been stated. The analysis therefore includes only the salt that occurs naturally in food and the salt which has been added by manufacturers, as for instance in bacon, canned vegetables, and in foods such as tuna, canned in brine. Manufactured or processed foods account for as much as 88 per cent of our total salt intake – clearly one good reason for returning to good home cooking!

PROTEIN Protein is essential for building new tissues and is therefore important during pregnancy. On the whole, our culture encourages us to eat more protein than we need. Although star rating has been given for protein, it is unlikely that anyone in this country will be eating less than the recommended intake for pregnancy, which is 60 g per day, unless they are on a particularly bizarre type of diet. Vegetarians and vegans with a staple diet that includes a balanced intake of pulses, bread, nuts, pasta, rice and other grains are likely to obtain sufficient protein for their needs during pregnancy.

CALCIUM, IRON AND FOLIC ACID (a B VITAMIN) These three nutrients are thought to be of particular importance during early pregnancy; calcium for bone formation, iron and folic acid for the production of red blood cells and therefore the prevention of anaemia.

STAR RATINGS

★ ★ ★ ★ A four star rating for calcium, iron, folic acid, protein and fibre means the recipe contains at least 50 per cent of the recommended daily amount (RDA). A four star rating for fat, saturated fat, salt and added sugar means the recipe contains less than 5 per cent of the maximum set in the guidelines for healthy eating.

★ ★ ★ This rating means the recipe contains at least 35 per cent of the RDA for calcium, iron, folic acid, protein and fibre. The recipe contains less than 10 per cent of the RDA for fat, saturated fat, salt and added sugar.

★ ★ The recipe contains at least 10 per cent of the RDA for calcium, iron, folic acid, protein and fibre, but less than a quarter of the RDA for fat, saturated fat, salt and added sugar.

★ The recipe contains at least 5 per cent of the RDA for calcium, iron, folic acid, protein and fibre, but less than one third of the RDA for fat, saturated fat, salt and added sugar.

No stars in the case of calcium, iron, folic acid, protein and fibre means the recipe contains less than 5 per cent of the RDA.

1

Breakfasts

The best way to start the day is with a sustaining breakfast that gives you the energy to get up and go. When you are pregnant your requirements for breakfast can vary from day to day. For a light yet nourishing breakfast, make up one of the satisfying drinks. When feeling hungry, prepare the wholesome scones or waffles, or try an egg dish with a difference.

NUTRITIONAL ANALYSIS
amount per portion
78 kcals/327 kJ
14 g Carbohydrate
4.5 g Protein ★
0.9 g Fat ★★★★
0.4 g Saturated Fat ★★★★
1.0 g Added Sugar ★★★★
1.4 g Fibre
152 mg Salt ★★★★
160 mg Calcium ★★★
0.7 mg Iron ★
22 mg Folic Acid

Strawberry Yogurt Drink

This creamy breakfast drink with its delicious blend of different fruits will act as a nutritious pick-me-up at other times of the day, too.

SERVES 4
175 g (6 oz) strawberries, hulled
300 ml (½ pint) low-fat natural yogurt
100 ml (4 fl oz) unsweetened orange juice
5 ml (1 tsp) clear honey
2.5-5 ml (½-1 tsp) chopped fresh mint
1 kiwi fruit, peeled and sliced
1 mandarin, peeled and segmented

1 Slice 4 of the strawberries and put to one side. Coarsely chop the remainder, place in a blender or food processor with the yogurt, orange juice, honey and mint and purée until smooth.
2 Pour into 4 glasses and decorate with the strawberry, kiwi and mandarin slices. Serve with long spoons.

NUTRITIONAL ANALYSIS
amount per portion
273 kcals/1141 kJ
14.2 g Carbohydrate
3.2 g Protein ★
23 g Fat ★
16.5 g Saturated Fat
0.0 g Added Sugar ★★★★
13.3 g Fibre ★★★
565 mg Salt ★★
115 mg Calcium ★★
2.4 mg Iron ★★
47 mg Folic Acid ★

Vegetable Vitality Drink

The high concentration of carotene in carrots, particularly in raw ones, converts to vitamin A in the body.

SERVES 1
50 g (2 oz) shredded coconut
225 g (8 oz) carrots, scrubbed and grated
juice of ½ lemon
5 ml (1 tsp) wheatgerm oil

1 Put the coconut in a heatproof jug, pour on 300 ml (½ pint) boiling water and stir well to mix. Leave to infuse for 30 minutes.
2 Purée the carrots with the lemon juice in a blender or food processor until broken down to a pulp. Strain the carrot pulp through a sieve into a jug.
3 Strain the milk from the coconut into the carrot. Add the oil and whisk vigorously to combine. Pour into a tall glass and serve immediately.

Date and Yogurt Scones (PAGE 35); *Plum and Apple Spread* (PAGE 37); *Mushrooms with Bacon* (PAGE 34);
Herrings in Oatmeal (PAGE 34)

Breakfast Vegetable Juice

Coriander adds a distinctive flavour and aroma to the juice. If coriander is not readily available use fresh parsley as an alternative.

SERVES 4

225 g (8 oz) carrots, scrubbed

225 g (8 oz) tomatoes

3 celery sticks, trimmed and chopped

15 ml (1 tbsp) chopped fresh coriander

6 ice cubes

200 ml (7 fl oz) unsweetened orange juice

salt and pepper, to taste

ice cubes, to serve

1 Place the carrots, tomatoes, celery, coriander and ice cubes into the juicing attachment of a food processor or food mixer. Blend until all the juice has been extracted.
2 Mix with the orange juice. Season. Serve, with extra ice cubes.

NUTRITIONAL ANALYSIS
amount per portion
43 kcals/180 kJ
9.8 g Carbohydrate
1.6 g Protein
0.0 g Fat ★★★★
0.1 g Saturated Fat ★★★★
0.0 g Added Sugar ★★★★
3.3 g Fibre ★★
277 mg Salt ★★★
64 mg Calcium ★★
1.0 mg Iron ★
47 mg Folic Acid ★

Baked Tarragon Eggs

Fresh tarragon, with its distinctive bitter-sweet taste, flavours this healthy start to the day.

SERVES 4

15 g (½ oz) polyunsaturated margarine

100 g (4 oz) mushrooms, sliced

2 tomatoes, chopped

25 ml (1½ tbsp) chopped fresh tarragon or 10 ml (2 tsp) dried

pepper, to taste

4 eggs

1 Melt the margarine in a saucepan and lightly cook the mushrooms for 3 minutes. Remove from the heat, add the tomatoes, tarragon and pepper.
2 Place the mixture in a shallow ovenproof dish and, using the back of a spoon, make 4 shallow hollows in the mixture. Carefully break an egg into each hollow.
3 Place the dish in a roasting tin with enough hot water to come halfway up the sides. Bake at 180°C (350°F) mark 4 for 10–12 minutes or until the eggs are set. Serve immediately with wholemeal toast.

NUTRITIONAL ANALYSIS
amount per portion
118 kcals/495 kJ
1.1 g Carbohydrate
7.9 g Protein ★★
9.2 g Fat ★★★
2.5 g Saturated Fat ★★★
0.0 g Added Sugar ★★★★
1.8 g Fibre ★
286 mg Salt ★★★
55 mg Calcium ★★
2.0 mg Iron ★★
31 mg Folic Acid ★

Cream of Parsley Soup (PAGE 42)*; Chinese Cabbage and Prawn Soup* (PAGE 45)*; Iced Sweet Pepper Soup* (PAGE 46)

NUTRITIONAL ANALYSIS
amount per portion
549 kcals/2294 kJ
14.8 g Carbohydrate
36.4 g Protein ★★★
38.5 g Fat
8.1 g Saturated Fat ★★
0.0 g Added Sugar ★★★★
2.3 g Fibre ★
388 mg Salt ★★★
111 mg Calcium ★★
2.9 mg Iron ★★
24 mg Folic Acid

Herrings in Oatmeal

This traditional Scottish dish is an excellent source of protein.

SERVES 4
4 small herrings, cleaned and heads removed
20 ml (4 tsp) Dijon mustard
1 egg, beaten
75 g (3 oz) fine oatmeal
lemon wedges and mustard and cress, to garnish

1 Remove the backbones from the fish (see page 108). Open out, place skin side down, and spread each fish with 5 ml (1 tsp) mustard.
2 Dip the fish in the beaten egg, then coat with oatmeal. Place the fish on a baking sheet, skin side down.
3 Bake at 220°C (425°F) mark 7 for 15-20 minutes or until golden brown. Serve hot, garnished with lemon wedges and mustard and cress.

NUTRITIONAL ANALYSIS
amount per portion
226 kcals/944 kJ
24.1 g Carbohydrate
11.4 g Protein ★★
10 g Fat ★★
4.2 g Saturated Fat ★★
0.0 g Added Sugar ★★★★
3.3 g Fibre ★★
1957 mg Salt
79 mg Calcium ★★
1.8 mg Iron ★★
28 mg Folic Acid ★

Mushrooms with Bacon

If available, serve this savoury breakfast dish on slices of Ciabatta, an Italian bread made with olive oil. It is very light and has an interesting texture.

SERVES 2
100 g (4 oz) oyster or flat black mushrooms, trimmed
30 ml (2 tbsp) Greek strained yogurt
5 ml (1 tsp) Worcestershire sauce
pepper, to taste
2 rashers streaky bacon
Ciabatta or French bread, warmed
parsley, to garnish

1 Heat the mushrooms with the yogurt, Worcestershire sauce and pepper in a small saucepan.
2 Grill the bacon until crisp. Cool slightly and snip into small pieces.
3 Add the bacon to the mushrooms and cook until just tender. Serve on slices of Ciabatta, garnished with parsley.

Date and Yogurt Scones

These scones are best eaten really fresh. Serve split and spread with a little low-fat soft cheese and sugar-reduced jam.

MAKES 10
50 g (2 oz) stoned dates, finely chopped
75 g (3 oz) plain white flour
150 g (5 oz) plain wholemeal flour
15 ml (1 tbsp) baking powder
pinch of grated nutmeg
50 g (2 oz) polyunsaturated margarine
50 g (2 oz) light muscovado sugar
150 ml (¼ pint) low-fat natural yogurt
semi-skimmed milk

1 Coat the dates in 25 g (1 oz) of the white flour. Place the remaining white and wholemeal flour in a bowl with the baking powder and nutmeg. Mix well.

2 Rub in the margarine until the mixture resembles fine breadcrumbs. Stir in the sugar and dates, then make a well in the centre of the mixture.

3 Place the yogurt in a small bowl, add 30 ml (2 tbsp) milk and whisk lightly until smooth. Pour into the well and mix with a palette knife to a soft dough. Leave to stand for about 5 minutes to allow the bran in the flour time to absorb the liquid. Lightly knead the dough on a floured surface until just smooth.

4 Roll out until 2 cm (¾ inch) thick. Using a 5 cm (2 inch) round cutter, stamp out 8 scones, re-rolling the dough as necessary. Place on a baking sheet, then brush with a little milk.

5 Bake at 230°C (450°F) mark 8 for about 10 minutes or until well risen and golden brown.

NUTRITIONAL ANALYSIS
amount per portion
153 kcals/639 kJ
25.8 g Carbohydrate
3.7 g Protein ★
4.7 g Fat ★★★
0.9 g Saturated Fat ★★★★
5.0 g Added Sugar ★★★
2.0 g Fibre ★
137 mg Salt ★★★★
53 mg Calcium ★★
0.9 mg Iron ★
12 mg Folic Acid

Walnut Waffles

Served with an apple and honey syrup, these nutty waffles make a satisfying breakfast treat.

NUTRITIONAL ANALYSIS
amount per portion
247 kcals/1034 kJ
34 g Carbohydrate
6.0 g Protein ★
10.8 g Fat ★★
2.0 g Saturated Fat ★★★★
15.2 g Added Sugar ★
1.5 g Fibre ★
105 mg Salt ★★★★
80 mg Calcium ★★
1.2 mg Iron ★
18 mg Folic Acid

SERVES 4

60 ml (4 tbsp) unsweetened apple juice
60 ml (4 tbsp) clear honey
40 g (1½ oz) self-raising wholemeal flour
40 g (1½ oz) self-raising white flour
15 ml (1 tbsp) light muscovado sugar
1 egg, separated
15 ml (1 tbsp) polyunsaturated oil, plus extra for greasing
150 ml (¼ pint) semi-skimmed milk
25 g (1 oz) walnuts, finely chopped

1 To make the syrup, gently heat the apple juice and honey in a saucepan until dissolved. Set aside to serve hot or cold.

2 To make the batter, mix the flours and sugar together in a bowl, making a well in the centre. Place the egg yolk in the centre with the oil, then gradually stir in the milk. Beat to give a thick pouring batter. Stir in the nuts.

3 Brush a waffle iron very lightly with oil and heat. (Follow the manufacturer's instructions for an electric iron.) Whisk the egg white until just stiff, then fold into the batter.

4 Pour enough batter into the hot iron to run just over the surface. Close the iron over the mixture and cook for about 2 minutes, turning the iron over if not electric, until golden brown and crisp and easily removed from the iron.

5 Serve immediately or place on a wire rack and keep warm in the oven. Continue until all the batter is used. Serve with the syrup. The syrup can be served cold or gently reheated, according to personal taste.

Plum and Apple Spread

The skin of the fruit is included to give this breakfast spread a chunky texture and increase the fibre content. For a smoother texture, roughly chop the fruit and cook with the skin, stones and cores, then sieve the purée before potting. This spread will keep for 2-3 weeks in the refrigerator, or may be frozen.

MAKES ABOUT 900 g (2 lb)
900 g (2 lb) ripe plums, such as Victoria, halved and stoned
900 g (2 lb) eating apples, quartered and cored
600 ml (1 pint) unsweetened red grape juice
2.5 ml (½ tsp) ground cinnamon

1 Put the plums and apples in a preserving pan or large, heavy-based saucepan with the grape juice and 300 ml (½ pint) cold water.
2 Bring slowly to the boil, lower the heat and simmer for about 50 minutes or until the fruit is reduced to a very thick purée. Stir frequently, pressing the fruit into the liquid with a wooden spoon so that it breaks up and becomes pulpy. Towards the end of the cooking time, stir continuously to ensure that the purée does not stick to the bottom of the pan.
3 Remove from the heat and leave for about 5 minutes or until the mixture has settled, then stir in the cinnamon.
4 Spoon the hot spread into warmed, clean, dry jars and leave until completely cold. Cover and seal the jars. Store in the refrigerator until required.

NUTRITIONAL ANALYSIS
amount per 25 g (1 oz)
27 kcals/112 kJ
6.9 g Carbohydrate
0.2 g Protein
0.0 g Fat ★★★★
0.0 g Saturated Fat ★★★★
0.0 g Added Sugar ★★★★
0.9 g Fibre
3.0 mg Salt ★★★★
5.0 mg Calcium
0.2 mg Iron
3.0 mg Folic Acid

Recipe for Shirred Eggs and Smoked Salmon

ollowing recent government health advice to pregnant women, we recommend that ggs in this recipe should be thoroughly cooked. *become overcooked.*

2 eggs, size 1, lightly beaten
15 ml (1 tbsp) single cream
ground coriander
salt and pepper, to taste
few coriander leaves
25 g (1 oz) slice smoked salmon
polyunsaturated margarine

1 Stir together the eggs and cream with a little coriander and seasoning in a bowl.
2 Lay a few coriander leaves on the smoked salmon and roll up. Slice into pinwheels.
3 Melt a small knob of margarine in a medium frying pan and pour in the egg. With a straight-edged wooden spatula, draw the egg across the pan until lightly set. Spoon on to a warmed plate, top with the salmon pinwheels and serve with fingers of wholemeal toast.

NUTRITIONAL ANALYSIS
amount per portion
282 kcals/1180 kJ
0.5 g Carbohydrate
22 g Protein ★★★
21.4 g Fat ★★
7.2 g Saturated Fat ★★
0.0 g Added Sugar ★★★★
0.9 g Fibre
1747 mg Salt
112 mg Calcium ★★
3.4 mg Iron ★★★
37 mg Folic Acid ★

Drop Scones with Raspberry Purée

This batter is made with oats and should be used immediately after mixing.

NUTRITIONAL ANALYSIS
amount per portion
82 kcals/341 kJ
14.3 g Carbohydrate
2.8 g Protein
1.9 g Fat ★★★★
0.5 g Saturated Fat ★★★★
0.0 g Added Sugar ★★★★
2.9 g Fibre ★
55 mg Salt ★★★★
41 mg Calcium ★
0.9 mg Iron ★
10 mg Folic Acid

MAKES ABOUT 10
225 g (8 oz) raspberries, thawed if frozen
finely grated rind and juice of 1 orange
50 g (2 oz) self-raising wholemeal flour
50 g (2 oz) porridge oats
1 egg, beaten
150 ml (¼ pint) semi-skimmed milk
polyunsaturated oil, for greasing
75 g (3 oz) raisins

1 To make the raspberry purée, purée the raspberries with the orange rind and juice in a blender or food processor. Transfer to a bowl. Cover and chill until ready to serve.

2 To make the batter, mix the flour and oats together in a bowl. Make a well in the centre, add the egg, then gradually stir in the milk, whisking lightly to make a smooth batter.

3 Lightly grease the base of a large heavy-based frying pan or griddle and heat until very hot.

4 Drop tablespoonfuls of the batter on to the frying pan, spacing well apart. Sprinkle a few raisins on to each one, then cook over low to moderate heat for about 2 minutes until bubbles appear on the surface. Turn over with a palette knife and continue cooking until golden brown underneath.

5 Remove the scones from the pan, wrap in a clean cloth and stand on a wire rack while making the remaining scones. Lightly grease the frying pan between each batch. Serve hot, with the chilled purée handed separately.

2

Soups

Homemade soups are appreciated by everyone – they are easy to prepare and full of goodness. And whether for a simple family meal or for a special occasion, they are the perfect start for a meal. There are many kinds of soups – thin and clear, thick and creamy, hot or chilled. Serve a thin soup with a hearty main course and a thicker one before a lighter meal. Soups make excellent snacks or light meals, served with wholemeal bread and cheese.

NUTRITIONAL ANALYSIS
amount per portion
89 kcals/373 kJ
12 g Carbohydrate
3.2 g Protein ★
3.5 g Fat ★ ★ ★ ★
0.7 g Saturated Fat ★ ★ ★ ★
0.0 g Added Sugar ★ ★ ★ ★
2.3 g Fibre ★
269 mg Salt ★ ★ ★
39 mg Calcium ★
2.1 mg Iron ★ ★
58 mg Folic Acid ★ ★

Tomato and Rice Soup

Adding brown rice to this soup gives an interesting contrast in textures as well as increasing the fibre content.

SERVES 4

30 ml (2 tbsp) long-grain brown rice

15 g (½ oz) polyunsaturated margarine

1 onion, skinned and chopped

1 garlic clove, skinned and crushed

2 celery sticks, trimmed and chopped

600 g (1¼ lb) canned tomatoes

30 ml (2 tbsp) tomato purée

5 ml (1 tsp) whole grain mustard

salt and pepper, to taste

5 ml (1 tsp) chopped fresh thyme or 2.5 ml (½ tsp) dried, plus extra to garnish

croûtons, to serve (optional)

1 Put the rice into a small saucepan with 150 ml (¼ pint) boiling water. Simmer gently for 10-15 minutes or until all the liquid has been absorbed and the rice is tender.
2 Meanwhile, melt the margarine in a large saucepan and cook the onion for 3-5 minutes until soft.
3 Add the garlic, celery, tomatoes with their juice, tomato purée and mustard. Season. Simmer gently for 20 minutes.
4 Cool slightly, then purée the soup in a blender or food processor until smooth. Return the soup to a clean pan. Add the thyme, rice and 300 ml (½ pint) boiling water. Simmer for a further 4-5 minutes to heat through. Garnish with thyme and serve with croûtons, if wished.

Cream of Celery Soup

This delicately flavoured soup is ideal to serve before a chicken dish. For special occasions, swirl a little Greek strained yogurt on the top.

SERVES 4

15 g (½ oz) polyunsaturated margarine

1 onion, skinned and finely chopped

1 garlic clove, skinned and crushed

6 celery sticks, trimmed

15 ml (1 tbsp) plain wholemeal flour

600 ml (1 pint) chicken stock

300 ml (½ pint) semi-skimmed milk

salt and pepper, to taste

celery leaves, to garnish

1 Melt the margarine in a saucepan and cook the onion for 4 minutes until soft. Add the garlic and celery and cook gently for a further 5 minutes.
2 Stir in the flour and cook for 1 minute. Gradually stir in the stock, milk and seasoning. Bring to the boil, lower the heat, cover and simmer gently for 25-30 minutes or until the celery is very soft.
3 Cool slightly, then purée the soup in a blender or food processor until smooth. Reheat gently. Serve hot, topped with celery leaves.

NUTRITIONAL ANALYSIS
amount per portion
90 kcals/376 kJ
8.5 g Carbohydrate
4.2 g Protein ★
4.6 g Fat ★★★★
1.5 g Saturated Fat ★★★★
0.0 g Added Sugar ★★★★
1.5 g Fibre
668 mg Salt ★★
132 mg Calcium ★★★
0.9 mg Iron ★
15 mg Folic Acid

Celeriac Soup with Dill

Prepare the celeriac just before frying as it discolours quickly. Make sure that the soup is well blended to give a smooth texture.

SERVES 3

25 g (1 oz) polyunsaturated margarine

225 g (8 oz) celeriac, peeled and chopped

1 medium onion, skinned and chopped

750 ml (1¼ pints) light stock

salt and pepper, to taste

45 ml (3 tbsp) single cream

lemon juice

10 ml (2 tsp) chopped fresh dill or pinch of dried dill weed

1 Melt the margarine in a medium saucepan and gently fry the celeriac and onion for 5 minutes.
2 Pour in the stock and season. Bring to the boil, lower the heat, cover and simmer for 30–40 minutes until tender.
3 Cool slightly, then purée in a blender or food processor until very smooth. Return the soup to a clean pan and reheat.
4 Remove from the heat, stir in the cream, a dash of lemon juice and the dill. Adjust the seasoning before serving accompanied by crusty wholemeal rolls.

NUTRITIONAL ANALYSIS
amount per portion
89 kcals/372 kJ
3.3 g Carbohydrate
2.1 g Protein
7.6 g Fat ★★★
2.4 g Saturated Fat ★★★
0.0 g Added Sugar ★★★★
2.9 g Fibre ★
706 mg Salt ★★
46 mg Calcium ★
1.0 mg Iron ★
6.0 mg Folic Acid

NUTRITIONAL ANALYSIS
amount per portion
143 kcals/597 kJ
16.6 g Carbohydrate
5.3 g Protein ★
6.6 g Fat ★★★
1.8 g Saturated Fat ★★★★
0.0 g Added Sugar ★★★★
3.8 g Fibre ★★
261 mg Salt ★★★
191 mg Calcium ★★★
2.4 mg Iron ★★
16 mg Folic Acid

Cream of Parsley Soup

With its piquant flavour and feathery green leaves, parsley is high in calcium, magnesium, sodium, iron and vitamins A, B and C.

SERVES 4
25 g (1 oz) polyunsaturated margarine
225 g (8 oz) floury potatoes, peeled and thinly sliced
1 onion, skinned and finely sliced
100 g (4 oz) fresh parsley, chopped
300 ml (½ pint) vegetable stock
300 ml (½ pint) semi-skimmed milk
salt and pepper, to taste
chopped fresh parsley, to garnish

1 Melt the margarine in a saucepan and cook the potatoes, onion and parsley for 5-10 minutes over a medium heat until the potatoes begin to soften, stirring constantly.
2 Add the stock, milk and seasoning and simmer for 30 minutes.
3 Cool slightly, then purée the soup in a blender or food processor until very smooth. Reheat and serve garnished with parsley.

NUTRITIONAL ANALYSIS
amount per portion
282kcals/1180 kJ
4.2 g Carbohydrate
7.4 g Protein ★★
26.3 g Fat ★
4.7 g Saturated Fat ★★
0.0 g Added Sugar ★★★★
2.3 g Fibre ★
375 mg Salt ★★★
75 mg Calcium ★★
1.4 mg Iron ★★
32 mg Folic Acid ★

Walnut Soup

Although this soup may sound unusual, it is quite delicious and full of flavour. The walnuts provide protein in the soup.

SERVES 4
1 garlic clove, skinned and crushed
175 g (6 oz) walnut halves
600 ml (1 pint) chicken stock
150 ml (¼ pint) Greek strained yogurt
salt and pepper, to taste
chopped walnuts and chives, to garnish

1 Work the garlic and walnuts in a blender or food processor until finely crushed. If using a blender, you may need to add a little stock to blend the walnuts. Very gradually pour in the stock and blend until smooth.
2 Pour the soup into a saucepan and bring to the boil, stirring continuously. Remove from the heat.
3 Stir in the yogurt, reserving about 60 ml (4 tbsp), and seasoning. Serve hot, garnished with a swirl of the remaining yogurt on top and sprinkled with a few walnuts and chives.

Chicken and Sweetcorn Chowder

If time is short, make a quick chicken chowder by using ready-cooked chicken, skinned, boned and cut into pieces. Simmer the chicken in 900 ml (1½ pints) stock with the vegetables and seasonings for 20 minutes. Drain, discarding the vegetables and seasonings and simmer the chicken pieces and stock with the sweetcorn for 5 minutes, then follow the recipe exactly as from step 4.

SERVES 6
1.6 kg (3½ lb) chicken
1 celery stick, trimmed and roughly chopped
1 parsley sprig
1 medium onion, skinned and roughly chopped
1 bay leaf
10 peppercorns
two 335 g (11.8 oz) cans sweetcorn, drained
6 hard-boiled eggs, chopped
45 ml (3 tbsp) chopped fresh parsley
salt and pepper, to taste
45 ml (3 tbsp) single cream

1 Place the chicken in a large saucepan with 1 litre (1¾ pints) water, the celery, parsley, onion, bay leaf and peppercorns. Bring to the boil, lower the heat and simmer gently for 1-1½ hours or until the chicken is completely tender.

2 When cooked, remove the chicken from the pan and cut the meat into large bite-size pieces. Discard the skin and bones.

3 Strain the chicken stock, return it to the pan and add the chicken flesh and sweetcorn and simmer for about 5 minutes.

4 Add the hard-boiled eggs to the soup with the chopped parsley and seasoning. Heat through gently, then pour into warmed individual bowls. Swirl cream into each portion and serve immediately.

NUTRITIONAL ANALYSIS
amount per portion
378 kcals/1581 kJ
19.2 g Carbohydrate
41.2 g Protein ★★★★
15.8 g Fat ★★
5.5 g Saturated Fat ★★
8.3 g Added Sugar ★★
7.4 g Fibre ★★
1334 mg Salt ★
83 mg Calcium ★★
3.7 mg Iron ★★★
60 mg Folic Acid ★★

Chicken Noodle Soup

The delicately scented fresh coriander leaves complements this satisfying Chinese-style soup.

NUTRITIONAL ANALYSIS
amount per portion
133 kcals/557 kJ
10 g Carbohydrate
16.7 g Protein ★★★
3.2 g Fat ★★★★
0.7 g Saturated Fat ★★★★
0.0 g Added Sugar ★★★★
1.6 g Fibre ★
848 mg Salt ★★
54 mg Calcium ★★
2.7 mg Iron ★★
13 mg Folic Acid

SERVES 4

2 chicken breasts, 100-175 g (4-6 oz) each, skinned, boned and cut into thin strips

900 ml (1½ pints) chicken stock

5 ml (1 tsp) mild curry powder

50 g (2 oz) Chinese egg noodles

3 spring onions, trimmed and chopped

30 ml (2 tbsp) chopped fresh coriander

salt and pepper, to taste

1 Place the chicken in a saucepan and add the stock. Bring to the boil, lower the heat, cover and simmer for 10 minutes or until the chicken is cooked.
2 Strain the chicken, reserving the cooking liquid. Return the chicken to the pan, add the curry powder and cook for 2-3 minutes over medium heat, stirring constantly so the curry powder coats all the chicken.
3 Gradually return the cooking liquid to the pan, then add the noodles, spring onions, coriander and seasoning. Simmer for 10 minutes or until the noodles are tender. Serve immediately.

Carrot Soup

This is a delicious soup, which can be served hot or chilled. If chilled, swirl a spoonful of yogurt on the top of each serving and sprinkle with chopped fresh mint.

NUTRITIONAL ANALYSIS
amount per portion
64 kcals/268 kJ
13.3 g Carbohydrate
2.9 g Protein
0.3 g Fat ★★★★
0.1 g Saturated Fat ★★★★
0.0 g Added Sugar ★★★★
3.6 g Fibre ★★
833 mg Salt ★★
99 mg Calcium ★★
1.4 mg Iron ★★
40 mg Folic Acid ★

SERVES 4

1 onion, skinned and finely chopped

450 g (1 lb) carrots, scrubbed and chopped

0.5 cm (¼ inch) piece fresh root ginger, peeled and crushed

5 cm (2 inch) piece cinnamon stick

750 ml (1¼ pints) chicken stock

200 ml (7 fl oz) fresh orange juice

finely grated rind of ½ orange

salt and pepper, to taste

60 ml (4 tbsp) thick set low-fat natural yogurt

orange rind, cut into matchstick strips, to garnish

1 Place the onion, carrots, ginger, cinnamon, stock, orange juice and rind and seasoning in a saucepan. Bring to the boil, lower the heat and simmer for 25 minutes.
2 Remove the cinnamon stick. Cool slightly, then purée the soup in a blender or food processor until smooth. Return the soup to a clean pan.
3 Beat together the yogurt and a little of the soup and stir, then return all the mixture to the soup. Heat through gently for 3-4 minutes but do not boil. Serve piping hot, garnished with orange rind.

Curried Potato and Apple Soup

Eating apples are used in this hearty, spiced soup. The curry powder may be adjusted to personal taste.

SERVES 4
25 g (1 oz) polyunsaturated margarine
4 medium old potatoes, peeled and diced
2 eating apples, peeled, cored and diced
10 ml (2 tsp) curry powder
1.1 litres (2 pints) vegetable stock or water
salt and pepper, to taste
150 ml (¼ pint) low-fat natural yogurt

1 Melt the margarine in a large saucepan and gently fry the potatoes and apples for about 10 minutes until lightly coloured, shaking the pan and stirring frequently.
2 Add the curry powder and fry gently for 1–2 minutes, stirring. Pour in the stock and bring to the boil. Season. Lower the heat, cover and simmer for 20–25 minutes or until the potatoes and apples are really soft.
3 Cool slightly, then sieve or purée the soup in a blender or food processor. Return the soup to a clean pan.
4 Stir the yogurt until smooth, then pour half into the soup. Heat through, stirring constantly, then taste and adjust the seasoning. Pour the hot soup into warmed individual bowls and swirl in the remaining yogurt. Serve immediately.

NUTRITIONAL ANALYSIS
amount per portion
217 kcals/908 kJ
38.5 g Carbohydrate
5.2 g Protein ★
5.9 g Fat ★★★
1.1 g Saturated Fat ★★★★
0.0 g Added Sugar ★★★★
4.2 g Fibre ★★
256 mg Salt ★★★
97 mg Calcium ★★
2.8 mg Iron ★★
23 mg Folic Acid

Chinese Cabbage and Prawn Soup

This is a clear soup full of vegetable goodness. The pale Chinese cabbage, also known as Chinese leaves, keeps very well in the bottom of the refrigerator.

SERVES 4
30 ml (2 tbsp) polyunsaturated oil
50 g (2 oz) French beans, trimmed and cut into 5 cm (2 inch) lengths
1 large carrot, scrubbed and cut into matchstick strips
1 small turnip, peeled and cut into matchstick strips
1.1 litres (2 pints) chicken stock
30 ml (2 tbsp) soy sauce, preferably naturally fermented shoyu
1.25 ml (¼ tsp) sweet chilli sauce
30 ml (2 tbsp) medium dry sherry
15 ml (1 tbsp) light muscovado sugar
175 g (6 oz) Chinese leaves, finely shredded
75 g (3 oz) peeled cooked prawns

1 Heat the oil in a saucepan and gently cook the beans, carrot and turnip for 5 minutes.
2 Add the stock, soy sauce, chilli sauce, sherry and sugar. Simmer for 15 minutes or until the vegetables are just tender.
3 Add the Chinese leaves and prawns and cook for 2-3 minutes until the leaves are tender but still crisp. Serve immediately.

NUTRITIONAL ANALYSIS
amount per portion
144 kcals/602 kJ
8.7 g Carbohydrate
7.6 g Protein ★★
8.1 g Fat ★★★
1.1 g Saturated Fat ★★★★
3.9 g Added Sugar ★★★
1.7 g Fibre ★
1509 mg Salt ★
137 mg Calcium ★★★
2.8 mg Iron ★★
49 mg Folic Acid ★

NUTRITIONAL ANALYSIS
amount per portion
31 kcals/131 kJ
4.4 g Carbohydrate
3.0 g Protein
0.4 g Fat ★★★★
0.1 g Saturated Fat ★★★★
0.0 g Added Sugar ★★★★
3.0 g Fibre ★★
680 mg Salt ★★
74 mg Calcium ★★
2.3 mg Iron ★★
26 mg Folic Acid ★

Iced Red Pepper Soup

Serve this iced soup as a refreshing start to a summer meal. Do not confuse the herb coriander with the spice of the same name. In this recipe, the fresh herb is used. Looking rather like frondy parsley, it is available at many supermarkets and also at continental and oriental specialist shops. Its flavour is highly aromatic, much stronger than parsley.

SERVES 4

60 ml (4 tbsp) chopped fresh coriander

225 g (8 oz) red peppers, seeded and sliced

1 medium onion, skinned and sliced

225 g (8 oz) ripe tomatoes, sliced

900 ml (1½ pints) vegetable or chicken stock

salt and pepper, to taste

1 To make coriander ice cubes, put the chopped coriander into an ice-cube tray, top up with water and freeze.

2 Place the peppers in a large saucepan with the onion, tomatoes and stock. Bring to the boil, lower the heat, cover and simmer for about 15 minutes or until the vegetables are tender. Drain, reserving the liquid.

3 Sieve the vegetables, or purée them in a blender or food processor, then sieve the purée to remove the tomato seeds.

4 Combine the reserved liquid and vegetable purée in a bowl with seasoning. Cool for 30 minutes, then chill for at least 2 hours before serving. Serve with coriander ice cubes.

Chilled Courgette Soup

The perfect start to a summer meal, this soup is enriched with blue Brie cheese. When buying courgettes, choose the smallest available – not longer than 15 cm (6 inches).

SERVES 4

25 g (1 oz) polyunsaturated margarine

450 g (1 lb) courgettes, trimmed and chopped

1 medium potato, peeled and diced

750 ml (1¼ pints) vegetable stock or water

5 ml (1 tsp) chopped fresh basil or 2.5 ml (½ tsp) dried

salt and pepper, to taste

100 g (4 oz) ripe pasteurised blue Brie

courgette slices and basil leaves, to garnish

1 Melt the margarine in a large heavy-based saucepan and gently fry the courgettes and potato, covered, for about 10 minutes until soft, shaking frequently.
2 Add the stock, basil and seasoning. Bring to the boil, stirring, then lower the heat and simmer for 20 minutes or until the vegetables are tender.
3 Remove the rind from the Brie and chop the cheese into small dice. Put into a blender or food processor, then pour in the soup. Purée until smooth. Transfer the soup to a bowl, cover and leave until cold. Chill.
4 To serve, whisk the soup vigorously to ensure an even consistency, then taste and adjust the seasoning. Pour into a chilled soup tureen or individual bowls and float the courgette slices and basil leaves on top.

NUTRITIONAL ANALYSIS
amount per portion
177 kcals/742 kJ
9.8 g Carbohydrate
7.7 g Protein ★ ★
12.2 g Fat ★ ★
5.3 g Saturated Fat ★ ★
0.0 g Added Sugar ★ ★ ★ ★
1.3 g Fibre
868 mg Salt ★ ★
72 mg Calcium ★ ★
1.2 mg Iron ★
45 mg Folic Acid ★

Iced Tzaziki Soup

This refreshing cucumber and yogurt soup is lightly flavoured with mint.

SERVES 4-6

1 medium cucumber, peeled

450 ml (¾ pint) low-fat natural yogurt

1 small garlic clove, skinned and crushed

30 ml (2 tbsp) chopped fresh mint

350 ml (12 fl oz) chicken stock

salt and pepper, to taste

mint leaves, to garnish

1 Quarter the cucumber lengthways and discard the seeds, using a teaspoon. Finely dice the cucumber, cutting 3 or 4 strips at a time.
2 Place the yogurt in a bowl and stir in cucumber, garlic and chopped mint.
3 Stir in the chicken stock and seasoning. Chill for 2-3 hours. Serve garnished with mint.

NUTRITIONAL ANALYSIS
amount per portion
72 kcals/301 kJ
9.1 g Carbohydrate
6.7 g Protein ★ ★
1.3 g Fat ★ ★ ★ ★
0.7 g Saturated Fat ★ ★ ★ ★
0.0 g Added Sugar ★ ★ ★ ★
0.4 g Fibre
572 mg Salt ★ ★
224 mg Calcium ★ ★ ★
0.7 mg Iron ★
17 mg Folic Acid

NUTRITIONAL ANALYSIS
amount per portion
159 kcals/663 kJ
23.7 g Carbohydrate
6.4 g Protein ★★
4.0 g Fat ★★★★
0.7 g Saturated Fat ★★★★
0.1 g Added Sugar ★★★★
7.1 g Fibre ★★
580 mg Salt ★★
92 mg Calcium ★★
3.2 mg Iron ★★
97 mg Folic Acid ★★

Vegetable and Bean Soup

Served with a sprinkling of grated cheese and slices of crusty bread, this soup is substantial enough to serve as a light meal.

SERVES 4
15 ml (1 tbsp) olive oil
1 onion, skinned and thinly sliced
1 garlic clove, skinned and crushed
8 tomatoes, chopped
45 ml (3 tbsp) tomato purée
600 ml (1 pint) vegetable or chicken stock
3 celery sticks, trimmed and finely chopped
2 potatoes, scrubbed and finely chopped
100 g (4 oz) green beans, trimmed and coarsely chopped
30 ml (2 tbsp) chopped fresh parsley
60 ml (4 tbsp) canned red kidney beans, drained and rinsed
salt and pepper, to taste
30 ml (2 tbsp) dry sherry (optional)

1 Heat the oil in a large saucepan and gently cook the onion for 3 minutes until soft but not brown.

2 Add the garlic, tomatoes, tomato purée and stock. Bring to the boil, lower the heat and simmer for 5 minutes, then add the celery, potatoes, green beans and parsley. Simmer for 10 minutes or until the vegetables are just tender.

3 Add the kidney beans, seasoning and sherry, if using. Heat through and serve.

Snacks

*Snacks often rely on using convenience foods or
'grabbing a sandwich'. In this chapter, however,
there are many healthy ideas to try instead. There are
snacks to nibble, such as toasted seeds or spiced
popcorn; or, when time permits, mouthwatering
morsels like sesame prawn toasts. Try the attractive
open sandwiches with their nutritious toppings or the
variations on the favourite jacket potato, full of
vitamin C and fibre.*

Open Sandwiches

Presentation is most important when preparing colourful open sandwiches – pay particular attention to arrangement of the food and garnishing.
Each makes 1 sandwich

1 NUTRITIONAL ANALYSIS
amount per portion
205 kcals/858 kJ
17.1 g Carbohydrate
14.4 g Protein ★★
9.3 g Fat ★★★
1.6 g Saturated Fat ★★★★
0.0 g Added Sugar ★★★★
1.5 g Fibre ★
2608 mg Salt
119 mg Calcium ★★
1.3 mg Iron ★
8 mg Folic Acid

2 NUTRITIONAL ANALYSIS
amount per portion
174 kcals/729 kJ
13.3 g Carbohydrate
10.0 g Protein ★★
9.4 g Fat ★★
2.4 g Saturated Fat ★★★
0.0 g Added Sugar ★★★★
1.9 g Fibre ★
677 mg Salt ★★
65 mg Calcium ★★
1.8 mg Iron ★★
33 mg Folic Acid ★

1 Prawns with Lemon and Coriander

Mix 10 ml (2 tsp) low-fat mayonnaise with a little chopped fresh coriander and spread it on crustless toast or dark rye bread. Cover with 50 g (2 oz) juicy prawns. Season to taste. Garnish with a twist of lemon and coriander.

2 Lumpfish Roe with Eggs

Lightly spread oblong wheat crackers or brown bread with polyunsaturated margarine and arrange a small bundle of fresh watercress or mustard and cress at one end. Fill the remainder with 5 ml (1 tsp) lumpfish roe topped with slices of hard-boiled egg.

3 Blue Brie, Bacon and Lamb's Lettuce

Lightly spread pumpernickel bread with polyunsaturated margarine. Arrange lamb's lettuce leaves along one long edge. Cover the bread with very thin slices of pasteurised blue Brie cheese, overlapping them on to the lettuce. Top the cheese with 1 slice of crisp, grilled back bacon.

4 Smoked Salmon on Pumpernickel

Spread pumpernickel bread with 25 g (1 oz) low-fat soft cheese mixed with horseradish sauce to taste. Cover with sliced smoked salmon, dill sprigs or celery leaves and lemon wedges.

5 Roast Beef and Mustard Mayonnaise

Spread lightly toasted, crustless bread with Dijon mustard and low-fat mayonnaise. Top with slices of rare roast beef and garnish with fine onion rings and bows of fresh chive stalks.

6 Hummus with Sesame

Spread crunchy crispbreads with hummus. Sprinkle liberally with toasted sesame seeds and garnish with olives and parsley.

7 Smoked Chicken with Orange

Stamp out rounds of light rye bread. Mix together equal quantities of low-fat natural yogurt and a low-fat soft cheese with herbs; spread thinly on the bread rounds. Top with thin slices of smoked chicken, orange segments and shreds of spring onion.

3 NUTRITIONAL ANALYSIS	4 NUTRITIONAL ANALYSIS	5 NUTRITIONAL ANALYSIS	6 NUTRITIONAL ANALYSIS	7 NUTRITIONAL ANALYSIS
amount per portion	amount per portion	amount per portion	amount per portion	amount per portion
277 kcals/1158 kJ	126 kcals/528 kJ	186 kcals/777 kJ	91 kcals/379 kJ	128 kcals/534 kJ
12.6 g Carbohydrate	13.0 g Carbohydrate	18.7 g Carbohydrate	9.1 g Carbohydrate	12.9 g Carbohydrate
16.2 g Protein ★★★	11.3 g Protein ★★	18.1 g Protein ★★★	2.7 g Protein	13.0 g Protein ★★
18.3 g Fat ★★	3.6 g Fat ★★★★	4.8 g Fat ★★★	5.3 g Fat ★★★	3.1 g Fat ★★★★
9.1 g Saturated Fat ★★	1.5 g Saturated Fat ★★★★	1.3 g Saturated Fat ★★★★	0.5 g Saturated Fat ★★★★	1.0 g Saturated Fat ★★★★
0.0 g Added Sugar ★★★★	0.0 g Added Sugar ★★★★	0.3 g Added Sugar ★★★★	0.1 g Added Sugar ★★★★	0.0 g Added Sugar ★★★★
3.5 g Fibre ★★	3.6 g Fibre ★★	1.5 g Fibre	1.9 g Fibre ★	1.7 g Fibre ★
2094 mg Salt	1715 mg Salt	615 mg Salt ★★	855 mg Salt ★★	1013 mg Salt ★★
91 mg Calcium ★★	37 mg Calcium ★	50 mg Calcium ★	68 mg Calcium ★★	44 mg Calcium ★
1.2 mg Iron ★	0.9 mg Iron ★	2.2 mg Iron ★★	1.4 mg Iron ★★	1.0 mg Iron ★
38 mg Folic Acid ★	19 mg Folic Acid	17 mg Folic Acid	13 mg Folic Acid	15 mg Folic Acid

Pan Bagna

If anchovy fillets are not to hand, substitute well drained canned tuna fish or pink or red salmon.

SERVES 4
30 ml (2 tbsp) olive oil
pepper, to taste
1 small garlic clove, skinned and crushed
100 g (4 oz) button mushrooms, sliced
50 g (2 oz) can anchovy fillets, well drained and chopped
50 g (2 oz) stoned black olives, chopped
30 ml (2 tbsp) chopped gherkins
15 ml (1 tbsp) capers, well drained
1 large wholemeal French stick
1 hard-boiled egg, thinly sliced
225 g (8 oz) tomatoes, thinly sliced
lettuce leaves, to garnish

NUTRITIONAL ANALYSIS
amount per portion
379 kcals/1582 kJ
49.1 g Carbohydrate
15.3 g Protein ★★★
14.9 g Fat ★★
2.7 g Saturated Fat ★★★
0.1 g Added Sugar ★★★★
10.7 g Fibre ★★★
3119 mg Salt
109 mg Calcium ★★
4.3 mg Iron ★★★
74 mg Folic Acid ★★

1 Place the olive oil in a small bowl and add pepper and the garlic. Add the mushrooms and toss until well coated. Mix in the anchovies, olives, gherkins and capers.

2 Cut the French stick into quarters, then split each piece almost in half and open out flat. Place the egg and tomato slices on the base of each piece of bread. Spread the mushroom mixture on each top half.

3 Fold the bread over to make 4 long sandwiches, pressing down well. Wrap each tightly in foil. Leave for 1 hour or overnight. Unwrap and cut each sandwich in half. Serve garnished with lettuce leaves.

NUTRITIONAL ANALYSIS
amount per portion
179 kcals/749 kJ
2.0 g Carbohydrate
10.8 g Protein ★★
14.3 g Fat ★★
4.8 g Saturated Fat ★★
0.0 g Added Sugar ★★★★
0.2 g Fibre
656 mg Salt ★★
147 mg Calcium ★★★
1.3 mg Iron ★★
27 mg Folic Acid ★

Courgette and Cheese Scramble

Ring the changes from the traditional scrambled egg on toast; try this version with courgettes and cheese.

SERVES 4

25 g (1 oz) polyunsaturated margarine

175 g (6 oz) courgettes, trimmed and coarsely grated

4 eggs, beaten

50 g (2 oz) Edam cheese, grated

60 ml (4 tbsp) semi-skimmed milk

salt and pepper, to taste

chopped fresh parsley, to garnish

1 Melt the margarine in a saucepan and gently cook the courgettes for about 3 minutes until soft.

2 Mix together the remaining ingredients. Add to the pan and cook gently for 5-7 minutes, stirring constantly until the mixture is thick but still creamy. Serve immediately, garnished with parsley, with wholemeal toast.

NUTRITIONAL ANALYSIS
amount per portion
268 kcals/1119 kJ
49.3 g Carbohydrate
10.8 g Protein ★★
4.5 g Fat ★★★★
2.7 g Saturated Fat ★★★
0.0 g Added Sugar ★★★★
6.2 g Fibre ★★
369 mg Salt ★★★
148 mg Calcium ★★★
2.0 mg Iron ★★
49 mg Folic Acid ★

Twice-Baked Potatoes with Herbs

These potatoes may be baked and filled ahead, then reheated when required. The herbs may be varied according to taste.

SERVES 4

4 large potatoes, scrubbed

30 ml (2 tbsp) chopped fresh mixed herbs such as chives, parsley, marjoram and basil

3 spring onions, trimmed and chopped

100 g (4 oz) low-fat soft cheese

2 tomatoes, finely chopped

salt and pepper, to taste

50 g (2 oz) low-fat Cheddar cheese, grated

herb sprigs, to garnish

1 Prick the potatoes all over with a fork. Bake at 200°C (400°F) mark 6 for about 1 hour or until tender.

2 Remove the potatoes from the oven and leave until cool enough to handle. Cut a thin slice horizontally from the top of each potato, then carefully scoop out most of the potato into a bowl, leaving shells about 0.5 cm (¼ inch) thick.

3 Mix the potato with the herbs, spring onions, soft cheese, tomatoes and seasoning. Spoon the mixture back into the potato shells and place in a shallow ovenproof dish.

4 Sprinkle the filling with the grated cheese. Return to the oven and bake for 25 minutes or until lightly golden. Garnish with herb sprigs and serve at once.

Baked Potato Skins with Spicy Tomato Sauce

Use the scooped out potato from the skins in another dish, such as Potato Scones (page 59).

NUTRITIONAL ANALYSIS
amount per portion
163 kcals/682 kJ
19.9 g Carbohydrate
3.7 g Protein ★
8.2 g Fat ★★★
1.5 g Saturated Fat ★★★★
0.0 g Added Sugar ★★★★
3.6 g Fibre ★★
314 mg Salt ★★★
51 mg Calcium ★★
2.3 mg Iron ★★
48 mg Folic Acid ★

SERVES 4

4 large baking potatoes, about 225 g (8 oz) each, scrubbed

400 g (14 oz) can tomatoes or 450 g (1 lb) fresh tomatoes

15 ml (1 tbsp) tomato purée

1 onion, skinned and finely chopped

1 garlic clove, skinned and crushed

30 ml (2 tbsp) chopped fresh mixed herbs

salt and pepper, to taste

2.5 ml (½ tsp) dried oregano

few drops of Tabasco sauce

40 g (1½ oz) polyunsaturated margarine, melted

1 Prick the potatoes all over with a fork. Bake at 200°C (400°F) mark 6 for about 1 hour or until just tender.

2 Meanwhile, combine all the remaining ingredients, except the margarine, in a saucepan. Cover and simmer for 10 minutes, then remove the lid and cook until reduced to a thick sauce.

3 Remove the potatoes from the oven and leave until cool enough to handle. Cut into quarters lengthways, then cut each quarter in half crossways. Scoop the potato from the skins, leaving a layer of potato about 0.3 cm (⅛ inch) thick on the skins. Brush the skins on both sides with the margarine and arrange them in a single layer on a baking sheet.

4 Increase the oven temperature to 240°C (475°F) mark 9 and bake the potato skins for 12-15 minutes or until crisp and just beginning to brown. Serve hot, with the sauce.

NUTRITIONAL ANALYSIS
amount per portion
222 kcals/928 kJ
14.6 g Carbohydrate
12.5 g Protein ★★
13.1 g Fat ★★
3.5 g Saturated Fat ★★★
0.0 g Added Sugar ★★★★
3.1 g Fibre ★★
321 mg Salt ★★★
73 mg Calcium ★★
2.5 mg Iron ★★
44 mg Folic Acid ★

Spanish Omelette

It is important to include eggs, in moderation, in our diets as they contain high quality protein, fat, iron and vitamins A, B and D.

SERVES 4
15 ml (1 tbsp) olive oil
50 g (2 oz) mushrooms, sliced
1 small red pepper, seeded and chopped
30 ml (2 tbsp) frozen peas
1 large potato, scrubbed and cut into 1 cm (½ inch) cubes
1 large onion, skinned and coarsely chopped
salt and pepper, to taste
6 eggs, lightly beaten
chopped fresh herbs, to garnish

1 Gently heat the oil in a medium non-stick frying pan and fry the mushrooms, pepper, peas, potato and onion with seasoning for 5 minutes, stirring occasionally.
2 Add 15 ml (1 tbsp) water to the pan, cover and cook for 10-15 minutes until the potato is tender. Remove the lid and increase the heat to evaporate any liquid.
3 Quickly stir in the eggs. Cook for 5 minutes, shaking the pan occasionally to prevent sticking. If liked, place under a hot grill to brown the top. Serve sprinkled with fresh herbs.

NUTRITIONAL ANALYSIS
amount per portion
175 kcals/730 kJ
14.7 g Carbohydrate
4.4 g Protein ★
11.1 g Fat ★★
2.2 g Saturated Fat ★★★
0.0 g Added Sugar ★★★★
2.7 g Fibre ★
95 mg Salt ★★★★
73 mg Calcium ★★
1.4 mg Iron ★★
56 mg Folic Acid ★★

Pesto-Stuffed Tomatoes

Basil and pine nuts are the classic ingredients of an Italian pesto sauce. Pine nuts have a delicate flavour reminiscent of almonds and pine. They have a high protein content, are rich in fat and low in carbohydrate.

SERVES 4
50 g (2 oz) burghul wheat
4 beefsteak tomatoes
30 ml (2 tbsp) chopped fresh basil
1 garlic clove, skinned and crushed
15 ml (1 tbsp) pine nuts
15 ml (1 tbsp) freshly grated Parmesan cheese
30 ml (2 tbsp) olive oil
pepper, to taste
basil leaves, to garnish

1 Put the burghul into a bowl and cover generously with boiling water. Leave to soak for 15 minutes.
2 Meanwhile, cut a slice from the base of each tomato. Scoop out the flesh and put in a sieve to remove the excess moisture, then finely chop. Set the tomato shells aside.
3 Place the basil, garlic, pine nuts and Parmesan cheese in a mortar or blender. Pound or blend until a fine paste is formed, then add the oil a little at a time.
4 Drain the burghul, pressing out excess water. Add the basil sauce, tomato flesh and pepper, mixing well. Pile into the tomato shells. Serve garnished with basil leaves.

Spiced Popcorn

Children love to watch the magic of making popcorn – a few grains turning into a panful of popcorn.
Choose one of the mixes to flavour the popcorn.

NUTRITIONAL ANALYSIS
amount per portion
138 kcals/579 kJ
16.8 g Carbohydrate
3.1 g Protein ★
7.4 g Fat ★★★
0.9 g Saturated Fat ★★★★
0.0 g Added Sugar ★★★★
2.8 g Fibre ★
192 mg Salt ★★★★
138 mg Calcium ★★★
9.6 mg Iron ★★★★
6.0 mg Folic Acid

SERVES 4

15 ml (1 tbsp) polyunsaturated oil

50 g (2 oz) popping corn

CURRY MIX

5 ml (1 tsp) ground turmeric

5 ml (1 tsp) ground ginger

10 ml (2 tsp) ground coriander

2.5 ml (½ tsp) cayenne pepper

5 ml (1 tsp) ground fenugreek

CHILLI MIX

5 ml (1 tsp) chilli powder

5 ml (1 tsp) garlic powder

5 ml (1 tsp) ground cloves

7.5 ml (1½ tsp) paprika

5 ml (1 tsp) ground cumin

SESAME MIX

15 ml (1 tbsp) sesame seeds, toasted

2.5 ml (½ tsp) ground mace

5 ml (1 tsp) ground cinnamon

2.5 ml (½ tsp) ground cloves

1 Make one of the spice mixtures. Mix together all the spices for the Curry mix or the Chilli mix. For the Sesame mix, crush the sesame seeds to a powder in a pestle and mortar; mix with the remaining spices. Set aside the mix.
2 To prepare the popcorn, heat the oil in a 3.4 litre (6 pint) saucepan with a tight-fitting lid. Add 3 kernels of the corn and heat with the lid on until the kernels pop.
3 Remove the pan from the heat and add the remaining corn. Cook, covered, over a medium heat for 2 minutes, shaking the pan, until the corn starts to pop. Reduce the heat slightly and continue to cook, still covered, shaking the pan, until the popping stops.
4 Remove from the heat and sprinkle the popcorn with one of mixes. Replace the lid and shake vigorously to coat the popcorn. Serve hot.

NUTRITIONAL ANALYSIS
amount per portion
51 kcals/212 kJ
5.1 g Carbohydrate
4.4 g Protein ★
1.6 g Fat ★★★★
0.2 g Saturated Fat ★★★★
0.0 g Added Sugar ★★★★
0.8 g Fibre
716 mg Salt ★★
37 mg Calcium ★
0.6 mg Iron
5.0 mg Folic Acid

Sesame Prawn Toasts

These mouthwatering Chinese snacks can also be served as a starter or as canapés for a cocktail party.

MAKES 16
2 spring onions, trimmed and finely chopped
1 cm (½ inch) piece fresh root ginger, peeled and grated
225 g (8 oz) peeled cooked prawns
25 g (1 oz) fresh wholemeal breadcrumbs
1 egg white, size 6
15 ml (1 tbsp) cornflour
1 garlic clove, skinned and crushed
30 ml (2 tbsp) lemon or lime juice
pepper, to taste
4 thin slices wholemeal bread
10 ml (2 tsp) polyunsaturated oil, for brushing
15 g (½ oz) sesame seeds

1 Purée the spring onions, ginger, prawns, breadcrumbs, egg white, cornflour, garlic and lemon juice in a blender or food processor until smooth. Season.
2 Trim the crusts from the bread and spread with the prawn mixture. Brush lightly with the oil and sprinkle with the sesame seeds. Place the toasts on a baking sheet.
3 Bake at 230°C (450°F) mark 8 for about 10 minutes until golden brown. Cut each slice into 4 triangles. Serve warm with soy sauce, preferably naturally fermented shoyu, for dipping.

NUTRITIONAL ANALYSIS
amount per portion
70 kcals/292 kJ
0.9 g Carbohydrate
5.8 g Protein ★
4.8 g Fat ★★★
0.7 g Saturated Fat ★★★★
0.1 g Added Sugar ★★★★
1.5 g Fibre
2416 mg Salt
49 mg Calcium ★
0.8 mg Iron ★
5.0 mg Folic Acid

Tapenade

This is a delicious, pungent mixture from Provence. In France, it is served like a pâté, spread on slices of toasted French bread with salad. It can also be accompanied with halved, hard-boiled eggs. Cook the eggs while preparing the Tapenade.

SERVES 6
175 g (6 oz) stoned black olives
50 g (1¾ oz) can anchovy fillets, drained
1 small garlic clove, skinned and crushed
99 g (3½ oz) can tuna in brine, drained
15 ml (1 tbsp) lemon juice
15 ml (1 tbsp) drained capers
5 ml (1 tsp) mustard powder
pepper, to taste
30 ml (2 tbsp) low-fat natural yogurt

1 Purée all the ingredients in a blender or food processor until smooth. Transfer to a small bowl.
2 Tapenade will keep in the refrigerator, covered, for up to 1 week.

Aubergine Dip

Ideal vegetables for dipping are celery, carrots and courgettes, cut into sticks. Mushrooms and florets of cauliflower or broccoli are also good.

SERVES 4

2 large aubergines, total weight about 700 g (1½ lb)

2 garlic cloves, skinned and crushed

10 ml (2 tsp) ground cumin

150 ml (¼ pint) low-fat natural yogurt

10 ml (2 tsp) ground coriander

30 ml (2 tbsp) tahini paste

about 30 ml (2 tbsp) lemon juice

salt and pepper, to taste

crudités, to serve

1 Prick the aubergines with a fork and place in a baking dish. Bake at 200°C (400°F) mark 6 for 1 hour or until soft. Leave until cool enough to handle.
2 Roughly chop the aubergines. Purée with the remaining ingredients in a blender or food processor until smooth. Season and add a little more lemon juice if necessary.
3 Turn the mixture into a serving bowl and chill. Serve as a dip with a selection of fresh vegetables.

NUTRITIONAL ANALYSIS
amount per portion
137 kcals/574 kJ
15.2 g Carbohydrate
8.6 g Protein ★★
5.3 g Fat ★★★
1.2 g Saturated Fat ★★★★
0.0 g Added Sugar ★★★★
5.0 g Fibre ★★
261 mg Salt ★★★
309 mg Calcium ★★★★
4.2 mg Iron ★★★
38 mg Folic Acid ★

Toasted Seeds

A healthy, high fibre snack as sunflower and pumpkin seeds are rich in proteins and minerals.

SERVES 4

45 ml (3 tbsp) pumpkin seeds

45 ml (3 tbsp) sunflower seeds

1 garlic clove, skinned and crushed

15 ml (1 tbsp) soy sauce, preferably naturally fermented shoyu

1 Dry-fry the pumpkin and sunflower seeds in a large saucepan over a medium heat for about 2 minutes, stirring constantly, until the seeds pop and 'jump' and colour lightly.
2 Add the garlic and soy sauce. Lower the heat and cook for 1 minute, stirring constantly, until thoroughly combined. Turn into a small serving bowl and serve warm or cold.
Variations can be made by mixing other spices with the cooked seeds.
SPICY TOASTED SEEDS
Stir in 1.25 ml (¼ tsp) chilli powder and 2.5 ml (½ tsp) ground cumin and cook over low heat for 1 minute, stirring constantly.
PAPRIKA TOASTED SEEDS
Stir in 5 ml (1 tsp) paprika and a large pinch of cayenne pepper and cook over low heat for 1 minute, stirring constantly.

NUTRITIONAL ANALYSIS
amount per portion
134 kcals/561 kJ
4.0 g Carbohydrate
5.6 g Protein ★
10.8 g Fat ★★
0.4 g Saturated Fat ★★★★
0.0 g Added Sugar ★★★★
0.7 g Fibre
7.0 mg Salt ★★★★
21 mg Calcium
2.6 mg Iron ★★
25 mg Folic Acid

NUTRITIONAL ANALYSIS
amount per portion
477 kcals/1995 kJ
45.3 g Carbohydrate
22.5 g Protein ★★★
24.6 g Fat ★
7.1 g Saturated Fat ★★
0.0 g Added Sugar ★★★★
6.7 g Fibre ★★
1782 mg Salt
232 mg Calcium ★★★
4.6 mg Iron ★★★
88 mg Folic Acid ★★

Quick Pizza

This colourful pizza is speedier to prepare as the base is made using a non-yeast dough.

SERVES 4

15 ml (1 tbsp) polyunsaturated oil

1 large onion, skinned and chopped

1 red pepper, seeded and chopped

1 green pepper, seeded and chopped

45 ml (3 tbsp) tomato purée

225 g (8 oz) can tomatoes

10 ml (2 tsp) chopped fresh basil or 5 ml (1 tsp) dried

pepper, to taste

225 g (8 oz) plain wholemeal flour

5 ml (1 tsp) baking powder

pinch of salt

50 g (2 oz) polyunsaturated margarine

1 egg, beaten

60 ml (4 tbsp) semi-skimmed milk

99 g (3½ oz) can tuna fish in brine, drained and flaked

40 g (1¾ oz) anchovy fillets, drained

100 g (4 oz) mozzarella cheese, grated

few black olives (optional)

1 Heat the oil in a saucepan and cook the onion and peppers over a low heat for about 5 minutes until soft. Stir in the tomato purée, canned tomatoes with juice, basil and pepper. Cook over a high heat for about 10 minutes until thickened. Cool.

2 Lightly grease a 32×22 cm (12½×8½ inch) baking sheet. Combine the flour, baking powder and salt in a bowl and rub in the margarine until the mixture resembles fine breadcrumbs. Bind to a soft dough with the egg and milk. Turn out on to a floured surface and knead until smooth. Roll out the dough to form a rectangle to fit the baking sheet. Lift on to the baking sheet.

3 Spread the tomato mixture over the pizza base to within 0.5 cm (¼ inch) of the edge. Arrange the tuna fish and anchovies on top and sprinkle with the cheese and olives. Bake at 200°C (400°F) mark 6 for 20-25 minutes until golden. Serve with a mixed salad.

Chicken Tacos

These spicy Mexican tacos are eaten with the fingers. Taco shells are available in most larger supermarkets.

NUTRITIONAL ANALYSIS
amount per portion
226 kcals/944 kJ
7.5 g Carbohydrate
23.4 g Protein ★★★
11.6 g Fat ★★
4.6 g Saturated Fat ★★
0.0 g Added Sugar ★★★★
1.8 g Fibre ★
441 mg Salt ★★★
126 mg Calcium ★★★
1.2 mg Iron ★
30 mg Folic Acid ★

SERVES 6

6 Mexican taco shells

15 g (½ oz) polyunsaturated margarine

1 medium onion, skinned and chopped

1 garlic clove, skinned and crushed

450 g (1 lb) cooked chicken, diced

4 tomatoes, skinned and chopped

30 ml (2 tbsp) chopped fresh coriander

salt and pepper, to taste

shredded lettuce

75 g (3 oz) Cheddar cheese, grated

Tabasco sauce

1 Put the taco shells in the oven to warm according to the instructions on the packet.
2 To make the filling, melt the margarine in a frying pan and fry the onion and garlic until soft but not coloured. Stir in the chicken, half the tomatoes, the coriander and seasoning. Cover and heat through.
3 Spoon 15-30 ml (1-2 tbsp) filling into each shell. Add a little lettuce, the remaining tomatoes and the cheese with a few drops of Tabasco sauce; serve the filled tacos immediately.

Potato Scones

Potatoes are best boiled in their skins, and peeled after they are cooked, because the goodness – vitamin C and minerals – lies just below the skin. Serve these delicious potato scones with cheese or no-added-sugar preserves.

NUTRITIONAL ANALYSIS
amount per portion
111 kcals/462 kJ
19.9 g Carbohydrate
2.8 g Protein
2.9 g Fat ★★★★
0.5 g Saturated Fat ★★★★
0.0 g Added Sugar ★★★★
2.3 g Fibre ★
74 mg Salt ★★★★
9.0 mg Calcium
0.8 mg Iron ★
15 mg Folic Acid

MAKES 8

450 g (1 lb) potatoes, scrubbed

25 g (1 oz) polyunsaturated margarine

salt and pepper, to taste

100 g (4 oz) self-raising wholemeal flour

1 Lightly grease a baking sheet. Cook the potatoes in a saucepan containing a small amount of boiling water for about 20 minutes until soft. Drain well and leave until cool enough to handle, then peel.
2 Mash the potatoes well with the margarine and seasoning. Beat in the flour to make a soft dough. Roll or pat out to an 18 cm (7 inch) round on a lightly floured surface. Place on the prepared baking sheet and mark into 8 wedges.
3 Bake at 220°C (425°F) mark 7 for 25-30 minutes until risen and a crisp golden brown. Serve warm, split and spread with polyunsaturated margarine.

NUTRITIONAL ANALYSIS
amount per portion
148 kcals/618 kJ
0.8 g Carbohydrate
15.3 g Protein ★★★
9.3 g Fat ★★★
3.3 g Saturated Fat ★★★
0.0 g Added Sugar ★★★★
0.0 g Fibre
1430 mg Salt ★
89 mg Calcium ★★
1.3 mg Iron ★
17 mg Folic Acid

Eggs Baked with Smoked Haddock

Here the fish is kept especially moist by the addition of some of the cooking juices.

SERVES 6
225 g (8 oz) smoked haddock fillet
100 ml (4 fl oz) semi-skimmed milk
1 bay leaf
pepper, to taste
polyunsaturated margarine, for greasing
6 eggs
25 g (1 oz) Cheddar cheese, grated

1 Place the haddock in a medium saucepan with the milk, bay leaf and pepper. Cover and simmer for about 12 minutes until the fish begins to flake.
2 Flake the fish, discarding the skin and bones. Divide the flesh between 6 individual greased ramekin dishes.
3 Boil the cooking liquor until reduced to about 60 ml (4 tbsp), then spoon into the ramekins. Carefully break an egg into each dish and top with the grated cheese.
4 Bake at 170°C (325°F) mark 3 for about 12 minutes or until the eggs are set. Serve immediately with fingers of toast.

Light Meals

*Quiches, pasta and vegetable dishes provide
refreshing new ideas for light meals. Many expectant
mothers only feel like eating lighter meals throughout
their entire pregnancy, so they need to be varied to
provide a range of different nutrients. In this chapter
you'll find a wide selection of delicous, easy-to-
prepare dishes that fit the bill perfectly.*

NUTRITIONAL ANALYSIS
amount per portion
223 kcals/930 kJ
3.4 g Carbohydrate
16.6 g Protein ★★★
16.0 g Fat ★★
5.5 g Saturated Fat ★★
0.0 g Added Sugar ★★★★
1.8 g Fibre ★
551 mg Salt ★★
163 mg Calcium ★★★
2.9 mg Iron ★★
48 mg Folic Acid ★

Eggs in Sauce Verte

Eggs are the original convenience food when it comes to quick, light, satisfying meals. Here they are made to look and taste particularly delicious by the addition of a glistening green sauce.

SERVES 2

large handful watercress sprigs, coarse stalks removed

1 medium leek, washed, trimmed and sliced

pinch of ground coriander

knob of polyunsaturated margarine

salt and pepper, to taste

4 eggs

15 ml (1 tbsp) Greek strained yogurt or fromage blanc

freshly grated Parmesan cheese

watercress sprigs, to garnish

---

1 Put the watercress, reserving a few sprigs for garnish, in a saucepan with the leek, coriander, margarine, seasoning and 60 ml (4 tbsp) water. Cover and cook until the watercress has softened.
2 Meanwhile boil the eggs in boiling water for 9 minutes. Remove the shells under cold water.
3 Purée the watercress mixture in a blender or food processor until smooth. Stir in the yogurt.
4 Serve the eggs in warmed dishes with the sauce, sprinkled with Parmesan and garnished with the reserved watercress sprigs. Accompany with crusty bread.

Curried Eggs

Garam masala, meaning 'hot spices', is a mixture of ground spices. It usually includes cardamom, cinnamon, cloves and black pepper.

SERVES 4	
30 ml (2 tbsp) polyunsaturated oil	*225 g (8 oz) can tomatoes*
1 medium onion, skinned and chopped	*15 ml (1 tbsp) tomato purée*
1 medium cooking apple, peeled, cored and chopped	*2.5 ml (½ tsp) chilli powder*
10 ml (2 tsp) garam masala	*salt and pepper, to taste*
300 ml (½ pint) vegetable stock or water	*300 ml (½ pint) low-fat natural yogurt*
	4 eggs, hard-boiled

1 Heat the oil in a large, heavy-based saucepan and gently fry the onion, apple and garam masala for about 5 minutes until soft, stirring frequently.
2 Pour in the stock and tomatoes and bring to the boil, stirring to break up the tomatoes as much as possible. Stir in the tomato purée with the chilli powder and seasoning. Lower the heat and simmer, uncovered, for 20 minutes to allow the flavours to develop.
3 Cool slightly, then purée the sauce and 150 ml (¼ pint) of the yogurt in a blender or food processor until smooth. Return to the rinsed-out pan.
4 Cut the eggs in half lengthways. Add them to the sauce, cut side up, then simmer very gently for 10 minutes. Taste the sauce and adjust the seasoning if necessary. Serve hot, with the remaining yogurt drizzled over the top, with boiled rice and a little mango chutney.

NUTRITIONAL ANALYSIS
amount per portion
225 kcals/942 kJ
12.3 g Carbohydrate
12 g Protein ★ ★
14.7 g Fat ★ ★
3.5 g Saturated Fat ★ ★ ★
0.0 g Added Sugar ★ ★ ★ ★
2.2 g Fibre ★
437 mg Salt ★ ★ ★
198 mg Calcium ★ ★ ★
4.0 mg Iron ★ ★ ★
41 mg Folic Acid ★

Chilled Ratatouille

Serve with French bread to complete this light meal. Versatile ratatouille, from Provence, also makes a tempting starter or accompaniment to fish or meat dishes.

SERVES 6	
350 g (12 oz) aubergine, trimmed	*1 green pepper, seeded and sliced*
salt and pepper, to taste	*100 g (4 oz) button mushrooms*
30 ml (2 tbsp) polyunsaturated oil	*150 ml (¼ pint) chicken stock*
450 g (1 lb) courgettes, trimmed and sliced	*30 ml (2 tbsp) tomato purée*
225 g (8 oz) leeks, washed, trimmed and sliced	*15 ml (1 tbsp) chopped fresh rosemary or 2.5 ml (½ tsp) dried*
450 g (1 lb) tomatoes, chopped	*chopped fresh herbs, to garnish*

1 Cut the aubergine into large bite-sized pieces. Put the aubergine pieces in a colander or sieve, sprinkle liberally with salt and set aside to drain for 30 minutes.
2 Rinse the aubergine under cold running water and pat dry with absorbent kitchen paper.
3 Heat the oil in a large frying pan and fry the aubergine and courgettes over high heat for 2-3 minutes, turning frequently. Stir in the remaining vegetables with the chicken stock, tomato purée, rosemary and seasoning.
4 Bring to the boil, lower the heat, cover and simmer for 8-10 minutes. The vegetables should be just tender with a hint of crispness, not mushy. Adjust the seasoning and pour into a bowl to cool for 30 minutes. Chill well for at least 4 hours.
5 Taste and adjust the seasoning, then transfer the ratatouille to a large serving bowl or individual dishes. Serve chilled, sprinkled with chopped herbs.

NUTRITIONAL ANALYSIS
amount per portion
99 kcals/414 kJ
9.5 g Carbohydrate
3.8 g Protein ★
5.3 g Fat ★ ★ ★
0.8 g Saturated Fat ★ ★ ★ ★
0.0 g Added Sugar ★ ★ ★ ★
4.9 g Fibre ★ ★
121 mg Salt ★ ★ ★ ★
59 mg Calcium ★ ★
2.0 mg Iron ★ ★
64 mg Folic Acid ★ ★

Pepper and Onion Flan

The warm, slightly bitter taste of the spice cumin has been used to enhance the flavour of this savoury vegetable flan.

	NUTRITIONAL ANALYSIS

NUTRITIONAL ANALYSIS

amount per portion

484 kcals/2022 kJ

47.3 g Carbohydrate

12.9 g Protein
★★

28.3 g Fat
★

9.5 g Saturated Fat
★★

0.0 g Added Sugar
★★★★

2.9 g Fibre
★

811 mg Salt
★★

306 mg Calcium
★★★★

2.1 mg Iron
★★

33 mg Folic Acid
★

SERVES 4

175 g (6 oz) plain wholemeal flour

pinch of salt

100 g (4 oz) polyunsaturated margarine

2 onions, skinned and thinly sliced

1 red pepper, seeded and sliced

30 ml (2 tbsp) plain white flour

5 ml (1 tsp) ground cumin

150 ml (¼ pint) semi-skimmed milk

150 ml (¼ pint) low-fat natural yogurt

2 egg yolks

30 ml (2 tbsp) freshly grated Parmesan cheese

1 To make the pastry, place the flour and salt into a bowl and rub in 75 g (3 oz) of the margarine until the mixture resembles fine breadcrumbs. Add sufficient cold water to form a dough. Knead until smooth.

2 Roll out the dough on a lightly floured surface and use to line a 20.5 cm (8 inch) plain flan ring placed on a baking sheet. Chill for 15-20 minutes.

3 Line with foil and baking beans. Bake blind at 200°C (400°F) mark 6 for 10-15 minutes until set but not browned.

4 Heat the remaining margarine in a frying pan and fry the onions and pepper, reserving a few slices for garnish, for 4-5 minutes. Remove with a slotted spoon and put into the flan case.

5 Stir the white flour and cumin into the pan. Cook for 2 minutes before adding the milk and yogurt. Bring to the boil, stirring briskly, simmer for 2-3 minutes. Beat in the egg yolks.

6 Pour over the onion and pepper and sprinkle with the Parmesan. Reduce the oven temperature to 190°C (375°F) mark 5 and bake for 35-40 minutes. Serve hot, garnished with the reserved pepper slices.

Open Sandwiches (PAGE 50); *Tapenade* (PAGE 56)

Cheese Tarts

In the filling for these tarts, choose red pepper, chives or olives for flavouring.

NUTRITIONAL ANALYSIS
amount per portion
226 kcals/947 kJ
20 g Carbohydrate
7.2 g Protein ★★
13.7 g Fat ★★
3.2 g Saturated Fat ★★★
0.0 g Added Sugar ★★★★
1.8 g Fibre ★
482 mg Salt ★★★
72 mg Calcium ★★
1.2 mg Iron ★
19 mg Folic Acid

MAKES 4

50 g (2 oz) plain wholemeal flour

50 g (2 oz) plain white flour

salt and pepper, to taste

50 g (2 oz) polyusaturated margarine

50 g (2 oz) low-fat soft cheese

1 egg, separated

100 ml (4 fl oz) semi-skimmed milk

one of the following flavourings:
1 small red pepper, seeded and finely chopped;
30 ml (2 tbsp) snipped fresh chives;
8 green and 8 black olives, stoned and chopped with
15 ml (1 tbsp) drained capers

1 Place the flours and salt into a bowl and rub in the margarine until the mixture resembles fine breadcrumbs. Add sufficient cold water to form a dough. Chill for 30 minutes.

2 Divide the dough into 4 pieces. Roll out each piece to a round and use to line 4 individual Yorkshire pudding tins. Prick with a fork. Bake blind at 200°C (400°F) mark 6 for 5 minutes.

3 Meanwhile, cream the cheese with a fork. Beat in the egg yolk and gradually add the milk. Season and add one of the flavourings. Whisk the egg white until stiff. Fold into the mixture.

4 Divide the filling between the pastry cases. Reduce the oven temperature to 190°C (375°F) mark 5 and bake for a further 25 minutes.

Courgette Pasticcio (PAGE 68); *Lamb Chops with Mint* (PAGE 82); *Mixed Leaf and Pinenut Salad*
(PAGE 130)

Pasta with Tuna and Olive Sauce

Made with storecupboard ingredients, this is ideal to serve when unexpected guests arrive.

NUTRITIONAL ANALYSIS
amount per portion
422 kcals/1762 kJ
61.6 g Carbohydrate
25.2 g Protein ★★★
9.5 g Fat ★★
1.5 g Saturated Fat ★★★★
0.0 g Added Sugar ★★★★
11.9 g Fibre ★★★
2358 mg Salt
81 mg Calcium ★★
5.3 mg Iron ★★★
71 mg Folic Acid ★★

SERVES 4

50 g (2 oz) can anchovy fillets

semi-skimmed milk, for soaking

15 ml (1 tbsp) polyunsaturated or olive oil

100 g (4 oz) onion, skinned and chopped

1 garlic clove, skinned and crushed

5 ml (1 tsp) dried marjoram

400 g (14 oz) can chopped tomatoes

350 g (12 oz) wholemeal pasta shapes

200 g (7 oz) can tuna fish in brine, well drained and flaked

50 g (2 oz) black or green olives

30 ml (2 tbsp) dry white wine

pepper, to taste

1 To remove the salt from the anchovies, drain well and place in a bowl. Cover with milk and soak for 20 minutes. Drain, pat dry and chop.

2 To make the sauce, heat the oil in a saucepan and gently cook the onion for 5 minutes. Add the garlic, marjoram and tomatoes with their juice. Bring to the boil and simmer for 15 minutes, stirring occasionally, until slightly thickened.

3 Meanwhile, cook the pasta in a large saucepan of boiling water for about 10 minutes or until just tender.

4 Add the tuna fish, anchovies and olives to the sauce. Return to the boil, stirring, then simmer for 2-3 minutes. Stir in the wine and pepper. Drain the pasta and serve hot with the sauce spooned over.

Vegetables in a Potato Crust

This satisfying vegetable dish is similar to a quiche as just before baking an egg, yogurt and curd cheese topping is poured over the vegetables.

NUTRITIONAL ANALYSIS
amount per portion
247 kcals/1032 kJ
21.4 g Carbohydrate
11.8 g Protein ★★
13.4 g Fat ★★
3.9 g Saturated Fat ★★★
0.0 g Added Sugar ★★★★
3.9 g Fibre ★★
600 mg Salt ★★
135 mg Calcium ★★★
2.3 mg Iron ★★
40 mg Folic Acid ★

SERVES 6

100 g (4 oz) plain wholemeal flour

50 g (2 oz) polyunsaturated margarine

175 g (6 oz) potatoes, scrubbed and coarsely grated

1 egg yolk

½ small cauliflower, cut into florets

2 carrots, scrubbed and grated

2 spring onions, trimmed and finely chopped

salt and pepper, to taste

3 eggs

200 ml (7 fl oz) low-fat natural yogurt

100 g (4 oz) curd cheese

30 ml (2 tbsp) chopped fresh mixed herbs

1 Put the flour into a bowl and rub in the margarine until the mixture resembles fine breadcrumbs. Add the potatoes and egg yolk and mix to a dough. Wrap and chill for 30 minutes.

2 Meanwhile, blanch the cauliflower florets in a saucepan of boiling water for 5 minutes. Drain thoroughly.

3 Roll out the dough on a lightly floured surface and use to line a 23 cm (9 inch) loose-based flan tin.

4 Mix the cauliflower florets with the carrots, spring onions and seasoning, then arrange in the flan case.

5 Combine the eggs, yogurt, curd cheese and herbs and beat until well blended. Spoon evenly over the vegetables. Bake at 190°C (375°F) mark 5 for 30-35 minutes. Serve warm.

NUTRITIONAL ANALYSIS
amount per portion
293 kcals/1225 kJ
28.4 g Carbohydrate
28.9 g Protein ★★★
8.1 g Fat ★★★
4.7 g Saturated Fat ★★
0.0 g Added Sugar ★★★★
5.1 g Fibre ★★
1571 mg Salt ★
307 mg Calcium ★★★★
3.7 mg Iron ★★★
113 mg Folic Acid ★★

Courgette Pasticcio

*A pasticcio is rather similar to a pizza. The grated courgettes are included in the pasticcio base.
This recipe serves 2 hungry people or can be stretched to serve 4.*

SERVES 2
400 g (14 oz) courgettes, trimmed and coarsely grated
100 g (4 oz) low-fat Cheddar cheese, grated
60 ml (4 tbsp) plain wholemeal flour
5 ml (1 tsp) chopped fresh basil or 2.5 ml (½ tsp) dried
pepper, to taste
4 egg whites, size 2
225 g (8 oz) can chopped tomatoes
10 ml (2 tsp) tomato purée
50 g (2 oz) button mushrooms, sliced
2.5 ml (½ tsp) dried oregano
parsley sprigs, to garnish

1 Combine the courgettes, 75 g (3 oz) of the cheese, the flour, basil and pepper in a large bowl. Whisk the egg whites until frothy but not stiff, then fold into the courgette mixture.

2 Place the mixture in a 23 cm (9 inch) loose-bottomed sandwich cake tin and smooth the surface. Bake at 180°C (350°F) mark 4 for 25 minutes or until slightly browned.

3 Mix the tomatoes and tomato purée together and spread over the cooked base. Scatter over the mushrooms and sprinkle the remaining cheese and oregano on top. Return to the oven and cook for a further 5 minutes. Garnish with parsley. Cut into wedges and serve hot.

Aubergine and Bean Gratin

A hearty filling makes these aubergines substantial enough for a vegetarian meal if served with a salad.

SERVES 4	
2 medium aubergines, trimmed	*225 g (8 oz) can cannellini beans, drained and rinsed*
15 g (½ oz) polyunsaturated margarine	*2 tomatoes, chopped*
1 onion, skinned and chopped	*pepper, to taste*
1 garlic clove, skinned and crushed	*30 ml (2 tbsp) freshly grated Parmesan cheese*
100 g (4 oz) button mushrooms	*parsley sprigs, to garnish*

1 Cook the aubergines in a saucepan of boiling water for about 10 minutes until tender.
2 Cut the aubergines in half lengthways and scoop out the flesh, leaving a 0.5 cm (¼ inch) shell. Finely chop the flesh and reserve the shells.
3 Melt the margarine in a saucepan and gently cook the onion, garlic and chopped aubergine flesh for 5 minutes. Add the mushrooms, beans, tomatoes and pepper.
4 Stuff the aubergine shells with the prepared mixture and sprinkle with the Parmesan cheese. Cook under a grill for 4-5 minutes until heated through. Serve hot, garnished with parsley.

NUTRITIONAL ANALYSIS
amount per portion
146 kcals/609 kJ
15.9 g Carbohydrate
7.6 g Protein ★★
5.6 g Fat ★★★
2.1 g Saturated Fat ★★★
0.0 g Added Sugar ★★★★
5.3 g Fibre ★★
265 mg Salt ★★★
131 mg Calcium ★★★
2.1 mg Iron ★★
45 mg Folic Acid ★

Haddock Quiche

Equally delicious served hot or cold, this tempting fish quiche uses both fresh and smoked haddock.

SERVES 6	
75 g (3 oz) plain white flour	*100 g (4 oz) smoked haddock fillet*
75 g (3 oz) plain wholemeal flour	*1 onion, skinned and chopped*
pinch of salt	*150 ml (¼ pint) semi-skimmed milk*
100 g (4 oz) polyunsaturated margarine	*1 egg*
225 g (8 oz) fresh haddock fillet	*15 ml (1 tbsp) chopped fresh parsley*
	25 g (1 oz) mature Cheddar cheese, grated

1 Put the flours and salt into a bowl and rub in 75 g (3 oz) of the margarine until the mixture resembles fine breadcrumbs. Add 25 ml (1 fl oz) chilled water and mix to make a soft dough. Add a little extra water if necessary.
2 Knead the dough on a lightly floured surface. Roll out and use to line a 20.5 cm (8 inch) loose-based flan tin. Chill for 30 minutes.
3 Meanwhile, place the fish in a saucepan with just enough water to cover.Simmer gently for 10 minutes. Drain, discard the skin and any bones and flake the fish into small pieces.
4 Melt the remaining margarine in a saucepan and gently cook the onion for 3-5 minutes until soft. Add the fish and heat through gently.
5 Spoon the filling into the flan case. Whisk together the milk, egg and parsley and pour over the fish. Sprinkle the cheese on top. Bake at 190°C (375°F) mark 5 for about 40 minutes until the filling is set. Serve hot or cold with salad.

NUTRITIONAL ANALYSIS
amount per portion
291 kcals/1218 kJ
20.1 g Carbohydrate
15.5 g Protein ★★★
17.2 g Fat ★★
4.0 g Saturated Fat ★★★
0.0 g Added Sugar ★★★★
2.0 g Fibre ★
1087 mg Salt ★★
116 mg Calcium ★★
1.6 mg Iron ★★
23 mg Folic Acid

NUTRITIONAL ANALYSIS
amount per portion
251 kcals/1049 kJ
44.8 g Carbohydrate
11.5 g Protein ★★
3.7 g Fat ★★★★
0.6 g Saturated Fat ★★★★
0.0 g Added Sugar ★★★★
13 g Fibre ★★★
316 mg Salt ★★★
109 mg Calcium ★★
4.0 mg Iron ★★★
111 mg Folic Acid ★★

Noodles and Crisp Vegetables

Shoyu, naturally fermented soy sauce, is made from soya beans with barley or wheat. Manufactured soy sauce usually contains sugar and other additives.

SERVES 4

225 g (8 oz) wholemeal noodles, such as soba buckwheat noodles or wholemeal fettucine

5 ml (1 tsp) polyunsaturated oil

2 onions, skinned and thinly sliced

100 g (4 oz) carrots, scrubbed and thinly sliced

450 g (1 lb) mixed fresh vegetables such as turnips, mushrooms, cabbage, fennel, peppers, swedes or broccoli florets, thinly sliced

75 g (3 oz) frozen or fresh peas, or mange-tout

15 ml (1 tbsp) soy sauce, preferably naturally fermented shoyu

15 ml (1 tbsp) dry sherry

dash of chilli oil (optional)

1 Cook the noodles according to the instructions on the packet and drain well.

2 Heat the oil in a large frying pan or wok and cook the onions and carrots over a medium heat for 5 minutes, stirring occasionally.

3 Add the remaining vegetables, soy sauce and 30 ml (2 tbsp) water. Raise the heat and cover the pan when the mixture begins to sizzle. Cook gently for 5 minutes, stirring occasionally.

4 Add the noodles, sherry and chilli oil, if using. Stir the mixture over a medium heat for 2-3 minutes to reheat the noodles. Serve at once.

Salmon and Dill Cakes

These are a healthy alternative to traditional fish cakes. Cooked in the oven, they are high in protein but low in fat.

SERVES 4
225 g (8 oz) potatoes, scrubbed
15 g (½ oz) polyunsaturated margarine
30 ml (2 tbsp) low-fat natural yogurt
two 200 g (7 oz) cans pink salmon, drained and flaked
40 ml (2½ tbsp) chopped fresh dill or 15 ml (1 tbsp) dried dill weed
15 ml (1 tbsp) grated onion
grated rind of 1 lemon
pepper, to taste
15 ml (1 tbsp) plain wholemeal flour
2 egg whites, beaten
75 g (3 oz) dried wholemeal breadcrumbs or rolled oats
45 ml (3 tbsp) low-fat mayonnaise
lemon wedges and fresh dill, to garnish

NUTRITIONAL ANALYSIS
amount per portion
371 kcals/1550 kJ
28.5 g Carbohydrate
21.3 g Protein ★★★
19.9 g Fat ★★
4.0 g Saturated Fat ★★★
0.0 g Added Sugar ★★★★
2.7 g Fibre ★
1384 mg Salt ★
103 mg Calcium ★★
2.4 mg Iron ★★
33 mg Folic Acid ★

1 Cook the potatoes in a saucepan of boiling water for 20 minutes or until tender. Drain and peel. Add the margarine and 15 ml (1 tbsp) of the yogurt. Mash until smooth. Turn into a bowl. Cool.

2 Add the salmon, 25 ml (1½ tbsp) of the fresh dill or 10 ml (2 tsp) dried dill, the onion, lemon rind and pepper. Mix well. Cover and chill for about 15 minutes until firm enough to handle.

3 Dust a work surface with the flour, then shape the salmon and potato mixture into 8 even-sized cakes. Dip into the egg white, then coat in the breadcrumbs. Place the fish cakes on a baking sheet. Cook at 200°C (400°F) mark 6 for 10-15 minutes until hot and crisp.

4 Meanwhile, mix the remaining yogurt and dill with the mayonnaise. Serve this sauce in a separate bowl with the cooked fish cakes. Garnish with lemon wedges and fresh dill.

NUTRITIONAL ANALYSIS
amount per portion
151 kcals/633 kJ
4.9 g Carbohydrate
9.4 g Protein ★★
10.6 g Fat ★★
3.8 g Saturated Fat ★★★
0.0 g Added Sugar ★★★★
6.8 g Fibre ★★
364 mg Salt ★★★
171 mg Calcium ★★★
1.9 mg Iron ★★
103 mg Folic Acid ★★

Cheesy Cauliflower

This is a colourful alternative to the usual cauliflower cheese and the nuts add a pleasant crunchy taste. It is important not to overcook the cauliflower so, if preferred, steam whole or divided into florets.

SERVES 4

1 cauliflower, about 900 g (2 lb), trimmed

2 tomatoes, finely chopped

50 g (2 oz) Brazil nuts, chopped

50 g (2 oz) button mushrooms, chopped

50 g (2 oz) Edam cheese, finely grated

salt and pepper, to taste

parsley sprigs, to garnish

1 Trim the base of the cauliflower and remove the outer leaves. Place the cauliflower in a large saucepan of boiling water and cook for 10–15 minutes, until tender, then drain.
2 Place the cauliflower in an ovenproof dish. Sprinkle the remaining ingredients over and cook at 190°C (375°F) mark 5 for 15 minutes or until the cheese is golden brown. Serve immediately, garnished with the parsley sprigs.

Spaghetti with Mushroom Sauce

Serve this delicious vegetarian pasta dish with freshly grated Parmesan cheese.

SERVES 4
350 g (12 oz) wholemeal spaghetti or other pasta
15 ml (1 tbsp) olive or corn oil
1 garlic clove, skinned and crushed
1 onion, skinned and finely chopped
900 g (2 lb) cup mushrooms, roughly chopped
1.25 ml (¼ tsp) paprika
1.25 ml (¼ tsp) grated nutmeg
salt and pepper, to taste
200 g (7 oz) natural Quark
45 ml (3 tbsp) chopped fresh parsley

1 Cook the spaghetti in boiling water for about 10 minutes, until just tender.
2 Meanwhile, heat the oil in a large saucepan and cook the garlic and onion for about 5 minutes, until soft.
3 Add the mushrooms, paprika, nutmeg and seasoning. Stir to mix well, then cover and cook over low heat for about 5 minutes or until the liquid just starts to run from the mushrooms. Do not overcook or the sauce will be too thin.
4 Spoon about three-quarters of the mushrooms and onions and the juices into a blender or food processor and purée. Return to the saucepan and stir in the Quark over low heat until melted. Stir in the parsley.
5 Drain the pasta and spoon on to 4 individual warmed plates. Spoon the sauce over.

NUTRITIONAL ANALYSIS
amount per portion
422 kcals/1763 kJ
61.7 g Carbohydrate
19.7 g Protein ★★★
12.3 g Fat ★★
4.4 g Saturated Fat ★★
0.0 g Added Sugar ★★★★
17.1 g Fibre ★★★★
416 mg Salt ★★★
140 mg Calcium ★★★
6.7 mg Iron ★★★
95 mg Folic Acid ★★

Chicken Stir-Fry Salad

The chicken is marinated in sesame oil, garlic, ginger and soy sauce before stir-frying. The cooked chicken is served over a mixed green salad.

SERVES 4	
450 g (1 lb) chicken breast fillets, skinned and cut into very thin strips	1 bunch watercress, trimmed
	½ head Chinese leaves, torn into bite-sized pieces
10 ml (2 tsp) sesame oil	½ head curly endive, torn into bite-sized pieces
2 garlic cloves, skinned and crushed	15 ml (1 tbsp) polyunsaturated oil
2 cm (¾ inch) piece fresh root ginger, peeled and grated	pepper, to taste
	radish roses, to garnish (optional)
45 ml (3 tbsp) soy sauce, preferably naturally fermented shoyu	

1 Put the chicken strips in a bowl. Add the sesame oil, garlic, ginger and soy sauce. Stir well and leave to marinate for 15 minutes.
2 Meanwhile, arrange the watercress, Chinese leaves and endive on a serving platter or individual plates.
3 Heat the oil in a large frying pan or wok and cook the chicken mixture over a high heat for 3-4 minutes, stirring constantly, until the chicken is cooked through.
4 Spoon the mixture over the leaves. Season and serve immediately, garnished with radish roses, if liked.

NUTRITIONAL ANALYSIS
amount per portion
214 kcals/896 kJ
5.0 g Carbohydrate
24.9 g Protein ★★★
10.7 g Fat ★★
2.3 g Saturated Fat ★★★
0.0 g Added Sugar ★★★★
1.2 g Fibre
252 mg Salt ★★★
187 mg Calcium ★★★
4.5 mg Iron ★★★
191 mg Folic Acid ★★★

Pasta with Pecan and Parsley Sauce

Tomato, spinach and plain pasta shapes are now increasingly available, both fresh and dried. This combination makes a colourful base for the rich green pecan and parsley sauce.

SERVES 4
50 g (2 oz) shelled pecan nuts
25 g (1 oz) fresh parsley
1 garlic clove, skinned and crushed
30 ml (2 tbsp) freshly grated Parmesan cheese
50 ml (2 fl oz) olive oil
150 g (5 oz) low-fat soft cheese
salt and pepper, to taste
350 g (12 oz) fresh or dried tricolour pasta

1 Work the nuts, parsley and garlic in a blender or food processor until fairly finely chopped. Blend in the Parmesan cheese, then add the oil, a little at a time. Stir in the cheese and seasoning.
2 Cook the pasta in a saucepan of boiling salted water until just tender. Drain and transfer to a warmed serving dish.
3 Heat the sauce gently, without boiling. Stir into the pasta. Serve with extra Parmesan, if liked.

NUTRITIONAL ANALYSIS
amount per portion
592 kcals/2476 kJ
69 g Carbohydrate
19.4 g Protein ★★★
28.5 g Fat ★
5.2 g Saturated Fat ★★
0.0 g Added Sugar ★★★★
5.2 g Fibre ★★
605 mg Salt ★★
166 mg Calcium ★★★
2.3 mg Iron ★★
25 mg Folic Acid ★

Meat and Offal
Main Courses

*Meat is a very important part of our diet, supplying
large quantities of protein, iron and vitamins,
especially the B group. When pregnant, women must
have an extra intake of protein and iron. Eating offal
once or twice a week, as well as meat, provides both.
Liver and kidneys also contain folic acid, another
vitamin believed beneficial during pregnancy. Always
select lean meat with little fat when choosing meat.*

NUTRITIONAL ANALYSIS
amount per portion
531 kcals/2220 kJ
20.9 g Carbohydrate
50.7 g Protein ★★★★
27.7 g Fat ★
6.6 g Saturated Fat ★★
0.0 g Added Sugar ★★★★
4.1 g Fibre ★★
905 mg Salt ★★
115 mg Calcium ★★
6.5 mg Iron ★★★
88 mg Folic Acid ★★

Beef, Walnut and Orange Casserole

Chuck steak is recommended for this casserole; although one of the more expensive cuts of beef for casseroling, it is worth buying in this case for its lean, tender flesh. From the shoulder of the animal, chuck steak is one of the best quality cuts of braising or stewing beef you can buy.

SERVES 4

900 g (2 lb) chuck steak, cut into 2.5 cm (1 inch) cubes

40 g (1½ oz) seasoned plain flour

30 ml (2 tbsp) polyunsaturated oil

1 onion, skinned and chopped

4 celery sticks, trimmed and roughly chopped

150 ml (¼ pint) unsweetened orange juice

600 ml (1 pint) beef stock

bouquet garni

2 garlic cloves, skinned and crushed

2 oranges

75 g (3 oz) walnut halves

salt and pepper, to taste

orange shreds, to garnish

1 Toss the meat in the seasoned flour. Heat the oil in a flameproof casserole and fry the onion and celery for about 5 minutes. Add the meat and fry for 5 minutes until browned. Add the orange juice, stock, bouquet garni and garlic.

2 Bring to the boil and cover. Cook at 170°C (325°F) mark 3 for 2 hours.

3 Meanwhile, peel the oranges over a plate, removing all the pith. Cut the flesh into segments.

4 Add the walnuts and orange segments to the casserole, together with any juice that may have collected on the plate. Continue to cook for a further 30 minutes until the meat is tender. Taste and adjust the seasoning. Serve the casserole garnished with orange shreds.

Bobotie

Serve this South African minced meat and fruit dish with boiled brown rice and chutney. Half the meat can be replaced with 225 g (8 oz) cooked pulses.

SERVES 4
15 ml (1 tbsp) polyunsaturated oil
1 onion, skinned and chopped
1 large garlic clove, skinned and crushed
25 ml (5 tsp) mild curry powder
450 g (1 lb) lean beef or lamb, minced
1 large slice wholemeal bread, soaked in 30 ml (2 tbsp) water and mashed
5 ready-to-eat dried apricots, rinsed and coarsely chopped
1 large banana, peeled and sliced
25 g (1 oz) sultanas
15 ml (1 tbsp) white wine or cider vinegar
salt and pepper, to taste
1 egg
150 ml (¼ pint) semi-skimmed milk
1.25 ml (¼ tsp) ground turmeric
2-3 bay leaves

NUTRITIONAL ANALYSIS
amount per portion
315 kcals/1316 kJ
23.8 g Carbohydrate
28.7 g Protein ★★★
12.3 g Fat ★★
3.8 g Saturated Fat ★★★
0.0 g Added Sugar ★★★★
5.5 g Fibre ★★
536 mg Salt ★★
134 mg Calcium ★★★
8.6 mg Iron ★★★★
33 mg Folic Acid ★

1 Heat the oil in a large saucepan and gently cook the onion for 5 minutes. Add the garlic and cook for 1 minute. Stir in the curry powder and cook for a further 1 minute.
2 Add the meat and cook, stirring, until browned. Add the bread, apricots, banana, sultanas, vinegar and seasoning. Stir well.
3 Transfer the mixture to a large ovenproof dish, pressing it down gently with the back of a spoon. Cover. Bake at 180°C (350°F) mark 4 for 20 minutes.
4 Beat the egg, milk and turmeric together in a bowl. Remove the dish from the oven and pour over the egg mixture. Arrange a few bay leaves in a pattern on the top. Bake for a further 40 minutes or until the top is firm and golden. Serve hot.

NUTRITIONAL ANALYSIS
amount per portion
206 kcals/863 kJ
2.8 g Carbohydrate
32.4 g Protein ★★★★
7.4 g Fat ★★★
3.3 g Saturated Fat ★★★
0.0 g Added Sugar ★★★★
0.1 g Fibre
321 mg Salt ★★★
80 mg Calcium ★★
3.3 mg Iron ★★
16 mg Folic Acid

Grilled Marinated Steak

The rump steak is marinated in an aromatic spiced yogurt. The spices are first dry-fried to release their flavours.

SERVES 4
700 g (1½ lb) rump steak
6 green cardamoms
4 cloves
6 black peppercorns
juice of 2 limes
150 ml (¼ pint) low-fat natural yogurt
2.5 ml (½ tsp) chilli powder
salt, to taste
lime slices or wedges, to serve

1 Cut off the fat around the edge of the steak, then cut the meat into serving pieces. Beat with a mallet until flat and thin.

2 Dry-fry the cardamoms, cloves and peppercorns in a heavy-based frying pan, then finely grind in a small electric mill or with a pestle and mortar. Transfer to a bowl and add half of the lime juice, the yogurt, chilli powder and salt. Stir well to mix.

3 Place the pieces of steak on 1-2 plates and brush with half of the marinade. Leave to stand at room temperature for at least 1 hour, then turn the steak pieces over the repeat on the other side.

4 Brush a grill pan with a little oil, then grill the steaks under a high heat until cooked to your liking.

5 Remove the steaks from the pan and arrange overlapping on a warmed serving dish. Pour the remaining lime juice into the juices collected in the grill pan, then pour into a small saucepan and bring quickly to the boil. Drizzle over the steak and garnish with lime slices or wedges. Serve immediately with a salad or a selection of vegetables.

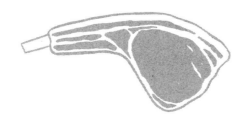

Carpaccio with Courgettes

This dish is named after a 15th-century Venetian painter. It can also be made with raw salmon marinated in the dressing for several hours.

SERVES 4
175 g (6 oz) fillet steak (not previously frozen)
2 small courgettes, trimmed
25 g (1 oz) piece Parmesan cheese, coarsely grated
2 small lemons, halved
30 ml (2 tbsp) olive oil
Worcestershire sauce
salt and pepper, to taste

1 Wrap the steak in foil and freeze for 1-2 hours until firm. Using a large very sharp knife, cut the steak into wafer-thin slices.
2 Using a potato peeler, cut the courgettes into long, thin ribbons.
3 Arrange the meat on 4 large serving plates. Sprinkle with the courgette, then the Parmesan cheese.
4 Squeeze the juice of half a lemon over each portion and drizzle over the olive oil. Add a little Worcestershire sauce and seasoning. Serve immediately.

NUTRITIONAL ANALYSIS
amount per portion
156 kcals/651 kJ
1.8 g Carbohydrate
11.6 g Protein ★ ★
11.4 g Fat ★ ★
3.1 g Saturated Fat ★ ★ ★
0.0 g Added Sugar ★ ★ ★ ★
1.7 g Fibre ★
327 mg Salt ★ ★ ★
116 mg Calcium ★ ★
1.2 mg Iron ★
10 mg Folic Acid

Cold Spiced Pork

The sweet spicy mixture seeps into the pork as it bakes. With plenty of accompanying vegetables, this recipe will serve 8.

SERVES 6
5 ml (1 tsp) juniper berries
2.5 ml (½ tsp) whole allspice berries
pinch of ground cloves
50 g (2 oz) light muscovado sugar
1.3 kg (2 lb 10 oz) smoked cured pork loin joint

1 Crush the juniper berries with the allspice and cloves. Stir in most of the sugar and spread this mixture over the pork loin.
2 Wrap the joint loosely in foil and place in a roasting tin.
3 Bake at 190°C (375°F) mark 5 for 45 minutes. Open the parcel, sprinkle the meat with the remaining sugar and bake for a further 15-20 minutes until golden brown and the meat is cooked through.
4 Leave to cool, then serve thinly sliced with salad, pickles and new potatoes when in season.

NUTRITIONAL ANALYSIS
amount per portion
210 kcals/880 kJ
8.7 g Carbohydrate
25.1 g Protein ★ ★ ★
8.6 g Fat ★ ★ ★
3.3 g Saturated Fat ★ ★ ★
8.3 g Added Sugar ★ ★
0.0 g Fibre
1057 mg Salt ★ ★
14 mg Calcium
1.2 mg Iron ★
6.0 mg Folic Acid

Seekh Kebabs

Every region in the Middle East boasts a traditional 'kofta' recipe of minced lamb or beef mixed to a soft paste with spices and fresh herbs. Buy the skewers (satay sticks) from Chinese supermarkets.

NUTRITIONAL ANALYSIS
amount per kebab
62 kcals/260 kJ
1.8 g Carbohydrate
8.7 g Protein ★★
2.3 g Fat ★★★★
0.9 g Saturated Fat ★★★★
0.0 g Added Sugar ★★★★
0.7 g Fibre
109 mg Salt ★★★★
53 mg Calcium ★★
2.6 mg Iron ★★
6.0 mg Folic Acid

SERVES 6-8

900 g (2 lb) lean minced beef or lamb
2 medium onions, skinned and grated
30 ml (2 tbsp) ground cumin
15 ml (1 tbsp) coarsely ground coriander
60 ml (4 tbsp) finely chopped fresh parsley
salt and pepper, to taste
olive oil
paprika
3 spring onions, trimmed and chopped
300 ml (½ pint) low-fat natural yogurt
15 ml (1 tbsp) chopped fresh mint
mint sprigs, onion rings and lemon wedges, to garnish

1 Ask your butcher to mince the meat 3 times, or chop it in a food processor until very fine. Knead the meat with the grated onion, cumin, coriander, parsley and seasoning to make smooth paste.

2 Take about 15-30 ml (1-2 tbsp) of the mixture and press a flat sausage shape on to the ends of wooden skewers. Brush them lightly with oil and sprinkle with a little paprika.

3 Grill about half at a time under a high heat for about 5 minutes. Turn, sprinkle with more paprika and grill the second side until well browned all over. (Keep the exposed wooden sticks away from the flame.) Keep the kebabs warm, loosely covered, until the remainder are cooked.

4 Meanwhile to make the sauce, mix the spring onions, reserving a few dark green shreds for garnish, with the yogurt and mint. Serve the kebabs garnished with mint sprigs, onion rings and reserved spring onion, with the sauce and lemon wedges handed separately.

Pork and Bean Stew

An anglicised version of the famous American dish Boston Baked Beans, this stew is a most economical way to feed as many as 6 people with hearty appetites. Don't worry about the small quantity of meat, because pulses are extremely nutritious: they are packed with protein, iron and vitamins (especially those from B group), plus the fact that they are very low in fat compared with other high-protein foods – yet very high in fibre.

NUTRITIONAL ANALYSIS
amount per portion
368 kcals/1536 kJ
35.6 g Carbohydrate
38 g Protein ★★★★
9.0 g Fat ★★★
3.2 g Saturated Fat ★★★
2.5 g Added Sugar ★★★
16.9 g Fibre ★★★★
1858 mg Salt
186 mg Calcium ★★★
6.8 mg Iron ★★★★
22 mg Folic Acid

SERVES 4-6

450 g (1 lb) lean belly pork

225 g (8 oz) dried black-eye or haricot beans, soaked overnight

15 ml (1 tbsp) black treacle

900 ml (1½ pints) chicken stock

1 onion, skinned and stuck with a few whole cloves

bouquet garni

3 medium carrots, scrubbed and sliced

2 leeks, washed, trimmed and sliced

30 ml (2 tbsp) Worcestershire sauce

15 ml (1 tbsp) tomato purée

salt and pepper, to taste

1 Cut the pork into chunky cubes, removing the rind and any bones. Fry the meat in a heavy based flameproof casserole over a high heat until the fat runs.

2 Drain the beans and add to the pork with the treacle, stock, onion and bouquet garni. Bring slowly to the boil, then lower the heat, cover and simmer for 1½ hours or until the beans are just becoming tender.

3 Add the carrots and leeks to the casserole, with the Worcestershire sauce, tomato purée and seasoning. Continue cooking for a further 30 minutes or until the beans are really tender. Discard the bouquet garni and taste and adjust the seasoning before serving.

Lamb and Date Casserole

The fresh dates add a natural sweetness to this spicy dish. Accompany with lemon-flavoured rice.

NUTRITIONAL ANALYSIS
amount per portion
471 kcals/1968 kJ
27.5 g Carbohydrate
39 g Protein ★★★★
23.6 g Fat ★
8.3 g Saturated Fat ★★
0.0 g Added Sugar ★★★★
2.2 g Fibre ★
666 mg Salt ★★
81 mg Calcium ★★
6.3 mg Iron ★★★
29 mg Folic Acid ★

SERVES 4

1.1 kg (2½ lb) chump end leg of lamb to yield
about 700 g (1½ lb) lean meat

15 ml (1 tbsp) seasoned flour

30 ml (2 tbsp) polyunsaturated oil

1 large onion, skinned and sliced

2.5 ml (½ tsp) ground cumin

7.5 ml (1½ tsp) ground coriander

300 ml (½ pint) light stock

30 ml (2 tbsp) tomato purée

salt and pepper, to taste

10-12 fresh dates, stoned

1 Remove the lean meat from the bone, trim and cut the lamb into 5 cm (2 inch) chunks. Toss in the seasoned flour.
2 Heat the oil in a flameproof casserole and brown the meat in batches; remove, using draining spoons.
3 Lower the heat, add the onion and spices and cook, stirring, for 3-4 minutes.
4 Stir in the stock and tomato purée. Replace the meat. Bring to the boil, lower the heat, cover and simmer gently for about 1 hour.
5 After 1 hour, adjust the seasoning, add the dates, cover and cook for a further 15 minutes.

Lamb Chops with Mint

Coat the cooked chops in the chopped mint while still warm to make sure that it sticks.

NUTRITIONAL ANALYSIS
amount per portion
224 kcals/936 kJ
3.9 g Carbohydrate
23.6 g Protein ★★★
12.8 g Fat ★★
5.5 g Saturated Fat ★★
2.5 g Added Sugar ★★★★
0.2 g Fibre
244 mg Salt ★★★★
22 mg Calcium
2.3 mg Iron ★★
3.0 mg Folic Acid

SERVES 4

12 small, lean rib lamb chops

15 ml (1 tbsp) olive oil

30 ml (2 tbsp) soy sauce, preferably naturally
fermented shoyu

20 ml (4 tsp) hoisin sauce

15 ml (1 tbsp) light muscovado sugar

90 ml (6 tbsp) chopped fresh mint

1 Trim the chops of all excess fat. Mix the oil, soy sauce and hoisin sauce with the sugar and spread lightly all over the chops.
2 Grill the chops under a high heat or cook on a cast-iron ribbed steak pan until golden brown.
3 Turn the chops. Brush the second side with any remaining marinade and cook until tender.
4 Dip in or sprinkle with mint while still warm. Serve hot with steamed vegetables or leave to cool and serve cold with salad.

Italian-Style Braised Pork

Cooking pork in milk may seem a very strange combination, but it is very popular in Italy. The milk and the long, slow cooking produce the most tender results. The loin used in this recipe is a tender cut of pork, but it can be rather dry if roasted in the normal way, because it is so lean. Braising loin of pork in milk ensures that the meat will be moist and succulent, and the flavour of garlic, juniper and rosemary gives the dish a unique aromatic taste.

SERVES 6

15 ml (1 tbsp) polyunsaturated oil
25 g (1 oz) polyunsaturated margarine
1 kg (2¼ lb) loin of pork, rinded
2 garlic cloves, skinned
1 large onion, skinned and chopped
568 ml (1 pint) semi-skimmed milk
5 juniper berries
2 rosemary sprigs
salt and pepper, to taste
rosemary sprigs, to garnish

1 Heat the oil and margarine in a large saucepan or flameproof casserole into which the meat will just fit and fry the pork, garlic and onion for about 15 minutes until the pork is browned on all sides. Add the milk, juniper berries, rosemary and seasoning.
2 Bring to the boil, cover, lower the heat and cook gently for 1½-2 hours until the pork is tender, turning and basting from time to time.
3 Transfer the pork to a warmed serving dish and carve into thick slices. Discard the garlic, juniper berries and rosemary.
4 The milky cooking juices will look curdled, so rub the sauce through a sieve or purée in a blender or food processor until smooth. Taste and adjust the seasoning. Pour a little of the sauce over the meat and serve the remaining sauce separately. Garnish with sprigs of rosemary. Serve with steamed or boiled new potatoes and green vegetables.

NUTRITIONAL ANALYSIS
amount per portion
369 kcals/1544 kJ
6.5 g Carbohydrate
38 g Protein ★★★★
21.4 g Fat ★★
9.3 g Saturated Fat ★★
0.0 g Added Sugar ★★★★
0.4 g Fibre
542 mg Salt ★★
137 mg Calcium ★★★
1.7 mg Iron ★★
18 mg Folic Acid

NUTRITIONAL ANALYSIS
amount per portion
294 kcals/1230 kJ
5.4 g Carbohydrate
23.3 g Protein ★★★
19.2 g Fat ★★
4.5 g Saturated Fat ★★
0.5 g Added Sugar ★★★★
0.7 g Fibre
299 mg Salt ★★★
26 mg Calcium ★
10.9 mg Iron ★★★★
257 mg Folic Acid ★★★★

Pan-Fried Liver and Tomato

Nutritious liver is an excellent source of iron, protein and B vitamins. Never over cook liver as it will harden.

SERVES 4

450 g (1 lb) lamb's liver, sliced

30 ml (2 tbsp) Marsala or sweet sherry

salt and pepper, to taste

225 g (8 oz) tomatoes, skinned

30 ml (2 tbsp) polyunsaturated oil

2 medium onions, skinned and finely sliced

pinch of ground ginger

150 ml (¼ pint) chicken stock

1 Using a very sharp knife, cut the liver into wafer-thin strips. Place in a shallow bowl with the Marsala and sprinkle with pepper. Cover and leave to marinate for several hours.

2 Cut the tomatoes into quarters and remove the seeds, reserving the juices. Slice the flesh into fine strips and set aside.

3 Heat the oil in a non-stick frying pan until very hot, and cook the liver strips, a few at a time, for about 30 seconds until the liver just changes colour, shaking the pan briskly.

4 Turn the slices and cook for a further 30 seconds only. Remove from the pan with a slotted spoon and keep warm while cooking the remaining batches.

5 Add the onions and ginger to the remaining oil in the pan and cook, uncovered, for about 5 minutes. Add the stock and seasoning, return the liver to the pan and add the tomatoes and their juice. Bring just to the boil, then turn into a warmed serving dish and serve immediately.

Calf's Liver with Vermouth

The initial browning should almost cook the liver, so simmer gently for 1-2 minutes only.

SERVES 4
30 ml (2 tbsp) polyunsaturated oil
450 g (1 lb) calf's liver, thinly sliced
15 ml (1 tbsp) green peppercorns in brine, finely chopped
75 ml (3 fl oz) dry vermouth
salt, to taste
30 ml (2 tbsp) single cream

1 Heat the oil in a medium frying pan and cook half the liver over moderate heat until browned on both sides. Remove from the pan with a slotted spoon. Repeat with the remaining liver.
2 Stir the peppercorns into the pan, then pour in the vermouth with 75 ml (3 fl oz) water. Bring to the boil and add salt.
3 Replace the liver and simmer for 1-2 minutes only or until just tender. Remove from the heat and stir in the cream.

NUTRITIONAL ANALYSIS
amount per portion
281 kcals/1176 kJ
4.3 g Carbohydrate
22.9 g Protein ★★★
17.4 g Fat ★★
4.4 g Saturated Fat ★★
0.7 g Added Sugar ★★★★
0.0 g Fibre
775 mg Salt ★★
17 mg Calcium
9.2 mg Iron ★★★★
270 mg Folic Acid ★★★★

Lamb and Olive Pilaff

This pilaff is simple to cook and is a complete meal in itself. Brown rice is best to use as it is rich in fibre and contains more calcium, iron and protein than white rice.

SERVES 2
225 g (8 oz) lamb neck fillet or boneless leg steaks
10 ml (2 tsp) olive oil
1 large onion, skinned and sliced
100 g (4 oz) button mushrooms, sliced
2.5 ml (½ tsp) ground coriander
5 ml (1 tsp) ground mixed spice
100 g (4 oz) long-grain brown rice
600 ml (1 pint) lamb or chicken stock
few rosemary sprigs
8 green olives
salt and pepper, to taste
100 g (4 oz) frozen peas

1 Trim the lamb and cut into bite-sized pieces. Heat the oil in a heavy based frying pan and fry the lamb, onion, mushrooms and spices until browned.
2 Stir the rice, stock, rosemary sprigs, olives and seasoning. Bring to the boil, lower the heat, cover and simmer for 25 minutes.
3 Stir in the peas and cook for a further 5 minutes or until the rice is tender and the stock absorbed.

NUTRITIONAL ANALYSIS
amount per portion
487 kcals/2037 kJ
48.4 g Carbohydrate
32.5 g Protein ★★★★
19.5 g Fat ★★
6.2 g Saturated Fat ★★
0.0 g Added Sugar ★★★★
11.4 g Fibre ★★★
2118 mg Salt
90 mg Calcium ★★
6.7 mg Iron ★★★
95 mg Folic Acid ★★

Lemon Veal

Unlike many veal escalope recipes, this one is healthier because the veal is grilled rather than fried.

NUTRITIONAL ANALYSIS
amount per portion
269 kcals/1123 kJ
25.6 g Carbohydrate
29.7 g Protein ★★★
6.1 g Fat ★★★
2.1 g Saturated Fat ★★★
0.0 g Added Sugar ★★★★
6.9 g Fibre ★★
1186 mg Salt ★★
146 mg Calcium ★★★
4.5 mg Iron ★★★
38 mg Folic Acid ★

SERVES 4
grated rind and juice of 2 lemons
60 ml (4 tbsp) chopped fresh parsley
15 ml (1 tbsp) dried oregano
5 ml (1 tsp) paprika
salt and pepper, to taste
4 veal escalopes, about 100 g (4 oz) each, beaten
1 egg, beaten
60 ml (4 tbsp) semi-skimmed milk
225 g (8 oz) fresh wholemeal breadcrumbs
watercress sprigs and lemon wedges, to garnish

1 Mix the lemon rind and juice, parsley, oregano, paprika and seasoning together and lay the veal escalopes in the mixture. Turn once or twice to ensure that they are evenly coated. Leave to stand in a cool place for 1 hour.

2 Mix the egg and milk together in a shallow dish. Spread out the breadcrumbs on a plate. One by one, dip the escalopes into the milk mixture and then into the breadcrumbs, patting the crumbs on gently. Cook under a grill for about 7½ minutes each side, until golden brown and cooked through. Garnish with watercress sprigs and lemon wedges and serve at once.

Veal Escalopes with Mushrooms

As this dish tastes quite rich, it is best accompanied simply with a mixed green salad.

NUTRITIONAL ANALYSIS
amount per portion
257 kcals/1076 kJ
5.3 g Carbohydrate
25.6 g Protein ★★★
10.9 g Fat ★★
2.3 g Saturated Fat ★★★
1.3 g Added Sugar ★★★★
1.2 g Fibre
499 mg Salt ★★★
48 mg Calcium ★
2.1 mg Iron ★★
23 mg Folic Acid

SERVES 4	juice of 1 lemon
30 ml (2 tbsp) corn or olive oil	150 ml (¼ pint) chicken stock
450 g (1 lb) veal escalopes, cut into thin strips	150 ml (¼ pint) dry white vermouth
1 onion, skinned and finely chopped	salt and pepper, to taste
100 g (4 oz) button mushrooms, halved	45 ml (3 tbsp) low-fat natural yogurt
2 courgettes, cut into thin strips	parsley sprig, to garnish
finely pared rind of 1 lemon, cut into matchstick strips	

1 Heat the oil in a frying pan and cook the veal strips for 2 minutes, until browned. Remove from the pan.

2 Add the onion, mushrooms and courgettes to the pan and cook for 3 minutes, until the onion is just beginning to soften.

3 Add the lemon rind to the pan with the lemon juice, stock, vermouth and seasoning. Cook, stirring occasionally, for 5-8 minutes, until the liquid is reduced by half.

4 Return the veal to the pan. Cover and cook for 3 minutes or until the veal is thoroughly reheated. Remove from the heat, swirl in the yogurt, garnish with parsley and serve at once.

Braised Veal with Oranges and Olives

Lean veal and orange segments combine to make an attractive fresh-tasting dish which is particularly good served with rice or pasta.

SERVES 4

450 g (1 lb) lean veal, trimmed of excess fat and cubed

10 ml (2 tsp) plain wholemeal flour

1 orange

15 ml (1 tbsp) olive oil

1 medium leek, trimmed and finely sliced

300 ml (½ pint) chicken or veal stock

salt and pepper, to taste

30 ml (2 tbsp) chopped fresh parsley

50 g (2 oz) black olives, stoned

1 Toss the meat in the flour. Finely grate 2.5 ml (½ tsp) of the orange rind and set aside. Pare all the rind and white pith from the orange and cut into segments between the membranes.
2 Heat the oil in a saucepan, add the veal and cook until lightly browned on all sides. Add the leek and stir well. Pour in the stock and cook for about 5 minutes, until the mixture has thickened slightly. Add the reserved orange rind and seasoning. Cover and simmer for 35-40 minutes, until the veal is tender.
3 Stir in the orange segments, parsley and olives and simmer for a further 5 minutes.

NUTRITIONAL ANALYSIS
amount per portion
197 kcals/824 kJ
5.5 g Carbohydrate
25.5 g Protein ★★★
8.3 g Fat ★★★
1.9 g Saturated Fat ★★★★
0.0 g Added Sugar ★★★★
2.6 g Fibre ★
1303 mg Salt ★
68 mg Calcium ★★
2.7 mg Iron ★★
20 mg Folic Acid

Tomato and Veal Casserole

Herbs, garlic and onion flavour this dish, cutting down on the need for salt. Serve with brown rice accompanied by a crisp green salad.

SERVES 4

15 ml (1 tbsp) olive oil

1 large onion, skinned and chopped

450 g (1 lb) lean veal, trimmed of excess fat and cubed

2.5 ml (½ tsp) dried oregano

5 ml (1 tsp) finely chopped fresh basil, or 2.5 ml (½ tsp) dried

1 garlic clove, skinned and crushed

175 g (6 oz) button mushrooms

15 ml (1 tbsp) tomato purée

400 g (14 oz) can tomatoes with juice

salt and pepper, to taste

finely chopped fresh parsley, to garnish

1 Put the oil and onion in a saucepan, cover and cook over a gentle heat for 6-8 minutes, until soft.
2 Increase the heat slightly and add the veal, stirring until all the pieces are lightly browned, then add the herbs, garlic and mushrooms. Mix well before stirring in the tomato purée and the tomatoes with the juices.
3 Bring to the boil, then cover, lower the heat and simmer for 40 minutes.
4 Uncover and continue cooking for about 10 minutes to reduce the sauce slightly, then season, sprinkle with the parsley and serve.

NUTRITIONAL ANALYSIS
amount per portion
189 kcals/792 kJ
5.1 g Carbohydrate
26.4 g Protein ★★★
7.1 g Fat ★★★
1.9 g Saturated Fat ★★★★
0.0 g Added Sugar ★★★★
2.7 g Fibre ★
413 mg Salt ★★★
40 mg Calcium ★
3.1 mg Iron ★★
53 mg Folic Acid ★★

NUTRITIONAL ANALYSIS
amount per portion
349 kcals/1459 kJ
12.3 g Carbohydrate
36.4 g Protein ★★★★
17.5 g Fat ★★
5.7 g Saturated Fat ★★
0.0 g Added Sugar ★★★★
2.9 g Fibre ★
776 mg Salt ★★
140 mg Calcium ★★★
3.0 mg Iron ★★
25 mg Folic Acid

Mustard Rabbit

Rabbit is a tasty and very lean meat; its flavour is complemented well by the sharpness of the mustard.

SERVES 4

15 g (½ oz) polyunsaturated margarine

15 ml (1 tbsp) polyunsaturated oil

2 carrots, scrubbed and sliced

2 leeks, washed, trimmed and sliced

1 large onion, skinned and chopped

900 g (2 lb) rabbit pieces

25 ml (1½ tbsp) plain wholemeal flour

600 ml (1 pint) chicken stock

30 ml (2 tbsp) Meaux mustard

150 ml (¼ pint) Greek strained yogurt

1 Melt the margarine and oil in a flameproof casserole and cook the carrots, leeks and onion for 5 minutes.

2 Toss the rabbit in the flour, shaking off the excess and reserving. Add the rabbit to the pan and cook for 5 minutes, turning, until sealed. Add the reserved flour, stock and mustard to the pan and stir well. Bring to the boil, lower the heat, cover and simmer for about 1 hour, stirring occasionally.

3 Using a slotted spoon, transfer the rabbit and vegetables on to a plate. Simmer the liquid until reduced by half, stirring occasionally. Remove from the heat, stir in the yogurt and return the rabbit and vegetables to the pan. Reheat gently and serve at once.

6

Chicken and Poultry Main Courses

Reasonably priced, chicken is an excellent source of protein in a very digestible form. It is also low in fats and calories. If using frozen poultry, thaw thoroughly before cooking. Remember, too, all poultry must be well cooked. Whether a casserole or stir-fry, there is a chicken dish to tempt everyone. When you want to cook a main meal with a difference, try one of the succulent game recipes.

NUTRITIONAL ANALYSIS
amount per portion
504 kcals/2108 kJ
14.1 g Carbohydrate
50.1 g Protein ★★★★
22.4 g Fat ★
6.4 g Saturated Fat ★★
0.0 g Added Sugar ★★★★
1.0 g Fibre
1213 mg Salt ★★
91 mg Calcium ★★
10.6 mg Iron ★★★★
18 mg Folic Acid

Guinea Fowl with Grapes

Guinea fowl are now reared on poultry farms and are available all year round. Their flavour is a cross between pheasant and chicken.

SERVES 4

350 g (12 oz) seedless white grapes

30 ml (2 tbsp) brandy

1 garlic clove, skinned and finely sliced

rosemary sprigs

salt and pepper, to taste

2 prepared guinea fowl

4 back bacon rashers, rinded

25 g (1 oz) polyunsaturated margarine

200 ml (7 fl oz) dry white wine

watercress, to garnish

1 Blanch the grapes in boiling water for 2 minutes, then remove the skins with a sharp knife.

2 Put the grapes in a bowl. Spoon over the brandy and leave to marinate, turning from time to time.

3 Put a few garlic slices, a sprig of rosemary and seasoning inside each bird. Wrap 2 bacon rashers round each one and secure with wooden cocktail sticks.

4 Place the guinea fowl in a casserole with the margarine. Season and sprinkle with a little extra rosemary. Cover and cook at 220°C (425°F) mark 7 for 15 minutes.

5 Bring the wine to the boil in a pan. Turn the guinea fowl over and pour over the wine. Cook, uncovered, for a further 15 minutes until the birds are tender.

6 Remove the guinea fowl to a warmed serving dish and keep hot. Skim off the fat, then add the grapes to the sauce and heat through.

7 Remove the bacon and cut the guinea fowl in half with poultry shears. Arrange the bacon over the halves, pour the sauce over and garnish with watercress.

Chicken and Tomato Casserole

Originating in Greece, this mouthwatering chicken dish is spiced with cinnamon, cloves and allspice berries. The flavour of these reddish brown berries is similar to nutmeg.

SERVES 4
4 chicken portions, skinned
salt and pepper, to taste
30 ml (2 tbsp) olive oil
1 small onion, skinned and chopped
3 garlic cloves, skinned and crushed
100 ml (4 fl oz) dry white wine
450 g (1 lb) ripe tomatoes, skinned, seeded and chopped
15 ml (1 tbsp) tomato purée
1 cinnamon stick
4 cloves
6 allspice berries
175 g (6 oz) can or jar artichoke hearts, drained
15-30 ml (1-2 tbsp) chopped fresh parsley or coriander

NUTRITIONAL ANALYSIS
amount per portion
292 kcals/1219 kJ
5.2 g Carbohydrate
32.4 g Protein ★★★★
14 g Fat ★★
3.2 g Saturated Fat ★★★
0.0 g Added Sugar ★★★★
1.6 g Fibre ★
585 mg Salt ★★
59 mg Calcium ★★
2.2 mg Iron ★★
55 mg Folic Acid ★★

1 Sprinkle the chicken with seasoning. Heat the oil in a large flameproof casserole and fry the chicken over moderate heat for about 5 minutes until well coloured on all sides. Remove from the pan with a slotted spoon and set aside.

2 Add the onion and garlic to the pan and fry gently for about 5 minutes until soft.

3 Return the chicken to the pan, pour in the wine, then add the tomatoes and tomato purée and mix well. Boil the mixture for a few minutes.

4 Meanwhile, pound the spices in a pestle and mortar. Add to the casserole with 150 ml (¼ pint) water and stir well to mix. Cover and simmer for about 45-60 minutes or until the chicken is tender.

5 Add the artichokes about 10 minutes before the end of the cooking time, to heat through. Taste and adjust the seasoning, stir in the parsley and serve immediately.

NUTRITIONAL ANALYSIS
amount per portion
300 kcals/1255 kJ
7.0 g Carbohydrate
28.3 g Protein ★ ★ ★
17.3 g Fat ★ ★
3.4 g Saturated Fat ★ ★ ★
0.1 g Added Sugar ★ ★ ★ ★
1.6 g Fibre ★
341 mg Salt ★ ★ ★
119 mg Calcium ★ ★
3.1 mg Iron ★ ★
39 mg Folic Acid ★

Shredded Sesame Chicken with Peppers

Serve this Chinese stir-fry for a quick evening meal. Once the ingredients are prepared, it only takes a few minutes to cook. Chinese egg noodles are the most suitable accompaniment.

SERVES 4
4 chicken breast fillets, skinned
30 ml (2 tbsp) polyunsaturated oil
1 large red pepper, seeded and sliced
1 large yellow pepper, seeded and sliced
6 spring onions, trimmed and chopped
2.5 cm (1 inch) piece fresh root ginger, peeled and coarsely grated
225 g (8 oz) can sliced bamboo shoots, drained
30 ml (2 tbsp) sesame seeds
30 ml (2 tbsp) soy sauce, preferably naturally fermented shoyu
30 ml (2 tbsp) dry sherry

1 Cut the chicken into thin strips. Heat the oil in a wok or large frying pan and stir-fry the chicken for 3 minutes.
2 Add the peppers, spring onions, ginger and bamboo shoots and stir-fry for 2 minutes. Stir in the sesame seeds and stir-fry for a further minute.
3 Add the soy sauce and sherry. Bring to the boil and boil for 1 minute, stirring all the time. Serve at once.

NUTRITIONAL ANALYSIS
amount per portion
491 kcals/2053 kJ
6.5 g Carbohydrate
33.1 g Protein ★ ★ ★ ★
37.3 g Fat
13.2 g Saturated Fat
1.3 g Added Sugar ★ ★ ★ ★
1.3 g Fibre
822 mg Salt ★ ★
114 mg Calcium ★ ★
7.2 mg Iron ★ ★ ★ ★
15 mg Folic Acid

Devilled Poussins

For this dish the poussins are cut in half. It is not difficult to do when using a sharp knife and scissors. However, ask your butcher to prepare them for you if preferred.

SERVES 6		60 ml (4 tbsp) no-sugar tomato ketchup
15 ml (1 tbsp) mustard powder		15 ml (1 tbsp) lemon juice
15 ml (1 tbsp) sweet paprika		50 g (2 oz) polyunsaturated margarine, melted
20 ml (4 tsp) ground turmeric		3 poussins, each weighing about 700 g (1½ lb)
20 ml (4 tsp) ground cumin		15 ml (1 tbsp) poppy seeds

1 Place the mustard powder, paprika, turmeric and cumin into a small bowl. Add the tomato ketchup and lemon juice. Beat well to form a thick, smooth paste. Slowly pour in the melted margarine, stirring all the time.
2 Place the poussins on a chopping board, breast side down. With a small sharp knife, cut right along the backbone of each bird through skin and flesh.
3 With scissors, cut through the backbone to open the birds up. Turn the birds over, breast side up.
4 Continue cutting alone the breast bone which will split the birds into 2 equal halves.
5 Lie the birds, skin side uppermost, on a large edged baking sheet. Spread the paste evenly over the surface of the birds and sprinkle with the poppy seeds. Cover loosely with cling film and leave in a cool place for at least 1-2 hours.
6 Uncover the poussins and cook on the baking sheet at 200°C (400°F) mark 6 for about 1 hour or until tender. Serve hot with a watercress salad.

Chicken Dhansak

This spicy chicken dish is full of protein as nutritious red lentils are included.

NUTRITIONAL ANALYSIS
amount per portion
436 kcals/1823 kJ
33.1 g Carbohydrate
44.7 g Protein ★★★★
14.9 g Fat ★★
3.3 g Saturated Fat ★★★
0.0 g Added Sugar ★★★★
7.4 g Fibre ★★
416 mg Salt ★★★
55 mg Calcium ★★
5.8 mg Iron ★★★
42 mg Folic Acid ★

SERVES 4

30 ml (2 tbsp) polyunsaturated oil

1 onion, skinned and chopped

2.5 cm (1 inch) piece fresh root ginger, peeled and crushed

1-2 garlic cloves, skinned and crushed

4 chicken portions

5 ml (1 tsp) ground coriander

2.5 cm (½ tsp) chilli powder

2.5 ml (½ tsp) ground turmeric

1.25 ml (¼ tsp) ground cinnamon

salt, to taste

225 g (8 oz) red lentils, washed (see page 118)

juice of 1 lime or lemon

fresh lime slices and coriander leaves, to garnish

1 Heat the oil in a flameproof casserole and gently fry the onion, ginger and garlic for 5 minutes until soft but not coloured.

2 Add the chicken portions and spices and fry for a few minutes more, turning the chicken constantly so that the pieces become coloured on all sides.

3 Pour enough water into the casserole to just cover the chicken. Add salt, then the red lentils.

4 Bring slowly to the boil, stirring, then lower the heat, cover and simmer for 40 minutes or until the chicken is tender when pierced with a skewer. During cooking, turn the chicken in the sauce occasionally, and check that the lentils have not absorbed all the water and become too dry – add water if necessary.

5 Remove the chicken from the casserole and leave until cool enough to handle. Take the meat off the bones, discarding the skin. Cut the meat into bite-sized pieces, return to the casserole and heat through thoroughly. Stir in the lime or lemon juice; taste and adjust the seasoning if necessary. Garnish with lime slices and coriander before serving.

Nasi Goreng

This colourful Indonesian dish can also be garnished with a thin plain omelette or strips of omelette.

NUTRITIONAL ANALYSIS
amount per portion
435 kcals/1819 kJ
52.1 g Carbohydrate
20.7 g Protein ★★★
17.4 g Fat ★★
3.5 g Saturated Fat ★★★
0.6 g Added Sugar ★★★★
6.2 g Fibre ★★
1089 mg Salt ★★
85 mg Calcium ★★
2.5 mg Iron ★★
72 mg Folic Acid ★★

SERVES 4

225 g (8 oz) long-grain brown rice

30 ml (2 tbsp) groundnut or polyunsaturated oil

1 large onion, skinned and chopped

1 garlic clove, skinned and crushed

1 green chilli, seeded and chopped

½ green pepper, seeded and cut into strips

50 g (2 oz) button mushrooms, sliced

100 g (4 oz) cooked chicken meat, skinned and diced

100 g (4 oz) peeled cooked prawns

50 g (2 oz) shelled unsalted peanuts

50 g (2 oz) frozen peas

2 spring onions, trimmed and finely chopped

15 ml (1 tbsp) soy sauce, preferably naturally fermented shoyu

2.5 ml (½ tsp) dark muscovado sugar

salt and pepper, to taste

shredded lettuce, to garnish

1 Put the rice in a saucepan containing 600 ml (1 pint) boiling water. Cover and simmer for 30 minutes or until the rice is just tender and the liquid has been absorbed.
2 Heat the oil in a large frying pan or wok and cook the onion, garlic, chilli and green pepper for 5 minutes until the onion is soft. Add the mushrooms and cook for a further 2-3 minutes, stirring occasionally.
3 Stir in the chicken, prawns, peanuts and cooked rice and cook for 3-4 minutes, stirring, until hot.
4 Add the remaining ingredients and continue cooking, stirring, for 1-2 minutes until heated through. Spoon on to a warmed serving dish, sprinkle with the shredded lettuce and serve immediately.

Casseroled Chicken with Figs

The casserole juices are rich and mildly sweet because of the addition of succulent fresh figs. Accompany with orange flavoured rice, or cook jacket potatoes alongside the casserole.

NUTRITIONAL ANALYSIS
amount per portion
810 kcals/3386 kJ
26.2 g Carbohydrate
48.7 g Protein ★ ★ ★ ★
54.7 g Fat
21.3 g Saturated Fat
0.0 g Added Sugar ★ ★ ★ ★
5.4 g Fibre ★ ★
855 mg Salt ★ ★
126 mg Calcium ★ ★ ★
3.3 mg Iron ★ ★
44 mg Folic Acid ★

SERVES 4

1.6 kg (3½ lb) chicken

salt and pepper, to taste

30 ml (2 tbsp) polyunsaturated oil

1 large onion, skinned and sliced

225 g (8 oz) carrots, scrubbed and sliced

45 ml (3 tbsp) plain white flour

150 ml (¼ pint) dry white wine

150 ml (¼ pint) chicken stock

finely grated rind and juice of 1 orange

30 ml (2 tbsp) chopped fresh lemon thyme or 5 ml (1 tsp) dried

8 ripe fresh figs, washed

1 Season the chicken inside with plenty of pepper.

2 Heat the oil in a flameproof casserole, carefully place the chicken into the dish, breast down, and brown all over.

3 Remove the chicken. Spoon all but 30 ml (2 tbsp) excess fat out of the dish. Add the onion and carrots and cook, stirring, until beginning to colour. Stir in the flour, then the wine, stock, orange rind and juice, thyme and seasoning. Bring to the boil and replace the chicken.

4 Cover the dish tightly. Cook at 190°C (375°F) mark 5 for about 1 hour or until the chicken is tender.

5 Add the figs to the casserole and continue to cook, covered, for 10-15 minutes.

6 Skim off excess fat, cut the chicken into joints and serve with orange flavoured rice.

NUTRITIONAL ANALYSIS
amount per portion
304 kcals/1272 kJ
2.4 g Carbohydrate
34.2 g Protein ★★★★
15.9 g Fat ★★
3.8 g Saturated Fat ★★★
0.0 g Added Sugar ★★★★
0.5 g Fibre
365 mg Salt ★★★
37 mg Calcium ★
6.4 mg Iron ★★★
365 mg Folic Acid ★★★★

Chicken Liver Kebabs

Herbs and grated orange rind flavour these nutritious kebabs. Serve with boiled brown rice and a salad for a really healthy main course.

SERVES 4

100 ml (4 fl oz) dry white wine
60 ml (4 tbsp) lemon juice
30 ml (2 tbsp) olive oil
1 garlic clove, skinned and crushed
15 ml (1 tbsp) chopped fresh tarragon or 10 ml (2 tsp) dried
finely grated rind of 1 orange
pepper, to taste
450 g (1 lb) boned chicken breasts, skinned and cubed
225 g (8 oz) chicken livers, halved
orange segments and watercress sprigs, to garnish

1 Mix the wine, lemon juice, olive oil, garlic, tarragon, orange rind and pepper together in a bowl.
2 Place the chicken and livers in a dish. Pour the marinade over, reserving about 75 ml (5 tbsp) for basting, and set aside for at least 4 hours, turning several times.
3 Thread the chicken pieces and livers alternately on to 4 long skewers.
4 Grill the kebabs for about 15 minutes, basting occasionally with the reserved marinade, and turning once during cooking. Garnish and serve hot.

NUTRITIONAL ANALYSIS
amount per portion
282 kcals/1180 kJ
23.2 g Carbohydrate
29.3 g Protein ★★★
9.1 g Fat ★★★
2.5 g Saturated Fat ★★★
0.0 g Added Sugar ★★★★
2.7 g Fibre ★
599 mg Salt ★★
43 mg Calcium ★
2.4 mg Iron ★★
30 mg Folic Acid ★

Turkey Paprika with Pasta

Paprika is a red pepper prepared from dried sweet peppers from Spain and Hungary. The flavours can vary from mild to hot. The best quality paprika is mild, sweet and bright red.

SERVES 4

15 ml (1 tbsp) polyunsaturated oil
1 small onion, skinned and sliced
450 g (1 lb) boned turkey breast, skinned and cut into strips
15 ml (1 tbsp) sweet paprika
450 ml (¾ pint) chicken stock
salt and pepper, to taste
1 green pepper, seeded and sliced
100 g (4 oz) small wholemeal pasta shapes
30 ml (2 tbsp) soured cream
sweet paprika, to garnish

1 Heat the oil in a large frying pan and fry the onion for 5 minutes until golden brown. Add the turkey and paprika to the pan and toss over moderate heat for 2 minutes.
2 Stir in the stock and seasoning and bring to the boil. Add the green pepper and pasta, cover and simmer gently for 15-20 minutes until the turkey and pasta are tender.
3 Stir in the soured cream and adjust the seasoning. To serve, garnish with a little paprika.

Pesto-stuffed Tomatoes (PAGE 54) *; Seekh Kebabs* (PAGE 80)*; Wild Rice and Thyme Salad* (PAGE 133)

Turkey and Ginger Stir-Fry

Quickly stir-frying these finely shredded pieces of vegetables and turkey uses less fat than other forms of frying. Also the vegetables retain more of their nutrients.

SERVES 4

30 ml (2 tbsp) polyunsaturated oil
4 spring onions, trimmed and roughly chopped
2.5 cm (1 inch) piece fresh root ginger, peeled and cut into thin strips
1 garlic clove, skinned and crushed
450 g (1 lb) boned turkey breast, skinned and cut into thin strips
1 red pepper, seeded and sliced
1 green pepper, seeded and cut into matchstick strips
1 leek, washed, trimmed and cut into thin strips
50 g (2 oz) shelled peanuts, unskinned
salt and pepper, to taste
15 ml (1 tbsp) sesame seeds
15 ml (1 tbsp) soy sauce, preferably naturally fermented shoyu

NUTRITIONAL ANALYSIS
amount per portion
305 kcals/1273 kJ
5.8 g Carbohydrate
29.7 g Protein ★★★
18.5 g Fat ★★
3.1 g Saturated Fat ★★★
0.0 g Added Sugar ★★★★
2.6 g Fibre ★
209 mg Salt ★★★★
81 mg Calcium ★★
2.5 mg Iron ★★
46 mg Folic Acid ★

1 Heat the oil in a large frying pan or wok and stir-fry the spring onions, ginger and garlic for 1 minute.

2 Add the turkey and stir-fry for 3-4 minutes until the turkey is evenly coloured. Stir in the peppers and leek and stir-fry for 2 minutes.

3 Add the peanuts, seasoning, sesame seeds and soy sauce and continue stir-frying for a further 2-3 minutes until the turkey is just tender. Serve piping hot.

Devilled Poussins (PAGE 92); *Cauliflower, Broccoli and Pepper Salad* (PAGE 135)

NUTRITIONAL ANALYSIS
amount per portion
370 kcals/1546 kJ
12.2 g Carbohydrate
27.4 g Protein ★★★
22.1 g Fat ★
2.5 g Saturated Fat ★★★
0.1 g Added Sugar ★★★★
8.5 g Fibre ★★★
796 mg Salt ★★
86 mg Calcium ★★
5.1 mg Iron ★★★
82 mg Folic Acid ★★

Stir-Fried Duck with Pecan Nuts

A mouthwatering, special occasion dish of strips of duck, spring onion and carrot stir-fried with crunchy pecan nuts and mange-tout. Simply serve with egg noodles.

SERVES 4

450 g (1 lb) duckling breast fillets, skinned

6 spring onions, trimmed

2 large carrots, scrubbed

30 ml (2 tbsp) polyunsaturated oil

1 garlic clove, skinned and crushed

225 g (8 oz) mange-tout

30 ml (2 tbsp) soy sauce, preferably naturally fermented shoyu

60 ml (4 tbsp) hoisin sauce

60 ml (4 tbsp) dry sherry

50 g (2 oz) pecan nuts

1 Thinly slice the duckling breasts. Cut the spring onions diagonally into similar sized strips. Cut the carrots into thick matchsticks.
2 Heat the oil with the garlic in a large frying pan or wok and stir-fry the duckling and carrots for 2-3 minutes, stirring all the time. Add the mange-tout and spring onions and fry for a further minute.
3 Add the soy sauce, hoisin sauce, dry sherry and pecan nuts, bring to the boil and boil for 1 minute. Serve hot with egg noodles.

NUTRITIONAL ANALYSIS
amount per portion
778 kcals/3251 kJ
6.1 g Carbohydrate
17.9 g Protein ★★★
74.8 g Fat
20.6 g Saturated Fat
0.0 g Added Sugar ★★★★
7.9 g Fibre ★★★
395 mg Salt ★★★
74 mg Calcium ★★
4.9 mg Iron ★★★
20 mg Folic Acid

Duck Breasts with Blackcurrant Sauce

Individual portions of duck are ideal for frying. Duck combines beautifully with fruit, as devotees of the classic duck with orange already know. Here blackcurrants are used but raspberries make an excellent alternative.

SERVES 2

2 duck breasts, with skins on

15 ml (1 tbsp) wine vinegar

30 ml (2 tbsp) dry white wine

213 g (7½ oz) can blackcurrants in unsweetened fruit juice

salt and pepper, to taste

1 Fry the duck breasts, skin side down, in a heavy based non-stick frying pan over high heat for 2-3 minutes. Turn the duck over and cook for a further 5 minutes until tender.
2 Slice the duck breasts neatly, then arrange on warmed serving plates.
3 Pour off any fat in the pan, then add the vinegar and boil rapidly for 1 minute, stirring in any sediment from the bottom of the pan. Stir in the wine. Lower the heat and stir in the blackcurrants with their juice. Season.
4 Heat gently, then pour the sauce over the duck. Serve hot with boiled new potatoes and a salad or green vegetable.

Turkey Tonnato

Turkey fillets are a low-fat substitute for the veal traditionally used in the Italian dish Vitello Tonnato. The chilling time ensures that the turkey will absorb the flavour of the tuna.

NUTRITIONAL ANALYSIS
amount per portion
319 kcals/1334 kJ
2.5 g Carbohydrate
33.3 g Protein ★★★★
18.6 g Fat ★★
3.4 g Saturated Fat ★★★
0.0 g Added Sugar ★★★★
1.2 g Fibre
1547 mg Salt ★
70 mg Calcium ★★
2.0 mg Iron ★★
33 mg Folic Acid ★

SERVES 4

450 g (1 lb) turkey fillets

60-90 ml (4-6 tbsp) dry white wine or cider

1 carrot, scrubbed and roughly chopped

2 celery sticks, trimmed

1 small onion, skinned and quartered

2 bay leaves

6 black peppercorns

100 g (3½ oz) can tuna in vegetable oil, drained

45 ml (3 tbsp) low-fat mayonnaise

45 ml (3 tbsp) lemon juice

pepper, to taste

50 g (2 oz) can anchovy fillets, drained and soaked in milk for 20 minutes

1 Place the turkey fillets into a heavy flameproof casserole or saucepan. Pour over 750 ml (1¼ pints) cold water and the wine. Add the carrot, celery, onion, bay leaves and peppercorns.

2 Bring slowly to the boil, lower the heat, cover and simmer gently for 10-15 minutes or until the turkey is just tender when pierced in the thickest part with a skewer.

3 Remove from the heat and leave the turkey to cool in the poaching liquid. Transfer the turkey to a board, reserving the poaching liquid, and cut into neat, thin slices. Arrange on a serving platter, cover and set aside.

4 Boil the poaching liquid rapidly until reduced to about 60 ml (4 tbsp). Strain and leave until cold.

5 Sieve the tuna into a bowl, pressing the fish through the sieve with the back of a spoon. Stir in the poaching liquid, mayonnaise, lemon juice and pepper and mix well until smooth. Spoon the dressing over the turkey, ensuring the meat is covered.

6 Drain and rinse the anchovies, pat dry with absorbent kitchen paper, then cut each one in half lengthways. Arrange the anchovies over the turkey in a lattice pattern, then sprinkle with the capers.

7 Cover and chill for 24-48 hours. Remove from the refrigerator at least 1 hour before serving.

NUTRITIONAL ANALYSIS
amount per portion
524 kcals/2191 kJ
8.5 g Carbohydrate
39.2 g Protein ★★★★
31.7 g Fat
6.8 g Saturated Fat ★★
0.0 g Added Sugar ★★★★
4.7 g Fibre ★★
2066 mg Salt
107 mg Calcium ★★
22.2 mg Iron ★★★★
48 mg Folic Acid ★

Pigeon and Cabbage Casserole

There is no close season for pigeons. They are available all the year but are best in August and September. Pink flesh and a plump breast are signs of tenderness.

SERVES 4

1 green, white or red cabbage, quartered

salt and pepper, to taste

6 streaky bacon rashers, rinded and chopped

2-4 pigeons, depending on size

8 small low-fat sausages, halved

2 onions, skinned and chopped

2.5 ml (½ tsp) ground cloves

300 ml (½ pint) red wine or wine and stock

1 Blanch the cabbage in a saucepan of boiling salted water for 5 minutes. Drain.

2 Fry the bacon in a large non-stick frying pan until the fat starts to run. Add the pigeons and sausages and fry for about 8 minutes until browned all over. Remove from the pan. Fry the onions in the fat remaining in the pan for 5 minutes until golden. Sprinkle the chopped bacon over the base of a casserole.

3 Shred the cabbage and mix with the onions and ground cloves. Spread half the cabbage mixture over the bacon, season with pepper and place the pigeons and sausages on top. Cover with the remaining cabbage, season with more pepper and pour over the wine.

4 Cover and cook at 170°C (325°F) mark 3 for about 1½ hours or until the birds are tender. Serve hot.

7

Fish and Shellfish Main Courses

Fish is full of protein, vitamins and minerals, and has the added benefit of being low in calories, too. White fish is also low in fats and easy to digest; oily fish is a rich source of vitamins A and D. Whatever fish you buy, make sure it is really fresh – pleasant smelling, firm fleshed and with bright eyes. The tempting recipes here show the many varied ways to present fish and shellfish from pies and casseroles to grills and bakes.

NUTRITIONAL ANALYSIS
amount per portion
252 kcals/1053 kJ
9.5 g Carbohydrate
37.6 g Protein ★★★★
5.6 g Fat ★★★
1.5 g Saturated Fat ★★★★
0.0 g Added Sugar ★★★★
0.5 g Fibre
724 mg Salt ★★
158 mg Calcium ★★★
1.1 mg Iron ★
24 mg Folic Acid

Plaice with Grapes

Poaching the plaice in this elegant recipe ensures none of the delicate flavour is lost, as the fish is topped with a sauce made from the poaching liquid.

SERVES 4

175 g (6 oz) green grapes, skinned, halved and seeded

8 large plaice or sole fillets, about 100 g (4 oz) each, skinned

100 ml (4 fl oz) dry white wine

100 ml (4 fl oz) fish stock

10 ml (2 tsp) finely chopped fresh basil or 5 ml (1 tsp) dried

2-3 bay leaves

5 ml (1 tsp) cornflour

100 ml (4 fl oz) semi-skimmed milk

salt and pepper, to taste

30 ml (2 tbsp) Greek strained yogurt

chopped fresh parsley, to garnish

1 Place 2-3 grape halves on the skinned side of each fillet. Roll up from the narrow end and arrange close together in a poaching pan or large saucepan.
2 Mix together the wine, stock, basil and bay leaves and pour over the fish. Bring to the boil, lower the heat, cover and poach gently for 10 minutes.
3 Using a slotted spoon, transfer the fish rolls to a serving dish, draining well, and keep warm. Simmer the cooking liquid for about 10 minutes to reduce by half. Remove the bay leaves.
4 Blend the cornflour with the milk, then stir into the cooking liquid. Season and bring back to the boil, stirring continuously until slightly thickened. Simmer for a further 5 minutes to give a pouring consistency. Stir in the yogurt.
5 Add the remaining grapes. Pour the sauce over the fish rolls and sprinkle with parsley. Serve at once.

Marinated Sole and Citrus Fruits

Yellow, orange and green citrus fruit rinds make a very attractive contrast to the white fish. Substitute any other flat fish fillets for the sole if you prefer in this vitamin C-rich main course.

SERVES 4
6 sole fillets, about 100 g (4 oz) each, skinned
finely grated rind and juice of 1 lime
finely grated rind and juice of 1 lemon
finely grated rind and juice of 1 orange
30 ml (2 tbsp) dry white wine
15 ml (1 tbsp) olive oil
30 ml (2 tbsp) chopped fresh parsley
1 shallot or small onion, skinned and finely chopped
salt and pepper, to taste
lime, lemon and orange wedges, to garnish

1 Cut the sole fillets in half widthways and place in a single layer in a shallow ovenproof dish. Mix the lime, lemon and orange rinds and juices with the wine, oil, parsley and shallot. Season and spoon over the fish. Cover and leave to marinate for at least 30 minutes.

2 Cover the fish tightly with foil. Bake at 200°C (400°F) mark 6 for 10-15 minutes or until tender.

3 Transfer the fish to a warmed serving dish and spoon over a little of the cooking liquid. Garnish with fruit wedges and serve with new potatoes and a green vegetable.

NUTRITIONAL ANALYSIS
amount per portion
170 kcals/711 kJ
2.0 g Carbohydrate
26.3 g Protein ★★★
5.9 g Fat ★★★
0.8 g Saturated Fat ★★★★
0.0 g Added Sugar ★★★★
0.8 g Fibre
373 mg Salt ★★★
56 mg Calcium ★★
1.5 mg Iron ★★
24 mg Folic Acid

Spanish Cod with Mussels

Mussels are at their best during the colder months, from October to March. Serve this colourful dish with hot crusty bread, followed by a crisp green salad.

SERVES 4
1 litre (1¾ pints) mussels, cleaned
300 ml (½ pint) dry white wine
700 g (1½ lb) cod fillet, skinned and cut into chunks
2 medium onions, skinned and sliced
1 red pepper, seeded and sliced
1-2 garlic cloves, skinned and crushed
450 g (1 lb) tomatoes, skinned and chopped
2.5 ml (½ tsp) Tabasco sauce, or to taste
1 bay leaf
salt and pepper, to taste

1 Put the mussels and wine in a large saucepan. Cover and cook for 4-5 minutes or until all the mussels have opened, shaking the pan occasionally. Drain, reserving the cooking liquid. Shell all but 8 mussels.

2 Layer the cod and vegetables in a casserole, then add the Tabasco sauce, bay leaf and seasoning. Pour over the reserved cooking liquid.

3 Cover and cook at 180°C (350°F) mark 4 for 45 minutes. Discard the bay leaf and add the mussels. Cover and cook for a further 15 minutes. Serve immediately.

NUTRITIONAL ANALYSIS
amount per portion
386 kcals/1613 kJ
8.0 g Carbohydrate
62.7 g Protein ★★★★
6.2 g Fat ★★★
1.2 g Saturated Fat ★★★★
0.0 g Added Sugar ★★★★
2.8 g Fibre ★
2218 mg Salt
291 mg Calcium ★★★★
16.2 mg Iron ★★★★
66 mg Folic Acid ★★

NUTRITIONAL ANALYSIS
amount per portion
328 kcals/1372 kJ
14.8 g Carbohydrate
41.4 g Protein ★★★★
8.1 g Fat ★★★
2.3 g Saturated Fat ★★★
5.0 g Added Sugar ★★★
1.8 g Fibre ★
1417 mg Salt ★
136 mg Calcium ★★★
4.2 mg Iron ★★★
32 mg Folic Acid ★

Steamed Mullet with Chilli Sauce

Silvery grey, with dark grey lines along its flank, the grey mullet is found in coastal waters and estuaries all over the world. First marinated then steamed, this flavoursome dish is served with a hot piquant sauce.

SERVES 2

1 grey mullet, about 550 g (1¼ lb), cleaned
75 ml (5 tbsp) no-sugar tomato ketchup
15 ml (1 tbsp) soy sauce, preferably naturally fermented shoyu
pinch of chilli powder
75 ml (5 tbsp) white wine
1 small red pepper, seeded and cut into matchsticks
1 small green pepper, seeded and cut into matchsticks
5 ml (1 tsp) cornflour
15 ml (1 tbsp) chopped fresh parsley
salt and pepper, to taste

1 Place the mullet in a shallow dish. Make 3 deep slashes along the length of the fish.
2 Whisk the tomato ketchup, soy sauce, chilli powder and wine together in a bowl. Pour the marinade over the fish. Cover and leave for 2 hours.
3 Drain off the marinade and reserve. Place the fish on a rack over a roasting tin half full of water. Cover tightly with foil. Steam the fish over a medium heat for 20-25 minutes. When cooked, the eyes should be white.
4 To make the chilli sauce, place the reserved marinade and the peppers in a saucepan. Stir in the cornflour mixed to a smooth paste with 15 ml (1 tbsp) water. Bring to the boil and simmer for 4-5 minutes. Stir in the parsley and seasoning.
5 Carefully lift the steamed mullet on to a warmed serving plate. Spoon over the sauce to serve.

Trout Poached in Wine

If you are unused to buying whole fresh fish at the fishmonger, you may find the different types of trout confusing. For this recipe you will need to buy freshwater trout, i.e. river, rainbow or lake trout, which are now becoming increasingly widely available, both fresh and frozen, at supermarkets. Look for shiny, slippery skin and bright eyes – both good indications of freshness.

SERVES 4
4 small trout, with heads on
salt and pepper, to taste
40 g (1½ oz) polyunsaturated margarine
1 large onion, skinned and sliced
2 celery sticks, trimmed and sliced
2 carrots, scrubbed and very thinly sliced
300 ml (½ pint) dry white wine
bouquet garni
15 ml (1 tbsp) plain white flour
lemon wedges and chopped fresh parsley, to garnish

1 Wash the trout under cold running water and drain. Pat dry and season the insides.
2 Melt 15 g (½ oz) of the margarine in a small saucepan, add the onion, celery and carrots and stir well to cover with margarine. Cover and sweat for 5 minutes.
3 Lay the vegetables in a greased casserole and arrange the fish on top. Pour over the wine and add the bouquet garni. Cover tightly.
4 Cook at 180°C (350°F) mark 4 for about 25 minutes until the trout are cooked. Transfer the trout and vegetables to a warmed serving dish and keep hot.
5 Pour the cooking juices into a small pan, discarding the bouquet garni. Blend together the remaining margarine and the flour. Whisk into the sauce and simmer gently, stirring, until thickened. Pour into a sauceboat or jug. Garnish the trout with lemon wedges and parsley.

NUTRITIONAL ANALYSIS
amount per portion
319 kcals/1332 kJ
7.9 g Carbohydrate
29.5 g Protein ★ ★ ★
13.7 g Fat ★ ★
2.7 g Saturated Fat ★ ★ ★
0.0 g Added Sugar ★ ★ ★ ★
2.1 g Fibre ★
653 mg Salt ★ ★
99 mg Calcium ★ ★
2.2 mg Iron ★ ★
16 mg Folic Acid

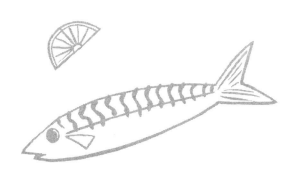

NUTRITIONAL ANALYSIS
amount per portion
230 kcals/962 kJ
3.2 g Carbohydrate
31.5 g Protein ★★★★
10.3 g Fat ★★
1.5 g Saturated Fat ★★★★
0.0 g Added Sugar ★★★★
0.8 g Fibre
387 mg Salt ★★★
71 mg Calcium ★★
1.1 mg Iron ★
31 mg Folic Acid ★

Marinated Cod Steaks

Sesame seeds give a pleasant crunch to the finished dish.

SERVES 4
30 ml (2 tbsp) grapeseed oil
30 ml (2 tbsp) white wine vinegar
10 ml (2 tsp) sesame seeds
pinch of mustard powder
salt and pepper, to taste
4 cod steaks, about 175 g (6 oz) each
1 large onion, skinned and thinly sliced

1 Whisk the oil, vinegar, sesame seeds, mustard powder and seasoning together in a jug.
2 Place the cod steaks in a shallow dish into which they just fit, add the onion rings and pour over the marinade. Cover and leave to marinate overnight in the refrigerator, turning once.
3 Line a grill pan with foil and carefully add the steaks and onion. Cook under a hot grill for about 4 minutes each side, brushing well with the marinade. Serve with mange-tout.

Monkfish with Mustard Seeds

The firm, white flesh of the monkfish comes from the tail end, as a third of the length of the fish is taken up by a large unattractive head.

SERVES 6
45 ml (3 tbsp) black mustard seeds
30 ml (2 tbsp) plain white flour
900 g (2 lb) monkfish fillet, skinned
30 ml (2 tbsp) mustard oil or polyunsaturated oil
1 medium onion, skinned and thinly sliced
300 ml (½ pint) low-fat natural yogurt
1 garlic clove, skinned and crushed
15 ml (1 tbsp) lemon juice
salt and pepper, to taste
whole prawns and coriander, to garnish

NUTRITIONAL ANALYSIS
amount per portion
261 kcals/1089 kJ
9.9 g Carbohydrate
28.6 g Protein ★★★
11.4 g Fat ★★
1.8 g Saturated Fat ★★★★
0.0 g Added Sugar ★★★★
1.0 g Fibre
580 mg Salt ★★
241 mg Calcium ★★★
1.5 mg Iron ★★
23 mg Folic Acid

1 Finely grind 30 ml (2 tbsp) of the mustard seeds in a small electric mill or with a pestle and mortar. Mix them with the flour.
2 Cut the monkfish into 2.5 cm (1 inch) cubes and toss in the flour and ground mustard seeds.
3 Heat the oil in a large heavy-based frying pan and fry the onion for about 5 minutes until golden.
4 Add the remaining mustard seeds to the pan with the monkfish. Fry over moderate heat for 3-4 minutes, turning very gently once or twice.
5 Gradually stir in the yogurt with the garlic, lemon juice and seasoning. Bring to the boil, lower the heat and simmer for 10-15 minutes or until the fish is tender.
6 Taste and adjust the seasoning. Turn into a warmed serving dish and garnish with the prawns and coriander. Serve immediately.

Fish Pie

A luxury salmon and cod mixture enclosed in a mouthwatering yeast pastry.

SERVES 4
1 egg, size 2, beaten
150 g (5 oz) strong wholemeal flour
2.5 ml (½ tsp) easy blend yeast
15 ml (1 tbsp) polyunsaturated oil
225 g (8 oz) salmon steak
225 g (8 oz) cod steak
200 ml (⅓ pint) semi-skimmed milk, plus a little extra, to mix
grated nutmeg
salt and pepper, to taste
25 g (1 oz) cornflour
100 g (4 oz) button mushrooms, chopped
2 eggs, size 2, hard-boiled and chopped
30 ml (2 tbsp) chopped fresh parsley

NUTRITIONAL ANALYSIS
amount per portion
404 kcals/1688 kJ
32.9 g Carbohydrate
31.8 g Protein ★★★★
17.3 g Fat ★★
4.1 g Saturated Fat ★★
0.0 g Added Sugar ★★★★
4.9 g Fibre ★★
473 mg Salt ★★★
148 mg Calcium ★★★
3.9 mg Iron ★★★
80 mg Folic Acid ★★

1 Lightly grease a baking dish or sheet. Reserving 15 ml (1 tbsp) beaten egg for the glaze, mix together the egg, flour, yeast, oil and about 45 ml (3 tbsp) warm water to make a soft, not sticky, dough. Knead for 5 minutes on a lightly floured surface, then cover and leave to rise in a warm place for 30 minutes.

2 Meanwhile, put the fish in a saucepan with the milk, 1.25 ml (¼ tsp) grated nutmeg and seasoning. Bring to the boil and simmer gently for 15 minutes. Strain the milk into a bowl and reserve. Cool the fish, then flake, discarding the skin and bones.

3 Mix the cornflour to a paste with a little cold milk. Add the reserved milk, mix well and return to the pan. Bring to the boil, stirring, until thickened. Remove from the heat and fold in the flaked fish, mushrooms, egg and parsley. Season with a little extra nutmeg and seasoning.

4 Knead the dough for 10 minutes on a lightly floured surface, then roll out thinly. Trim into a neat 30 cm (12 inch) square, reserving trimmings for decoration. Transfer the pastry square to the prepared dish or sheet and place the fish mixture in the centre.

5 Brush some cold water around the edge of the square. Draw up the points of the square to the middle to form an envelope shape and seal the edges together well.

6 Mix the reserved egg with 5 ml (1 tsp) water and glaze the top of the pie. Decorate with the dough trimmings and glaze the decorations. Prick a couple of holes in the top. Bake at 200°C (400°F) mark 6 for 20-25 minutes until golden brown. Serve hot with a mixed salad.

NUTRITIONAL ANALYSIS
amount per portion
453 kcals/1892 kJ
2.1 g Carbohydrate
32.7 g Protein ★★★★
35.1 g Fat
7.1 g Saturated Fat ★★
0.0 g Added Sugar ★★★★
2.2 g Fibre ★
650 mg Salt ★★
112 mg Calcium ★★
5.1 mg Iron ★★★
0.0 mg Folic Acid

Spiced Grilled Mackerel

Like all oily fish, mackerel are a good source of vitamins A and D. However, because of their oil content, they deteriorate quickly, so choose ones with rigid bodies and with bright eyes and gills.

SERVES 4

4 fresh mackerel, about 275 g (10 oz) each, cleaned
juice of 1 lemon
60 ml (4 tbsp) chopped fresh coriander
10 ml (2 tsp) garam masala
5 ml (1 tsp) ground cumin
5 ml (1 tsp) chilli powder
salt and pepper, to taste
30 ml (2 tbsp) polyunsaturated oil
lemon wedges, to serve

1 First bone the mackerel. With a sharp knife, cut off the heads just behind the gills. Extend the cut along the belly to both ends of the fish so that the fish can be opened out.
2 Place the fish on a board, skin side facing upwards. With the heel of your hand, press along the backbone to loosen it.
3 Turn the fish over and lift out the backbone, using the tip of the knife if necessary to help pull the bone away from the flesh cleanly. Discard the bone.
4 Remove the tail and cut each fish in half lengthways, then wash under cold running water and pat dry with absorbent kitchen paper. Score the skin side in several places with a knife.
5 Mix the lemon juice, half of the coriander, the garam masala, cumin, chilli powder and seasoning together in a jug.
6 Put the mackerel in a grill pan and pour over the marinade. Cover and leave at cool room temperature for 2 hours, turning the fish once and brushing with the marinade.
7 When ready to cook, brush half the oil over the skin side of the mackerel. Cook under moderate grill for 5 minutes, then turn the fish over and brush with the remaining oil. Grill for a further 5 minutes.
8 Transfer the fish to a warmed serving platter and sprinkle with the remaining coriander. Serve immediately, accompanied by lemon wedges.

Tempura

A special occasion dish of seafood and vegetables deep-fried in batter, then served with a piquant dipping sauce.

SERVES 4

75 g (3 oz) plain wholemeal flour

75 g (3 oz) plain white flour

1 egg, size 3

60 ml (4 tbsp) soy sauce, preferably naturally fermented shoyu

30 ml (2 tbsp) sesame or polyunsaturated oil

30 ml (2 tbsp) dry sherry

2 fresh green chillies, seeded and finely chopped

2 garlic cloves, skinned and crushed

1 cm (½ inch) piece fresh root ginger, peeled and finely chopped

1 spring onion, trimmed and chopped

polyunsaturated or groundnut oil, for deep-frying

225 g (8 oz) large raw prawns, shelled and deveined

8 scallops, shelled and cleaned

1 carrot, scrubbed and cut into 0.5 cm (¼ inch) sticks

1 courgette, trimmed and cut into 0.5 cm (¼ inch) sticks

16 button mushrooms

spring onions, to garnish

NUTRITIONAL ANALYSIS
amount per portion
565 kcals/2360 kJ
30.7 g Carbohydrate
36.9 g Protein ★ ★ ★ ★
32.6 g Fat
6.0 g Saturated Fat ★ ★
0.1 g Added Sugar ★ ★ ★ ★
4.1 g Fibre ★ ★
2856 mg Salt
236 mg Calcium ★ ★ ★
5.6 mg Iron ★ ★ ★
46 mg Folic Acid ★

1 To make the batter, put the flours into a bowl and beat in the egg and 225 ml (8 fl oz) cold water to make a stiff batter. Cover and refrigerate for 30 minutes.

2 Meanwhile to make the sauce, mix the soy sauce, oil and sherry together. Add the chillies, garlic, ginger and spring onion. Stir the mixture well. Set aside.

3 Heat the oil in a deep-fat fryer to 180°C (350°F). Coat the seafood and vegetables in the batter, shaking off any surplus, and deep-fry in batches for about 2-3 minutes until golden brown. As the food is cooked, place in an ovenproof dish lined with absorbent kitchen paper. Keep warm in the oven.

4 Arrange the tempura on a large dish. Garnish with spring onions. Stir the sauce and divide between 4 saucers. Let everyone help themselves to tempura with a fork or chopsticks and dip into their own portion of sauce. Serve with noodles and stir-fried vegetables.

Mediterranean Fish Stew

Serve sprinkled with parsley and with lots of crusty wholemeal bread to soak up the delicious juices.

NUTRITIONAL ANALYSIS
amount per portion
409 kcals/1709 kJ
6.5 g Carbohydrate
53.2 g Protein ★★★★
13.2 g Fat ★★
2.0 g Saturated Fat ★★★
0.0 g Added Sugar ★★★★
2.2 g Fibre ★
3658 mg Salt
242 mg Calcium ★★★
9.5 mg Iron ★★★★
55 mg Folic Acid ★★

SERVES 4

450 g (1 lb) fresh mussels

30 ml (2 tbsp) olive oil

1 onion, skinned and thinly sliced

1 garlic clove, skinned and crushed

450 g (1 lb) tomatoes, skinned, seeded and chopped

300 ml (½ pint) dry white wine

450 ml (¾ pint) fish stock

15 ml (1 tbsp) chopped fresh dill or 5 ml (1 tsp) dried dill weed

10 ml (2 tsp) chopped fresh rosemary or 5 ml (1 tsp) dried

15 ml (1 tbsp) tomato purée

salt and pepper, to taste

450 g (1 lb) monkfish fillet, skinned and cut into large chunks

4 jumbo prawns, peeled

225 g (8 oz) squid, cleaned and cut into rings

1 To clean the mussels, put in a large bowl and scrape well under cold running water. Cut off the 'beards'. Discard any that are open. Rinse until there is no trace of sand in the bowl.

2 Heat the oil in a large saucepan or flameproof casserole and gently cook the onion for 3-4 minutes. Add the garlic and tomatoes and cook for a further 3-4 minutes.

3 Add the white wine, stock, herbs, tomato purée and seasoning. Bring to the boil, lower the heat and simmer for a further 5 minutes.

4 Add the monkfish and simmer for 5 minutes. Add the prawns and squid and simmer for a further 5 minutes. Add the prepared mussels, cover the pan and cook for 3-4 minutes until the shells open. Discard any of the mussels that do not open. Ladle the stew into individual bowls and serve.

Lettuce and Smoked Mackerel Dolmas

A refreshing yogurt and cucumber sauce is served with these lettuce parcels filled with a nutritious mackerel, egg and brown rice mixture.

SERVES 6	
1 large Batavia or Cos lettuce	45 ml (3 tbsp) lemon juice
salt and pepper, to taste	150 ml (¼ pint) set low-fat natural yogurt
100 g (4 oz) long-grain brown rice, cooked	105 ml (7 tbsp) fish stock
2 eggs, hard-boiled and chopped	150 ml (¼ pint) low-fat natural yogurt
225 g (8 oz) smoked mackerel fillet, skinned, boned and flaked	¼ cucumber, finely grated
	5 ml (1 tsp) chopped fresh mint or coriander

1 Ease off 12 lettuce leaves and cut out the tough stalk from the core end. Blanch a few at a time in a saucepan of boiling salted water for 1 minute. Drain.
2 Mix the rice, egg, mackerel, 30 ml (2 tbsp) of the lemon juice and set yogurt together in a bowl. Season. Divide the filling into 12.
3 Wrap each portion in a blanched lettuce leaf to make a neat parcel. Pack, seam side down, in a single layer in an ovenproof dish. Pour over the stock and cover tightly.
4 Cook at 200°C (400°F) mark 6 for about 20 minutes.
5 While the dolmas are cooking, make the sauce. Mix the yogurt, remaining lemon juice, cucumber and mint together and season. Serve the dolmas hot with the sauce handed separately.

NUTRITIONAL ANALYSIS
amount per portion
170 kcals/711 kJ
9.7 g Carbohydrate
13.8 g Protein ★★
8.8 g Fat ★★★
1.4 g Saturated Fat ★★★★
0.0 g Added Sugar ★★★★
1.4 g Fibre
433 mg Salt ★★★
125 mg Calcium ★★
1.7 mg Iron ★★
33 mg Folic Acid ★

Poached Skate with Capers

There are many varieties of skate available from Mediterranean waters. Only the wings of the skate are eaten and are sold either ready-skinned or with the skin on, which you remove after cooking.

SERVES 4
1 onion, skinned and chopped
1 bay leaf
1 clove
90 ml (6 tbsp) cider vinegar
2 parsley sprigs
6 black peppercorns
700 g (1½ lb) skate, cut into 4 pieces
30 ml (2 tbsp) lemon juice
15 ml (1 tbsp) capers
lemon slices and parsley, to garnish

1 Put the onion in a wide saucepan with 1.1 litres (2 pints) water, the bay leaf, clove, cider vinegar, parsley and peppercorns. Bring to the boil and simmer for 20 minutes.
2 Slip the skate pieces into the simmering liquid and cook gently for 15-20 minutes until the fish is tender and flakes easily when tested with a fork.
3 Lift the fish from the liquid using a fish slice. If necessary, remove the skin from both sides using a small sharp knife.
4 Place the fish on a warmed serving platter and sprinkle with the lemon juice and capers. Serve garnished with lemon slices and parsley.

NUTRITIONAL ANALYSIS
amount per portion
172 kcals/718 kJ
2.1 g Carbohydrate
31.5 g Protein ★★★★
4.3 g Fat ★★★★
0.5 g Saturated Fat ★★★★
0.1 g Added Sugar ★★★★
0.6 g Fibre
415 mg Salt ★★★
32 mg Calcium ★
1.1 mg Iron ★
28 mg Folic Acid ★

Prawns and Rice with Dill

Uncooked Mediterranean prawns are expensive but their flavour and texture are superior to the smaller cooked prawns.

NUTRITIONAL ANALYSIS
amount per portion
387 kcals/1616 kJ
38.1 g Carbohydrate
29.5 g Protein ★★★
13.9 g Fat ★★
2.0 g Saturated Fat ★★★
0.0 g Added Sugar ★★★★
2.3 g Fibre ★
4766 mg Salt
190 mg Calcium ★★★
2.5 mg Iron ★★
56 mg Folic Acid ★★

SERVES 4

175 g (6 oz) long-grain brown rice

salt and pepper, to taste

450 g (1 lb) raw prawns, in their shells without heads

30 ml (2 tbsp) polyunsaturated oil

1 large bulb fennel, trimmed and thinly sliced

2 large courgettes, trimmed and roughly chopped

150 ml (¼ pint) fish or vegetable stock

15 g (½ oz) polyunsaturated margarine

30 ml (2 tbsp) chopped fresh dill

1 garlic clove, skinned and crushed

1 Cook the rice in a saucepan of boiling salted water for about 30 minutes or until tender. Rinse with boiling water and drain well.

2 Meanwhile, peel the prawns, cut down their backs and remove the black intestine. Wash well and dry on absorbent kitchen paper. Halve, or divide into 3 if large.

3 Heat the oil in a large frying pan and stir-fry the prawns quickly until pink. Remove from the pan with a slotted spoon.

4 Add the fennel to the pan and stir-fry for 2-3 minutes until slightly softened. Mix in the courgettes and stir-fry briefly. Stir in the rice and seasoning and heat through thoroughly, stirring.

5 Return the prawns to the pan with the stock and bring to the boil. Cover and cook gently for 3-4 minutes or until the prawns are cooked and just firm.

6 Adjust the seasoning. Just before serving, stir in the margarine, dill and garlic.

Swedish Herrings

The herring is a firm, meaty fish which is rich in oil. This traditional Scandinavian recipe would make an excellent summer dish, served with warm crusty bread and salad.

SERVES 4
8 herring fillets
salt and pepper, to taste
4 whole cloves
2 dried chillies
12 peppercorns
1 bay leaf
1 blade mace
60 ml (4 tbsp) malt vinegar
75 ml (5 tbsp) tarragon vinegar
1 shallot or small onion, skinned and finely chopped
chopped fresh dill and lemon slices, to garnish
150 ml (¼ pint) Greek strained yogurt, to serve

NUTRITIONAL ANALYSIS
amount per portion
516 kcals/2158 kJ
1.5 g Carbohydrate
35.9 g Protein ★★★★
40.8 g Fat
10.2 g Saturated Fat ★
0.0 g Added Sugar ★★★★
0.0 g Fibre
348 mg Salt ★★★
111 mg Calcium ★★
1.6 mg Iron ★★
13 mg Folic Acid

1 Sprinkle the herring fillets, skin side down, with seasoning, then roll up from the head end.

2 Arrange the rolled herrings in a casserole and add the cloves, chillies, peppercorns, bay leaf and mace. Cover with the vinegars and 150 ml (¼ pint) water. Sprinkle the shallot on top.

3 Cover and cook at 170°C (325°F) mark 3 for about 45 minutes or until the herring fillets are tender.

4 Transfer the fish carefully to a serving dish and strain or pour the liquor over. Leave to cool for about 2-3 hours.

5 Garnish with dill and lemon slices and serve cold with yogurt.

NUTRITIONAL ANALYSIS
amount per portion
341 kcals/1427 kJ
1.5 g Carbohydrate
38.9 g Protein ★★★★
18.8 g Fat ★★
3.6 g Saturated Fat ★★★
1.0 g Added Sugar ★★★★
0.0 g Fibre
599 mg Salt ★★
84 mg Calcium ★★
2.2 mg Iron ★★
17 mg Folic Acid

Grilled Red Mullet

Fish is an excellent source of protein and low in saturated fat – try to eat it at least twice a week if not more often.

SERVES 4
4 red mullet, cleaned
pepper, to taste
fresh rosemary sprigs
juice of 1 lemon
30 ml (2 tbsp) red wine vinegar
10 ml (2 tsp) Worcestershire sauce
10 ml (2 tsp) clear honey
45 ml (3 tbsp) corn oil
10 ml (2 tsp) chopped fresh rosemary

1 Remove the scales from the fish by scraping from tail to head with the back of a knife; rinse well. Sprinkle pepper inside each fish and put 1 sprig of rosemary in each. Arrange in a dish.

2 Mix together the lemon juice, vinegar, Worcestershire sauce, honey, oil and chopped rosemary then pour over the fish. Cover and leave to marinate for 30 minutes, turning once.

3 To grill, place more rosemary sprigs on top of the drained fish. Cook under a medium grill for 10-15 minutes, turning carefully once and brushing with the marinade.

4 Discard the cooked rosemary sprigs and use fresh sprigs to garnish. Serve hot with brown rice and fresh peas.

West Country Cod

Use homemade fish stock for the best flavour.

NUTRITIONAL ANALYSIS
amount per portion
160 kcals/671 kJ
3.8 g Carbohydrate
31.1 g Protein ★★★★
1.3 g Fat ★★★★
0.2 g Saturated Fat ★★★★
0.0 g Added Sugar ★★★★
0.6 g Fibre
490 mg Salt ★★★
51 mg Calcium ★★
1.2 mg Iron ★
31 mg Folic Acid ★

SERVES 4

4 cod fillets, each about 175 g (6 oz), skinned

1 onion, skinned and thinly sliced

pepper, to taste

thinly pared rind of 1 orange, cut into 7.5 cm (3 inch) strips

juice of 1 small orange

150 ml (¼ pint) medium-dry cider

100 ml (4 fl oz) fish or vegetable stock

10 ml (2 tsp) chopped fresh coriander

coriander sprigs, to garnish

1 Wipe the fish with absorbent kitchen paper and put in a shallow 1.1 litre (2 pint) ovenproof dish. Cover the fish with the onion, seasoning and orange rind.

2 Mix the orange juice with the cider and fish stock. Pour over the fish, cover and cook at 190°C (375°F) mark 5 for 20-25 minutes or until the fish is cooked through and flakes easily when tested with a fork. Place the fish, onion and orange strips on a serving dish and keep warm.

3 Strain the cooking liquid into a small saucepan and boil rapidly for 5 minutes or until reduced by half. Pour over the fish and sprinkle with the coriander. Garnish and serve hot.

8

Vegetarian Main Courses

There are some excellent main courses to try without using meat, poultry or fish. These colourful, nutritious dishes include nuts, cheese, pulses, vegetables and grains. Pulses are an important source of protein but, for a complete protein meal, a grain, such as brown rice, wholemeal bread or pasta, must be served as well. This can either be included in the dish or served as an accompaniment.

Buckwheat and Lentil Casserole

Buckwheat consists of tiny, brown seeds. They are high in protein and contain most of the B vitamins. The grains are gluten free.

SERVES 4

150 g (5 oz) buckwheat

salt and pepper, to taste

30 ml (2 tbsp) polyunsaturated oil

1 red or green pepper, seeded and cut into strips

1 medium onion, skinned and finely chopped

350 g (12 oz) courgettes, trimmed and sliced

175 g (6 oz) mushrooms, sliced

225 g (8 oz) red lentils, washed (see page 118)

3 bay leaves

30 ml (2 tbsp) lemon juice

1 garlic clove, skinned and crushed

2 rosemary sprigs

5 ml (1 tsp) cumin seeds

600 ml (1 pint) vegetable stock

chopped fresh parsley, to garnish

NUTRITIONAL ANALYSIS
amount per portion
413 kcals/1726 kJ
67.1 g Carbohydrate
19.4 g Protein ★★★
9.3 g Fat ★★★
3.3 g Saturated Fat ★★★★
0.0 g Added Sugar ★★★★
8.5 g Fibre ★★★
406 mg Salt ★★★
59 mg Calcium ★★
6.5 mg Iron ★★★
58 mg Folic Acid ★★

1 Bring 450 ml (¾ pint) water to the boil in a saucepan, sprinkle in the buckwheat, add a pinch of salt and return to the boil. Boil rapidly for 1 minute. Lower the heat, cover and cook gently, without stirring, for 12 minutes or until the water has been absorbed. Transfer to a greased casserole.

2 Heat the oil in a flameproof casserole or saucepan and fry the pepper and onion for 5 minutes. Add the courgettes and mushrooms and fry for 5 minutes. Stir in the lentils, bay leaves, lemon juice, garlic, rosemary, cumin and stock. Add to the buckwheat and stir well.

3 Simmer for 45 minutes until the lentils are cooked, stirring occasionally. Adjust the seasoning and sprinkle with parsley. Serve with boiled rice and grated cheese, if liked.

Spiced Red Lentils with Aubergine and Mushrooms

The seeds of cumin, black mustard and fennel are quickly fried to release their aromas, then mixed into the lentils and vegetables at the end of the cooking time to add the spicy flavour.

NUTRITIONAL ANALYSIS
amount per portion
224 kcals/935 kJ
33.6 g Carbohydrate
15.2 g Protein ★★★
4.1 g Fat ★★★★
0.5 g Saturated Fat ★★★★
0.4 g Added Sugar ★★★★
8.8 g Fibre ★★★
85 mg Salt ★★★★
56 mg Calcium ★★
6.3 mg Iron ★★★
36 mg Folic Acid ★

SERVES 6
350 g (12 oz) red lentils
5 ml (1 tsp) ground turmeric
2 garlic cloves, skinned and crushed
1 aubergine, trimmed
225 g (8 oz) mushrooms, halved
salt and pepper, to taste
2.5 ml (½ tsp) light muscovado sugar
15 ml (1 tbsp) polyunsaturated oil
5 ml (1 tsp) cumin seeds
5 ml (1 tsp) black mustard seeds
2.5 ml (½ tsp) fennel seeds
5 ml (1 tsp) garam masala
chopped fresh coriander, to garnish

1 Pick over the lentils and remove any grit or discoloured pulses. Put into a sieve and wash thoroughly under cold running water. Drain well.

2 Put the lentils in a large saucepan with the turmeric and garlic. Cover with 1.4 litres (2½ pints) water. Bring to the boil, lower the heat and simmer for about 25 minutes.

3 Meanwhile, cut the aubergine into 2.5 cm (1 inch) cubes. Add the aubergine and mushrooms to the lentils with seasoning and the sugar. Continue simmering gently for 15-20 minutes until the vegetables are tender.

4 Heat the oil in a separate small saucepan and fry the remaining spices for 1 minute or until the mustard seeds begin to pop.

5 Stir the spice mixture into the lentils, cover the pan with a tight-fitting lid and remove from the heat. Leave to stand for 5 minutes for the flavours to develop. Turn into a warmed serving dish and garnish with coriander. Serve hot with boiled rice.

Mixed Vegetable Loaf

Carrots, courgettes and leeks make a delicious combination for this baked vegetable loaf. It is accompanied by a well flavoured tomato sauce.

SERVES 4

10 ml (2 tsp) polyunsaturated oil

350 g (12 oz) carrots, scrubbed and grated

350 g (12 oz) courgettes, trimmed and grated

225 g (8 oz) leeks, washed, trimmed and finely shredded

1 garlic clove, skinned and crushed

150 g (5 oz) fresh wholemeal breadcrumbs

75 g (3 oz) Cheddar cheese, grated

3 eggs, size 2, beaten

45 ml (3 tbsp) low-fat natural yogurt

30 ml (2 tbsp) chopped fresh parsley

salt and pepper, to taste

TOMATO SAUCE

1 kg (2¼ lb) ripe tomatoes, skinned and coarsely chopped

1 small onion, skinned and finely chopped

1 carrot, scrubbed and chopped

2 celery sticks, trimmed and finely chopped

1 garlic clove, skinned and crushed

30 ml (2 tbsp) chopped fresh parsley

15 ml (1 tbsp) chopped fresh basil or 7.5 ml (1½ tsp) dried

NUTRITIONAL ANALYSIS
amount per portion
345 kcals/1441 kJ
34.8 g Carbohydrate
20.8 g Protein ★★★
14.5 g Fat ★★
6.3 g Saturated Fat ★★
0.0 g Added Sugar ★★★★
12.3 g Fibre ★★★
1559 mg Salt ★
404 mg Calcium ★★★★
7.3 mg Iron ★★★★
133 mg Folic Acid ★★★

1 Lightly grease a 900 g (2 lb) loaf tin and line the base with greased greaseproof paper. Heat the oil in a saucepan and gently cook the vegetables and garlic for 5 minutes. Drain off the liquid and discard. Mix the vegetables with the breadcrumbs, cheese, eggs, yogurt, parsley and seasoning.

2 Transfer the mixture to the loaf tin and cover with greased foil. Stand the tin in a roasting tin and add enough hot water to come halfway up the sides of the loaf tin. Bake at 180°C (350°F) mark 4 for 55-60 minutes until set.

3 While the loaf is cooking make the sauce. Put all the ingredients into a saucepan. Cover and simmer for about 45 minutes until the vegetables are soft. Cool slightly, then purée the sauce in a blender or food processor. Reheat gently.

4 Ease the cooked loaf away from the tin with a palette knife and invert on to a warmed serving dish. Serve sliced with the sauce.

Filo Spinach Pie

Feta is the best known Greek cheese. Traditionally made from sheep or goat's milk, it is curdled naturally without rennet.

NUTRITIONAL ANALYSIS
amount per portion
452 kcals/1889 kJ
47.2 g Carbohydrate
23.5 g Protein ★★★
20.4 g Fat ★★
9.4 g Saturated Fat ★★
1.4 g Added Sugar ★★★★
4.1 g Fibre ★★
3129 mg Salt
671 mg Calcium ★★★★
40.2 mg Iron ★★★★
452 mg Folic Acid ★★★★

SERVES 4
15 ml (1 tbsp) olive oil plus 5 ml (1 tsp)
1 onion, skinned and chopped
1-2 garlic cloves, skinned and crushed
2.5 ml (½ tsp) ground cinnamon
1.4 kg (3 lb) fresh spinach, washed, trimmed and roughly chopped, or three 225 g (8 oz) packets frozen spinach
15 ml (1 tbsp) chopped fresh oregano or marjoram or 7.5 ml (1½ tsp) dried
grated nutmeg, to taste
salt and pepper, to taste
100 g (4 oz) feta cheese, crumbled
100 g (4 oz) cottage cheese
30 ml (2 tbsp) freshly grated Parmesan cheese
1 egg, beaten
225 g (8 oz) filo pastry, thawed if frozen
sesame seeds

1 Lightly grease a 25 cm (10 inch) shallow, round baking dish and set aside. Heat 15 ml (1 tbsp) of the oil in a large saucepan and cook the onion and garlic for 5 minutes until soft, stirring frequently. Stir in the cinnamon and cook for 1 minute, stirring constantly.

2 Add the spinach. If using fresh, cook with just the water clinging to the leaves for about 5 minutes until wilted, stirring frequently. Cook for 10 minutes if using frozen spinach.

3 Stir in the herbs, nutmeg and seasoning. Cook for 3-4 minutes until the moisture evaporates. Stir in the cheeses and egg and mix thoroughly. Set aside.

4 Use half of the pastry to line the baking dish, trimming it with kitchen scissors so that it overlaps the dish by about 5 cm (2 inches) all the way around.

5 Spoon in the filling and level the surface. Bring the overlapped pastry up over the filling. Cut the remaining pastry in half and place on top of the pie, one piece on top of the other, tucking under the edges to enclose the filling completely.

6 Brush the pie with the remaining oil, score the top into squares and sprinkle with sesame seeds. Bake at 180°C (350°F) mark 4 for about 45 minutes until golden brown. Serve hot or cold.

Vegetables Baked with a Feta Cheese Crust

Serve with hot garlic bread and a spinach or mixed green salad.

NUTRITIONAL ANALYSIS	
amount per portion	
274 kcals/1144 kJ	
21.3 g Carbohydrate	
12.6 g Protein	★★
15.9 g Fat	★★
7.0 g Saturated Fat	★★
0.0 g Added Sugar	★★★★
6.2 g Fibre	★★
2248 mg Salt	
369 mg Calcium	★★★★
2.7 mg Iron	★★
91 mg Folic Acid	★★

SERVES 6

2 large aubergines, total weight about 700 g
(1½ lb), trimmed and roughly chopped

450 g (1 lb) tomatoes, chopped

2 medium onions, skinned and chopped

4 celery sticks, trimmed and roughly chopped

2 bay leaves

5 ml (1 tsp) dried marjoram

45 ml (3 tbsp) tomato purée

150 ml (¼ pint) vegetable stock

400 g (14 oz) can artichoke hearts, drained and
quartered

100 g (4 oz) stoned black olives

salt and pepper, to taste

50 g (2 oz) polyunsaturated margarine

50 g (2 oz) plain white flour

600 ml (1 pint) semi-skimmed milk

100 g (4 oz) feta cheese, crumbled

2 eggs, separated

1 Put the aubergines, tomatoes, onions, celery, bay leaves, marjoram, tomato purée and stock in a large shallow flameproof casserole. Bring to the boil, cover and simmer for 15 minutes or until the vegetables are softened. Add the artichoke hearts, olives and seasoning.

2 Melt the margarine in a saucepan, stir in the flour and cook, stirring, for 1-2 minutes. Gradually stir in the milk off the heat, then bring to the boil, stirring, and simmer for 2-3 minutes. Remove from the heat, stir in the cheese and egg yolks. Whisk the egg whites until stiff and fold in. Season with pepper.

3 Spoon the mixture over the vegetables to cover completely. Bake at 180°C (350°F) mark 4 for about 50 minutes until golden brown. Serve hot.

NUTRITIONAL ANALYSIS
amount per portion
187 kcals/780 kJ
6.3 g Carbohydrate
7.1 g Protein ★★
15 g Fat ★★
3.5 g Saturated Fat ★★★
0.0 g Added Sugar ★★★★
2.5 g Fibre ★
307 mg Salt ★★★
110 mg Calcium ★★
1.0 mg Iron ★
26 mg Folic Acid ★

Spicy Nut Burgers

Serve these healthy burgers with low-fat natural yogurt and a mixed salad, to contrast with the richness of the spiced nut mixture.

MAKES 6
15 ml (1 tbsp) polyunsaturated oil
1 medium onion, skinned and finely chopped
1 medium carrot, scrubbed and grated
2.5 ml (½ tsp) cumin seeds
2.5 ml (½ tsp) ground coriander
1 garlic clove, skinned and crushed
100 g (4 oz) finely chopped mixed nuts
50 g (2 oz) soft brown breadcrumbs
50 g (2 oz) Cheddar cheese, grated
salt and pepper, to taste
1 egg

1 Heat the oil in a saucepan and fry the onion, carrot, cumin, coriander and garlic for 5 minutes until the onion is soft.
2 Add the nuts, breadcrumbs and cheese. Season and stir well to mix. Beat in the egg to bind the mixture together. Divide into 6 and shape into burgers.
3 Place the burgers on a lightly greased baking sheet and brush with a little oil. Bake at 200°C (400°F) mark 6 for 20 minutes or until golden brown. Serve hot.

NUTRITIONAL ANALYSIS
amount per portion
534 kcals/2233 kJ
71.6 g Carbohydrate
25.8 g Protein ★★★
17.9 g Fat ★★
8.4 g Saturated Fat ★★
2.2 g Added Sugar ★★★★
17.1 g Fibre ★★★★
862 mg Salt ★★
613 mg Calcium ★★★★
7.7 mg Iron ★★★★
108 mg Folic Acid ★★

Wholewheat with Vegetables

Wholewheat grain or berry is the most nutritious form of wheat, with none of the wheatgerm or outer layers removed. When cooked, wholewheat grain is chewy and satisfying.

SERVES 4
275 g (10 oz) wholewheat grain
salt and pepper, to taste
15 ml (1 tbsp) polyunsaturated oil
350 g (12 oz) carrots, scrubbed and cut into chunks
350 g (12 oz) parsnips, peeled and cut into chunks
15 ml (1 tbsp) mild curry powder
30 ml (2 tbsp) sweet chutney
350 g (12 oz) leeks, washed, trimmed and thickly sliced
175 g (6 oz) Emmenthal cheese, grated

1 Cook the wholewheat grain in a saucepan of boiling salted water for about 25 minutes or until just tender. Drain, reserving 300 ml (½ pint) of the cooking liquid.
2 Heat the oil in a flameproof casserole and gently cook the carrots, parsnips, wheat and curry powder for 2-3 minutes, stirring occasionally.
3 Pour in the reserved stock then add the chutney, leeks and seasoning. Cover and simmer for about 25 minutes or until the vegetables are tender. Uncover, and boil rapidly to evaporate any excess juices, if necessary. Adjust the seasoning and serve topped with the cheese.

Vegetable Pie

Curd cheese, a medium-fat soft cheese available from supermarkets and delicatessens, is used to enrich the sauce for the vegetables.

NUTRITIONAL ANALYSIS
amount per portion
537 kcals/2244 kJ
62.2 g Carbohydrate
22.8 g Protein ★★★
23.7 g Fat ★
5.7 g Saturated Fat ★★
0.0 g Added Sugar ★★★★
16.9 g Fibre ★★★★
955 mg Salt ★★
301 mg Calcium ★★★★
7.8 mg Iron ★★★★
155 mg Folic Acid ★★★

SERVES 4

75 g (3 oz) plain wholemeal flour

100 g (4 oz) plain white flour

75 g (3 oz) polyunsaturated margarine, chilled

350 g (12 oz) carrots, scrubbed and chopped

350 g (12 oz) cauliflower, cut into florets

225 g (8 oz) courgettes, trimmed and chopped

1 red pepper, seeded and chopped

175 g (6 oz) leeks, washed, trimmed and sliced

200 g (7 oz) can chick-peas, rinsed and drained

100 g (4 oz) fresh parsley, chopped

1 small onion, skinned and chopped

75 g (3 oz) curd cheese

salt and pepper, to taste

1 egg, size 6, beaten

15 g (½ oz) natural roasted peanuts, finely chopped

1 To make the pastry, mix the wholemeal and 75 g (3 oz) of the white flour in a bowl and rub in the margarine until the mixture resembles fine breadcrumbs. Add about 60 ml (4 tbsp) cold water to make a soft dough. Wrap and chill for 30 minutes.

2 Meanwhile, prepare the vegetables. Cook the carrots in a saucepan of boiling water for 3 minutes. Add the remaining vegetables, except the chick-peas, and cook for a further 3 minutes. Drain the vegetables, reserving 300 ml (½ pint) liquid, and mix with the chick-peas. Place in a rimmed 1.7 litre (3 pint) pie dish.

3 To make the sauce, put the parsley, onion and reserved liquid into a saucepan. Simmer gently for 8-10 minutes. Cool slightly, then purée in a blender or food processor with the curd cheese until smooth. Blend the remaining flour with 45 ml (3 tbsp) water, and add to the parsley purée with the seasoning. Return to the saucepan and bring to the boil, stirring until thickened. Pour the sauce evenly over the vegetables.

4 Roll out the dough on a lightly floured surface. Cut off a band about 2 cm (¾ inch) wide and press on to the lightly greased rim of the pie dish. Brush with beaten egg. Carefully lay the large piece of pastry over the pie dish and filling, then trim around the edge. Pinch to seal. Glaze with the remaining egg and decorate with pastry trimmings. Glaze and sprinkle with the peanuts.

5 Bake at 190°C (375°F) mark 5 for about 35 minutes until golden brown.

NUTRITIONAL ANALYSIS
amount per portion
638 kcals/2666 kJ
98.6 g Carbohydrate
32.6 g Protein ★★★★
15.2 g Fat ★★
7.9 g Saturated Fat ★★
0.0 g Added Sugar ★★★★
8.4 g Fibre ★★★
858 mg Salt ★★
460 mg Calcium ★★★★
16.6 mg Iron ★★★★
224 mg Folic Acid ★★★

Spinach and Ricotta Cannelloni

This is a perfect dish to cook in advance and freeze. Reheat just before serving, for a quick meal.

SERVES 4

450 g (1 lb) fresh spinach, washed and stalks removed, or 225 g (8 oz) frozen spinach, thawed, chopped and drained
275 g (10 oz) ricotta cheese
1 egg, size 2, beaten
5 ml (1 tsp) grated nutmeg
salt and pepper, to taste
16 cannelloni tubes
two 400 g (14 oz) cans tomatoes
1 garlic clove, skinned and crushed
1 small onion, skinned and finely chopped
5 ml (1 tsp) dried mixed herbs
100 g (4 oz) mozzarella cheese, thinly sliced
basil sprigs, to garnish

1 Lightly oil an ovenproof dish. If using fresh spinach, cook only in the water that clings to the leaves for 5 minutes. Drain well and coarsely chop. Frozen spinach does not require cooking.

2 Put the spinach, ricotta cheese, egg and nutmeg in a bowl, mix well and season. Fill the cannelloni tubes with the mixture. Arrange in a single layer in the prepared dish.

3 Roughly chop the tomatoes and put into a saucepan with their juice, the garlic, onion and herbs. Season, bring to the boil, lower the heat and simmer for 15-20 minutes until slightly thickened.

4 Cool slightly, then purée the mixture in a blender or food processor. Pour over the cannelloni. Cover with foil. Cook at 200°C (400°F) mark 6 for 35 minutes.

5 Remove the foil and arrange the cheese slices over the top. Return to the oven, cook for a further 10 minutes until bubbling and golden brown. Garnish with basil and serve with a green salad.

Tofu and Vegetables in Coconut Sauce

Tofu is made from soya bean curd. Silken tofu is lightly pressed and firm tofu is more heavily pressed.

SERVES 4

75 g (3 oz) creamed coconut

225 g (8 oz) firm or pressed tofu

polyunsaturated oil, for deep frying, plus 15 ml (1 tbsp)

6 spring onions, trimmed and finely chopped

2.5 cm (1 inch) piece fresh root ginger, peeled and finely chopped

1 garlic clove, skinned and crushed

2.5 ml (½ tsp) ground turmeric

2.5 ml (½ tsp) chilli powder

30 ml (2 tbsp) soy sauce, preferably naturally fermented shoyu

4 medium carrots, scrubbed and cut into matchstick strips

225 g (8 oz) cauliflower florets, separated into small sprigs

175 g (6 oz) French beans, trimmed

175 g (6 oz) beansprouts

salt and pepper, to taste

NUTRITIONAL ANALYSIS
amount per portion
363 kcals/1519 kJ
11 g Carbohydrate
9.8 g Protein ★★
32 g Fat
7.1 g Saturated Fat ★★
0.0 g Added Sugar ★★★★
5.2 g Fibre ★★
204 mg Salt ★★★★
379 mg Calcium ★★★★
4.3 mg Iron ★★★
62 mg Folic Acid ★★

1 First make the coconut milk. Cut the creamed coconut into small pieces and place in a measuring jug. Pour in boiling water up to the 900 ml (1½ pint) mark. Stir until dissolved, then strain through a muslin-lined sieve. Set aside.

2 Drain the tofu and cut into cubes. Pat thoroughly dry with absorbent kitchen paper. Heat the oil to 190°C (375°F) in a wok or deep-fat fryer. Deep-fry the cubes of tofu in the hot oil until golden brown on all sides, turning them frequently with a slotted spoon. Remove and drain on absorbent kitchen paper.

3 Heat the 15 ml (1 tbsp) oil in a heavy-based saucepan or flameproof casserole and gently fry the spring onions, ginger and garlic for about 5 minutes until soft.

4 Add the turmeric and chilli powder and stir-fry for 1-2 minutes, then add the coconut milk and soy sauce and bring to the boil, stirring all the time. Add the carrots and cauliflower. Simmer, uncovered, for 10 minutes.

5 Add the French beans and simmer for a further 5 minutes, then add the tofu and beansprouts and heat through. Add seasoning, then turn into a warmed serving dish. Serve immediately with egg noodles.

Chick-Pea and Parsnip Soufflés

For ease of serving, the soufflé mixture is baked in individual dishes. If using one larger dish, increase the cooking time by about 20 minutes, covering lightly after about 30 minutes if necessary.

SERVES 4
50 g (2 oz) freshly grated Parmesan cheese
175 g (6 oz) chick-peas, soaked overnight and drained
450 g (1 lb) parsnips, peeled and cut into chunks
salt and pepper, to taste
50 g (2 oz) polyunsaturated margarine
45 ml (3 tbsp) plain white flour
300 ml (½ pint) semi-skimmed milk
3 eggs, separated
10 ml (2 tsp) mild curry powder

1 Lightly grease 4 deep 450 ml (¾ pint) ovenproof dishes and coat with a little of the Parmesan cheese.

2 Boil the chick-peas in water to cover for 10 minutes, then drain and cover again with fresh water. Bring to the boil and simmer for 1½ hours or until tender.

3 Meanwhile, cook the parsnips in a saucepan of boiling salted water until just tender. Drain.

4 Melt the margarine in a saucepan, stir in the flour and cook, stirring, for 1-2 minutes. Gradually stir in the milk off the heat, then bring to the boil, stirring, and simmer for 2-3 minutes. Remove from the heat, cool slightly then stir in the egg yolks, seasoning, curry powder and all but 30 ml (2 tbsp) of the remaining cheese.

5 Purée the parsnips, chick-peas and sauce mixture together in a food processor or blender until almost smooth. Turn out into a large bowl and add seasoning.

6 Lightly whisk the egg whites until stiff but not dry, then fold through the mixture. Spoon into the prepared dishes and sprinkle over the remaining Parmesan cheese.

7 Bake at 200°C (400°F) mark 6 for about 20 minutes or until the soufflés are well risen, golden brown and just set. Serve immediately.

NUTRITIONAL ANALYSIS
amount per portion
464 kcals/1940 kJ
47.6 g Carbohydrate
24.7 g Protein ★★★
20.7 g Fat ★★
6.7 g Saturated Fat ★★
0.0 g Added Sugar ★★★★
12.4 g Fibre ★★★
859 mg Salt ★★
391 mg Calcium ★★★★
5.8 mg Iron ★★★
109 mg Folic Acid ★★

Vegetable Paella

The combination of chick-peas and rice makes this a balanced protein, meatless meal. Serve with a salad and low-fat natural yogurt.

NUTRITIONAL ANALYSIS
amount per portion
665 kcals/2780 kJ
106.9 g Carbohydrate
22.9 g Protein ★ ★ ★
19.1 g Fat ★ ★
2.7 g Saturated Fat ★ ★ ★
0.0 g Added Sugar ★ ★ ★ ★
17.6 g Fibre ★ ★ ★ ★
1324 mg Salt ★
119 mg Calcium ★ ★
5.8 mg Iron ★ ★ ★
111 mg Folic Acid ★ ★

SERVES 4

225 g (8 oz) chick-peas, soaked overnight and drained

30 ml (2 tbsp) olive oil

1 medium Spanish onion, skinned and finely chopped

2 garlic cloves, skinned and crushed

1.25 ml (¼ tsp) ground turmeric

1 green chilli, seeded and finely chopped

350 g (12 oz) long-grain brown rice

350 g (12 oz) tomatoes, chopped

750 ml (1¼ pints) vegetable stock

1 red pepper, seeded and chopped

1 green pepper, seeded and chopped

salt and pepper, to taste

50 g (2 oz) whole blanched almonds, 50 g (2 oz) black olives and fresh coriander, to garnish

1 Boil the chick-peas in water to cover for 10 minutes, then drain and cover again with fresh water. Bring to the boil and simmer for 1½ hours or until tender.

2 Meanwhile, heat the oil in a heavy-based saucepan and cook the onion and garlic, stirring, for 3 minutes. Add the turmeric and chilli and stir well. Mix in the rice and cook for 1 minute, stirring, until coated with oil.

3 Add the tomatoes and stock and stir well. Bring to the boil, lower the heat and simmer, half covered, for 25-30 minutes.

4 Drain the chick-peas and add to the rice mixture with the red and green peppers and seasoning. Cook for 5-10 minutes until all the liquid has been absorbed and all the ingredients are tender. Garnish with the almonds, olives and fresh coriander.

NUTRITIONAL ANALYSIS
amount per portion
371 kcals/1549 kJ
74.9 g Carbohydrate
16.1 g Protein ★★★
2.9 g Fat ★★★★
0.5 g Saturated Fat ★★★★
0.0 g Added Sugar ★★★★
13.3 g Fibre ★★★★
355 mg Salt ★★★
69 mg Calcium ★★
5.1 mg Iron ★★★
97 mg Folic Acid ★★

Spaghetti with Ratatouille Sauce

Salting aubergines before cooking them removes their bitter juices and draws out any excess moisture.

SERVES 4
1 aubergine, trimmed and diced
salt and pepper, to taste
1 green pepper, seeded and sliced into thin strips
1 red pepper, seeded and sliced into thin strips
3 medium courgettes, trimmed and sliced into thin strips
1 onion, skinned and chopped
1 garlic clove, skinned and crushed
350 g (12 oz) tomatoes, skinned and chopped
10 ml (2 tsp) chopped fresh basil
400 g (14 oz) wholewheat spaghetti
freshly grated Parmesan cheese, to serve

1 Spread out the aubergine on a plate and sprinkle with salt. Leave to dégorge for 30 minutes.

2 Tip the diced aubergine into a sieve and rinse under cold running water. Put into a large, heavy-based saucepan with the prepared vegetables, basil and seasoning. Cover and cook over moderate heat for 30 minutes. Shake the pan and stir the vegetables frequently during this time, to encourage the juices to flow.

3 Meanwhile, plunge the spaghetti into a large saucepan of boiling salted water. Simmer, uncovered, for 12 minutes or according to packet instructions.

4 Drain the spaghetti thoroughly and turn into a warmed serving dish. Taste and adjust the seasoning of the ratatouille sauce, then pour over the spaghetti. Serve immediately, with the Parmesan cheese handed separately.

Monkfish with Mustard Seeds (PAGE 106); *Spiced Grilled Mackerel* (PAGE 108)

Vegetable Accompaniments

Fresh vegetables are important in a healthy diet for they provide a variety of vitamins, minerals and fibre. As the vitamin content is reduced during cooking, keep the cooking time brief and either use minimum of liquid or steam the vegetables. Whenever possible, eat vegetables raw. Vary the selection of vegetables you use during the week as each one is nutritionally different. The exciting salad recipes have been included to introduce variety to both summer and winter meals.

French Fruit Tart (PAGE 141); *Kheer* (PAGE 151); *Almond Baked Apples* (PAGE 142)

NUTRITIONAL ANALYSIS
amount per portion
115 kcals/482 kJ
13.3 g Carbohydrate
7.8 g Protein ★★
2.6 g Fat ★★★★
1.0 g Saturated Fat ★★★★
0.0 g Added Sugar ★★★★
8.0 g Fibre ★★★
97 mg Salt ★★★★
66 mg Calcium ★★
2.5 mg Iron ★★
49 mg Folic Acid ★

Summer Vegetables with Warm Basil Dressing

This aromatic dressing will enhance any fresh young garden vegetables. Young peas, beans and broccoli need a brief blanching.

SERVES 4
3 peppers, yellow, green and red
450 g (1 lb) broad beans, shelled
100 g (4 oz) tiny button mushrooms
1 or 2 beefsteak tomatoes, sliced
4 crisp lettuce hearts, halved or quartered
75 ml (5 tbsp) vegetable stock
75 ml (5 tbsp) dry white wine
45 ml (3 tbsp) fromage frais
salt and pepper, to taste
12 small basil leaves

1 Cook the peppers under a hot grill until the skins are charred, turning them frequently. Cool slightly, then peel off the skins. Cut off the tops and remove the seeds, then slice into strips.
2 Blanch the broad beans in a saucepan of boiling water for 2 minutes. Drain. Arrange the vegetables in groups on a large serving plate.
3 To make the dressing, place the stock and wine in a small saucepan and bring to the boil. Boil rapidly to reduce it by half. Cool slightly, then stir in the fromage frais, seasoning and basil. Whisk until smooth, then pour over the vegetables and serve immediately.

NUTRITIONAL ANALYSIS
amount per portion
169 kcals/707 kJ
3.8 g Carbohydrate
1.7 g Protein
16.5 g Fat ★★
2.2 g Saturated Fat ★★★
1.9 g Added Sugar ★★★★
1.3 g Fibre
29 mg Salt ★★★★
19 mg Calcium
1.2 mg Iron ★
83 mg Folic Acid ★★

Mixed Leaf and Pine Nut Salad

For the crispest salad, remember to toss the leaves and dressing together at the very last minute.

SERVES 4
1 small head radicchio
1 small bunch lamb's lettuce
½ head oak leaf lettuce
½ head curly endive
25-50 g (1-2 oz) alfalfa sprouts
50 ml (2 fl oz) grapeseed oil
30 ml (2 tbsp) white wine vinegar
10 ml (2 tsp) runny honey
salt and pepper, to taste
25 g (1 oz) pine nuts, toasted

1 Wash the salad leaves and shred roughly. Rinse the alfalfa sprouts in a sieve or colander. Pat the salad leaves and the alfalfa sprouts dry with absorbent kitchen paper.
2 To make the dressing, whisk together the grapeseed oil, white wine vinegar and honey. Season.
3 Toss the salad leaves, alfalfa sprouts, pine nuts and dressing together in a large salad bowl. Serve immediately.

Fruit and Cheese Salad

A refreshing, colourful salad full of goodness – its low-fat dressing has no oil or egg yolk, just juice and seasonings.

SERVES 4
225 g (8 oz) green cabbage, finely shredded
4 courgettes, trimmed and shredded or coarsely grated
90 ml (6 tbsp) unsweetened orange juice
1.25 ml (¼ tsp) grated nutmeg
salt and pepper, to taste
30 ml (2 tbsp) finely chopped fresh parsley
15 ml (1 tbsp) snipped fresh chives
1 garlic clove, skinned and crushed
350 g (12 oz) cottage cheese
100 g (4 oz) black grapes, halved and seeded
2 eating apple, quartered, cored and sliced
2 oranges, peeled and segmented
1 bunch watercress, trimmed and divided into small sprigs

NUTRITIONAL ANALYSIS
amount per portion
182 kcals/761 kJ
22.8 g Carbohydrate
16 g Protein ★★★
3.6 g Fat ★★★★
2.2 g Saturated Fat ★★★
0.2 g Added Sugar ★★★★
5.6 g Fibre ★★
1070 mg Salt ★★
188 mg Calcium ★★★
2.2 mg Iron ★★
134 mg Folic Acid ★★★

1 Mix the cabbage and courgettes together in a bowl. To make the dressing, mix the orange juice, nutmeg, seasoning, parsley, chives and garlic together in another bowl.
2 Add all but 15 ml (1 tbsp) of the dressing to the shredded vegetables and toss together. Spoon the shredded vegetables on to a shallow dish or platter.
3 Make 4 hollows in the vegetables and spoon in the cottage cheese. Arrange the grapes, apples, oranges and watercress sprigs over and around the vegetables. Spoon over the remaining dressing and serve.

Mixed Mushroom and Chicken Liver Salad

An interesting salad of hot fried liver and mushrooms spooned over crisp salad leaves.

NUTRITIONAL ANALYSIS
amount per portion
335 kcals/1398 kJ
1.4 g Carbohydrate
25.2 g Protein ★★★
25.4 g Fat ★
4.6 g Saturated Fat ★★
0.0 g Added Sugar ★★★★
5.8 g Fibre ★★
558 mg Salt ★★
124 mg Calcium ★★
14.4 mg Iron ★★★★
692 mg Folic Acid ★★★★

SERVES 2

a selection of salad leaves, such as radicchio, watercress, frisée, oakleaf or lamb's lettuce

15 ml (1 tbsp) hazelnut oil

25 g (1 oz) polyunsaturated margarine

225 g (8 oz) chicken livers, halved

225 g (8 oz) mixed mushrooms, such as oysters, button or cup

60 ml (4 tbsp) chopped fresh parsley

2 spring onions, trimmed and chopped

15 ml (1 tbsp) white wine vinegar

salt and pepper, to taste

1 Wash the salad leaves and shake dry. Arrange on 2 plates.
2 Heat the oil and margarine in a large frying pan and fry the chicken livers for 2-3 minutes until well browned. Add the mushrooms and fry for a further 5 minutes.
3 Stir in the parsley, onions, vinegar and seasoning.
4 Divide the mixture between the salad leaves and serve immediately with crusty bread.

Warm Potato Salad

Warm potato salad makes a delightful change from the usual cold variety, and leaving the skins on adds nutrients and fibre.

NUTRITIONAL ANALYSIS
amount per portion
229 kcals/955 kJ
40.2 g Carbohydrate
7.3 g Protein ★★
5.5 g Fat ★★★
1.5 g Saturated Fat ★★★★
0.0 g Added Sugar ★★★★
4.4 g Fibre ★★
188 mg Salt ★★★★
156 mg Calcium ★★★
1.2 mg Iron ★
45 mg Folic Acid ★

SERVES 4

700 g (1½ lb) potatoes, scrubbed

15 ml (1 tbsp) olive oil

150 ml (¼ pint) low-fat natural yogurt

15 ml (1 tbsp) freshly grated Parmesan cheese

10 ml (2 tsp) lemon juice

45-60 ml (3-4 tbsp) chopped fresh herbs, including chives or spring onions

pepper, to taste

½ green or red pepper, seeded and chopped

watercress sprigs, to garnish

1 Cook the potatoes in a tightly covered saucepan with 2 cm (¾ inch) boiling water for about 20 minutes until tender.
2 Drain the potatoes and cut into large chunks. Pour the oil over and set aside to cool slightly.
3 To make the dressing, mix the yogurt, cheese, lemon juice, herbs, seasoning and green or red pepper together in a serving bowl. Add the potatoes and toss gently to avoid breaking. Garnish with watercress and serve warm.

Wild Rice and Thyme Salad

Expensive wild rice is not actually rice at all, but is the seed from a wild grass.

NUTRITIONAL ANALYSIS
amount per portion
166 kcals/696 kJ
24.6 g Carbohydrate
3.2 g Protein ★
6.8 g Fat ★★★
0.9 g Saturated Fat ★★★★
0.0 g Added Sugar ★★★★
2.6 g Fibre ★
17 mg Salt ★★★★
18 mg Calcium
0.9 mg Iron ★
20 mg Folic Acid

SERVES 8

150 g (5 oz) French beans, trimmed and halved

150 g (5 oz) broad beans

salt and pepper, to taste

50 g (2 oz) wild rice

175 g (6 oz) long-grain brown rice

30 ml (2 tbsp) grapeseed oil

50 g (2 oz) small button mushrooms, halved

30 ml (2 tbsp) chopped fresh thyme

15 ml (1 tbsp) walnut oil

30 ml (2 tbsp) white wine vinegar

15 ml (1 tbsp) Dijon mustard

1 Cook the French beans in a saucepan of boiling water for 10-12 minutes until just tender. Drain and refresh under cold running water and set aside to cool completely.
2 Cook the broad beans in a pan of boiling, salted water for 5-7 minutes. Drain and refresh under cold running water, slipping off their outer skins if wished, and set aside to cool completely.
3 Place the wild rice in a large pan of boiling, salted water. Boil for 10 minutes before adding the brown rice. Boil together for a further 25-30 minutes or until both are just tender. Drain and refresh the rice under cold running water.
4 Stir together the French beans, broad beans and rice in a large bowl.
5 Heat the grapeseed oil in a small frying pan and fry the mushrooms with the thyme for 2-3 minutes. Remove from the heat, stir in the walnut oil, vinegar, mustard and seasoning. Spoon into the rice mixture and stir well. Adjust the seasoning. Cool, cover and refrigerate until required.

NUTRITIONAL ANALYSIS
amount per portion
243 kcals/1016 kJ
9.4 g Carbohydrate
5.3 g Protein ★
20.8 g Fat ★★
2.8 g Saturated Fat ★★★
0.0 g Added Sugar ★★★★
3.5 g Fibre ★★
21 mg Salt ★★★★
53 mg Calcium ★★
1.7 mg Iron ★★
114 mg Folic Acid ★★

Avocado and Peanut Salad

The peanuts and avocado provide a range of amino acids, making this salad a good source of protein.

SERVES 4

½ small head curly endive, separated into sprigs

2 oranges, peeled and segmented

30 ml (2 tbsp) natural roasted peanuts

¼ cucumber, halved, seeded and chopped

45 ml (3 tbsp) orange juice

15 ml (1 tbsp) olive oil

salt and pepper, to taste

1 garlic clove, skinned and crushed

15 ml (1 tbsp) chopped fresh mint

1 ripe avocado, peeled and stoned

1 Put the endive into a serving bowl and add the orange segments, peanuts and cucumber.
2 To make the dressing, mix the orange juice, olive oil, seasoning, garlic and mint together in another bowl.
3 Cut the avocado into thin slices. Toss gently in the dressing, then add with the dressing to the salad. Toss lightly together and serve.

NUTRITIONAL ANALYSIS
amount per portion
82 kcals/343 kJ
3.9 g Carbohydrate
11 g Protein ★★
2.6 g Fat ★★★★
0.3 g Saturated Fat ★★★★
0.0 g Added Sugar ★★★★
3.9 g Fibre ★★
469 mg Salt ★★★
77 mg Calcium ★★
1.6 mg Iron ★★
65 mg Folic Acid ★★

Celeriac and Crab Salad

Most supermarkets and fishmongers sell ready-dressed crab; alternatively use frozen crab meat, half brown, half white.

SERVES 4

175 g (6 oz) celeriac, peeled

45 ml (3 tbsp) lemon juice

10 ml (2 tsp) whole grain mustard

salt and pepper, to taste

2 small dressed crabs, about 175 g (6 oz) crab meat

large bunch watercress

350 g (12 oz) tomatoes

1 Coarsely grate the celeriac and immediately mix with the lemon juice, mustard and seasoning.
2 Flake the crab meat with a fork, then mix into the celeriac. Adjust the seasoning. Cover and chill for 1-2 hours
3 Rinse and drain the watercress, discarding any coarse stalks. Dry on absorbent kitchen paper. Thinly slice the tomatoes and roughly chop the end pieces.
4 To serve, arrange the watercress and sliced tomatoes on individual serving plates. Top with the crab and celeriac mixture, then sprinkle with chopped tomato.

Sesame Aubergines with Olives

When buying aubergines, look for firm, smooth and glossy ones which have a uniform colour.

SERVES 4
45 ml (3 tbsp) sesame seeds
15 ml (1 tbsp) olive oil
1 large onion, skinned and thinly sliced
1 garlic clove, skinned and crushed
3 tomatoes, roughly chopped
2 aubergines, trimmed and diced
50 g (2 oz) large black olives, stoned
chopped fresh parsley, to garnish

1 Dry-fry the sesame seeds in a frying pan over medium heat until golden brown, stirring frequently. Remove from the heat and cool.
2 Heat the oil in a saucepan and cook the onion for 3 minutes until soft. Add the garlic and tomatoes and cook for 1 minute. Stir in the aubergines, olives and half of the sesame seeds. Cook for further 5-10 minutes or until the aubergine is tender.
3 Turn the mixture into a warmed serving dish and sprinkle with the remaining sesame seeds. Garnish with parsley. Serve hot or cold.

NUTRITIONAL ANALYSIS
amount per portion
150 kcals/626 kJ
9.8 g Carbohydrate
4.0 g Protein ★
11.4 g Fat ★★
1.6 g Saturated Fat ★★★★
0.0 g Added Sugar ★★★★
5.4 g Fibre ★★
868 mg Salt ★★
159 mg Calcium ★★★
2.8 mg Iron ★★
56 mg Folic Acid ★★

Cauliflower, Broccoli and Pepper Salad

Parboiled so they are still crisp, cauliflower and broccoli florets are teamed with strips of bright yellow and red peppers, then coated with a tahini dressing.

SERVES 6
225 g (8 oz) broccoli, cut into florets
225 g (8 oz) cauliflower, cut into florets
1 small yellow pepper, seeded and thinly sliced
1 small red pepper, seeded and thinly sliced
1 garlic clove, skinned and crushed
60 ml (4 tbsp) tahini
90 ml (6 tbsp) lemon juice
salt and pepper, to taste
sesame seeds, to garnish

1 Blanch the broccoli and cauliflower in a saucepan of boiling water for 3 minutes, then drain and leave to cool. Place the broccoli, cauliflower and peppers in a salad bowl.
2 To make the dressing, whisk the garlic, tahini, 60 ml (4 tbsp) water, lemon juice and seasoning together in a small bowl.
3 Pour the dressing over the salad and toss gently to coat. Cover and chill. Sprinkle with sesame seeds just before serving.

NUTRITIONAL ANALYSIS
amount per portion
83 kcals/346 kJ
4.9 g Carbohydrate
4.5 g Protein ★
5.4 g Fat ★★★
0.8 g Saturated Fat ★★★★
0.0 g Added Sugar ★★★★
3.2 g Fibre ★★
24 mg Salt ★★★★
152 mg Calcium ★★★
3.0 mg Iron ★★
70 mg Folic Acid ★★

NUTRITIONAL ANALYSIS
amount per portion
75 kcals/315 kJ
9.9 g Carbohydrate
3.1 g Protein ★
2.8 g Fat ★★★★
1.8 g Saturated Fat ★★★★
0.0 g Added Sugar ★★★★
4.3 g Fibre ★★
343 mg Salt ★★★
79 mg Calcium ★★
0.6 mg Iron
125 mg Folic Acid ★★★

Hot Beetroot with Dill

Leaving the skin on the beetroot during cooking preserves the vitamins.

SERVES 4

550 g (1¼ lb) raw beetroot

15 ml (1 tbsp) chopped fresh dill or 10 ml (2 tsp) dried dill weed

30 ml (2 tbsp) lemon juice

75 ml (3 fl oz) low-fat natural yogurt

50 ml (2 fl oz) soured cream

salt and pepper, to taste

1 Place the beetroot in a saucepan of boiling water and simmer for about 45 minutes or until just tender. Drain. When cool enough to handle, peel the beetroot, then cut into thin slices. Arrange in a dish and keep warm.
2 To make the dressing, mix the dill with the lemon juice in a bowl. Stir in the yogurt and soured cream. Season. Spoon the dressing over the beetroot and serve at once.

NUTRITIONAL ANALYSIS
amount per portion
63 kcals/264 kJ
12.3 g Carbohydrate
1.8 g Protein
0.2 g Fat ★★★★
0.0 g Saturated Fat ★★★★
2.6 g Added Sugar ★★★
1.4 g Fibre
88 mg Salt ★★★★
45 mg Calcium ★
1.0 mg Iron ★
40 mg Folic Acid ★

Courgettes in Orange Sauce

Serve this colourful side dish with pork, gammon or any grilled meat.

SERVES 4

350 g (12 oz) courgettes, trimmed and quartered

4 spring onions, trimmed and finely chopped

5 ml (1 tsp) grated fresh root ginger

45 ml (3 tbsp) cider vinegar

15 ml (1 tbsp) soy sauce, preferably naturally fermented shoyu

10 ml (2 tsp) light muscovado sugar

30 ml (2 tbsp) dry sherry

45 ml (3 tbsp) vegetable stock

finely grated rind and juice of 1 orange

7.5 ml (1½ tsp) cornflour

1 orange, peeled and segmented

1 Cook the courgettes in a saucepan of boiling water for 4-5 minutes until just tender.
2 Meanwhile, put the remaining ingredients, except the cornflour and orange segments, into a saucepan. Bring to the boil, lower the heat and gently simmer for 4 minutes.
3 Mix the cornflour with a little water to make a smooth paste, then stir into the sauce and cook for 2 minutes, stirring continuously, until the sauce thickens.
4 Drain the courgettes and return them to the pan. Pour over the sauce and add the orange segments. Heat through briefly and serve.

Warm Cucumber with Herbs

Although the cucumber pieces are sprinkled with salt to extract any bitterness, rinsing them thoroughly afterwards removes the salt.

SERVES 4

1 cucumber

salt and pepper, to taste

25 g (1 oz) polyunsaturated margarine

1 small onion, skinned and finely chopped

15 ml (1 tbsp) chopped fresh dill or 7.5 ml (½ tbsp) dried dill weed

2.5 ml (½ tsp) light muscovado sugar

60 ml (4 tbsp) Greek strained yogurt

chopped fresh dill or dill weed, to garnish

1 Score the skin of the cucumber with a fork. Cut into 5 cm (2 inch) lengths, then cut into quarters.
2 Scoop out the seeds, then put the cucumber in a colander and sprinkle with salt. Cover with a plate, weigh down, and leave to drain for 30 minutes. Rinse thoroughly and pat dry with absorbent kitchen paper.
3 Melt the margarine in a large frying pan and gently cook the onion for 5 minutes until soft. Add the cucumber, dill, sugar and seasoning. Cook for 5 minutes. Remove from the heat and stir in the yogurt. Garnish with the dill and serve.

NUTRITIONAL ANALYSIS
amount per portion
82 kcals/343 kJ
4.0 g Carbohydrate
1.7 g Protein
6.7 g Fat ★★★
1.9 g Saturated Fat ★★★★
0.6 g Added Sugar ★★★★
0.6 g Fibre
182 mg Salt ★★★★
48 mg Calcium ★
0.4 mg Iron
20 mg Folic Acid

Sliced Potato Baked with Fennel

This side dish makes a good accompaniment to beef and poultry dishes.

SERVES 4

25 g (1 oz) polyunsaturated margarine

700 g (1½ lb) potatoes, scrubbed

1 bulb fennel, trimmed

1.25 ml (¼ tsp) grated nutmeg

salt and pepper, to taste

300 ml (½ pint) semi-skimmed milk

25 g (1 oz) mature Cheddar cheese, finely grated

1 Lightly grease a 1.7 litre (3 pint) shallow ovenproof dish with a little of the margarine.
2 Cut the potatoes and fennel into very thin slices. Layer, reserving a third of the potato slices, in the prepared dish, sprinkling each layer with the nutmeg and seasoning. Pour the milk over.
3 Arrange the reserved potato slices in a neat overlapping layer on top. Melt the remaining margarine and brush over the potatoes. Cover the dish with foil.
4 Bake at 180°C (350°F) mark 4 for 1 hour. Remove the foil. Sprinkle the grated cheese over the top and cook for a further 45 minutes until golden and tender. Serve hot.

NUTRITIONAL ANALYSIS
amount per portion
263 kcals/1101 kJ
40.6 g Carbohydrate
8.2 g Protein ★★
8.7 g Fat ★★★
3.1 g Saturated Fat ★★★
0.0 g Added Sugar ★★★★
4.0 g Fibre ★★
359 mg Salt ★★★
167 mg Calcium ★★★
1.2 mg Iron ★
49 mg Folic Acid ★

NUTRITIONAL ANALYSIS
amount per portion
89 kcals/371 kJ
12.8 g Carbohydrate
8.6 g Protein ★★
1.0 g Fat ★★★★
0.5 g Saturated Fat ★★★★
0.0 g Added Sugar ★★★★
15.8 g Fibre ★★★★
164 mg Salt ★★★★
75 mg Calcium ★★
3.4 mg Iron ★★★
134 mg Folic Acid ★★★

Peas with Tomato

This is a spicy and unusual way of preparing peas and would make an excellent accompaniment to any grilled meat or oily fish.

SERVES 4
2 onions, skinned and chopped
400 g (14 oz) can tomatoes
1 garlic clove, skinned and crushed
10 ml (2 tsp) mild chilli powder
450 g (1 lb) frozen peas
30 ml (2 tbsp) tomato purée
pepper, to taste
thinly sliced onion rings, to garnish

1 Put the onions, tomatoes with their juice, garlic and chilli powder into a saucepan. Bring to the boil, lower the heat and simmer for 15 minutes, crushing the tomatoes occasionally.

2 Add the peas, tomato purée and pepper. Cook for a further 5 minutes until the peas are just tender. Serve garnished with onion rings.

Desserts

Fruits are included in most of these sumptuous desserts as they are full of vitamins, fibre and natural sweetness. The significant amounts of vitamin C present in many fruits help the body absorb iron in other foods. Vitamin C cannot be stored in the body, so some fruit should be taken each day.

NUTRITIONAL ANALYSIS
amount per portion
426 kcals/1779 kJ
53.8 g Carbohydrate
10.4 g Protein ★★
20.3 g Fat ★★
4.6 g Saturated Fat ★★
7.4 g Added Sugar ★★
3.7 g Fibre ★★
545 mg Salt ★★
168 mg Calcium ★★★
2.4 mg Iron ★★
37 mg Folic Acid ★

Pineapple Tart

To test whether a fresh pineapple is ready to eat, grasp the crown of leaves and move it gently; the amount of movement will indicate the ripeness of the fruit. When a leaf can be pulled out easily, the pineapple is fully ripe.

SERVES 4

75 g (3 oz) plain wholemeal flour

100 g (4 oz) plain white flour

75 g (3 oz) polyunsaturated margarine

15 ml (1 tbsp) light muscovado sugar

1 egg yolk

1 egg, size 2, beaten

300 ml (½ pint) semi-skimmed milk

5 ml (1 tsp) vanilla essence

1 small pineapple, about 700 g (1½ lb), peeled, sliced and cored

30 ml (2 tbsp) reduced-sugar apricot jam

15 ml (1 tbsp) lemon juice

1 Place an 18 cm (7 inch) fluted flan ring on a baking sheet. Put the wholemeal flour and 75 g (3 oz) of the white flour into a bowl and rub in the margarine until the mixture resembles fine breadcrumbs. Stir in 5 ml (1 tsp) of the sugar.

2 Beat the egg yolk with 30 ml (2 tbsp) cold water and use about half of it to to mix the flours and margarine to a firm but pliable dough. Knead on a lightly floured surface until smooth. Roll out and use to line the flan ring. Chill for 15 minutes.

3 Line the pastry case with greaseproof paper and baking beans. Bake blind at 190°C (375°F) mark 5 for 15 minutes. Remove the paper and beans and bake for a further 5-10 minutes or until the pastry case is cooked. Allow to cool, then remove the flan ring carefully and place the pastry case on a serving plate.

4 Put the remaining 25 g (1 oz) flour in a small bowl. Add the remaining egg yolk and water mixture and the beaten egg. Beat well until smooth.

5 Warm the milk in a small saucepan and gradually stir into the flour and egg mixture. Strain back into the rinsed pan and cook over a gentle heat for about 4 minutes, stirring until the pastry cream has thickened and is free from lumps. Remove from the heat and beat in the remaining sugar and the vanilla essence. Cool slightly, then pour into the pastry case. Leave until cold.

6 Arrange the sliced pineapple decoratively on top of the pastry cream. Heat the apricot jam and lemon juice together and sieve. Use to glaze the top of the tart. Leave for at least 5 minutes before serving.

French Fruit Tart

Use alternative fruits in season if those suggested below are not available.

NUTRITIONAL ANALYSIS
amount per portion
288 kcals/1202 kJ
37.1 g Carbohydrate
5.0 g Protein ★
14.4 g Fat ★★
2.4 g Saturated Fat ★★★
2.4 g Added Sugar ★★★★
3.9 g Fibre ★★
371 mg Salt ★★★
71 mg Calcium ★★
1.8 mg Iron ★★
22 mg Folic Acid

MAKES 6 SLICES

100 g (4 oz) plain wholemeal flour

100 g (4 oz) plain white flour

100 g (4 oz) polyunsaturated margarine

60 ml (4 tbsp) thick set low-fat natural yogurt

225 g (8 oz) strawberries, hulled

2 peaches, halved, stoned and sliced

2 kiwi fruit, peeled and sliced

30 ml (2 tbsp) reduced-sugar jam

10 ml (2 tsp) lemon juice

1 Mix the flours together in a bowl and rub in the margarine until the mixture resembles fine breadcrumbs. Add 15-30 ml (1-2 tbsp) chilled water and mix to a soft dough. Roll out and use to line a 10×30 cm (4×12 inch) rectangular loose-bottomed tin. Chill for 15 minutes.

2 Line the pastry case with greaseproof paper and baking beans. Bake blind at 190°C (375°F) mark 5 for 15 minutes. Remove the paper and beans and bake for a further 5-10 minutes. Allow to cool, then remove the flan tin and place the pastry case on a serving plate or board.

3 Spread the yogurt over the base of the pastry case and arrange the fruit in an attractive pattern. Mix together the jam and lemon juice and spoon evenly over the fruits. Serve sliced.

Plum Clafoutis

Serve the clafoutis hot, straight from the oven, or chilled.

NUTRITIONAL ANALYSIS
amount per portion
185 kcals/772 kJ
9.5 g Carbohydrate
5.5 g Protein ★
14.1 g Fat ★★
2.7 g Saturated Fat ★★★
4.2 g Added Sugar ★★★
2.9 g Fibre ★
348 mg Salt ★★★
61 mg Calcium ★★
1.0 mg Iron ★
16 mg Folic Acid

SERVES 6

450 g (1 lb) plums, halved and stoned

50 g (2 oz) low-fat soft cheese

50 g (2 oz) ground almonds

25 g (1 oz) light muscovado sugar

2 eggs

60 ml (4 tbsp) semi-skimmed milk

50 g (2 oz) polyunsaturated margarine, melted

1 Lightly grease a 20.5 cm (8 inch) round flan dish and arrange the plums in it in a circular pattern.

2 To make the batter, beat the cheese, ground almonds and sugar together, then gradually whisk in the eggs and milk. Fold in the margarine. Pour the batter over the plums.

3 Bake at 200°C (400°F) mark 6 for 25-30 minutes until golden and set.

NUTRITIONAL ANALYSIS
amount per portion
220 kcals/921 kJ
31.9 g Carbohydrate
3.4 g Protein ★
9.7 g Fat ★★
1.1 g Saturated Fat ★★★★
3.8 g Added Sugar ★★★
9.6 g Fibre ★★★
129 mg Salt ★★★★
93 mg Calcium ★★
1.9 mg Iron ★★
23 mg Folic Acid

Almond Baked Apples

The almond coating and fig filling makes these baked apples with a difference.

SERVES 4
75 g (3 oz) dried figs, rinsed and chopped
grated rind of 1 lime or ½ lemon
4 cookings apples, about 225 g (8 oz) each, left whole, peeled and cored
50 g (2 oz) ground almonds
15 ml (1 tbsp) light muscovado sugar
15 ml (1 tbsp) polyunsaturated margarine, melted

1 Put the figs in a bowl, cover with boiling water and leave to soak for 5 minutes. Drain, then mix in the grated rind. Use the mixture to fill the centre of each apple, packing down firmly.

2 Mix the ground almonds and sugar together in a bowl. Brush each apple with the melted margarine, then roll the apples in the ground almond mixture. Place in a shallow 1.1 litre (2 pint) ovenproof dish.

3 Bake at 180°C (350°F) mark 4 for about 45-50 minutes or until the apples are cooked through and tender when pricked with a skewer. Serve hot.

NUTRITIONAL ANALYSIS
amount per portion
132 kcals/552 kJ
14.6 g Carbohydrate
5.5 g Protein ★
6.3 g Fat ★★★
4.0 g Saturated Fat ★★★
3.8 g Added Sugar ★★★
2.3 g Fibre ★
41 mg Salt ★★★★
79 mg Calcium ★★
0.5 mg Iron
44 mg Folic Acid ★

Orange Mousses

This mousse is quick and easy to make and looks pretty served in the orange shells.

SERVES 4
4 sweet oranges
15 ml (1 tbsp) powdered gelatine
15 ml (1 tbsp) light muscovado sugar
75 ml (3 fl oz) Greek strained yogurt
50 ml (2 fl oz) whipping cream
few orange segments and mint sprigs, to decorate

1 Over a large bowl, cut the top third off the oranges to make a zigzag edge. Remove all the flesh from the oranges and press through sieve, then make the juice up to 300 ml (½ pint) with a little water if necessary. Reserve the orange shells.

2 Put half the juice into a saucepan, add the gelatine and leave for 5 minutes. Over a low heat, dissolve the gelatine by stirring, then add the sugar, stirring until dissolved. Pour into a bowl. Stir in the remaining juice and leave until the mixture sets around the edges of the bowl.

3 Fold the yogurt into the orange mixture. Whip the cream until it forms soft peaks and fold in to the mixture. Leave for 10-15 minutes until it holds its shape. Pile into the reserved orange shells. Chill for 2-3 hours or until set. Serve chilled, decorated with orange segments and mint sprigs.

Strawberry Shortcake

This tempting variation of an American favourite uses low-fat natural yogurt to replace some of the cream.

SERVES 4
50 g (2 oz) plain wholemeal flour
175 g (6 oz) self-raising white flour
50 g (2 oz) polyunsaturated margarine
15 ml (1 tbsp) light muscovado sugar
75 ml (3 fl oz) semi-skimmed milk
45 ml (3 tbsp) whipping cream
45 ml (3 tbsp) thick set low-fat natural yogurt
2.5 ml (½ tsp) clear honey (optional)
225 g (8 oz) fresh strawberries, hulled and sliced if large

1 Lightly grease a baking sheet. Put the flours into a bowl and rub in the margarine until the mixture resembles fine breadcrumbs. Stir in the sugar and add enough milk to make a soft, pliable dough.

2 Roll out on a floured surface to 1 cm (½ inch) thick, then cut out 4 rounds with a 10 cm (4 inch) fluted pastry cutter. Put on the prepared baking sheet. Bake at 200°C (400°F) mark 6 for 12-15 minutes or until cooked. Set aside to cool.

3 Meanwhile, prepare the filling. Whip the cream until stiff, then mix with the yogurt and honey, if using.

4 Split the scone shortcakes in half and place the cream mixture on the bases, reserving 20 ml (4 tsp). Cover the cream with the strawberries, reserving 4 slices. Put on the tops and decorate with the reserved cream and fruit.

NUTRITIONAL ANALYSIS
amount per portion
361 kcals/1508 kJ
51.1 g Carbohydrate
8.0 g Protein ★★
15.3 g Fat ★★
4.6 g Saturated Fat ★★
4.2 g Added Sugar ★★★
4.1 g Fibre ★★
753 mg Salt ★★
225 mg Calcium ★★★
1.9 mg Iron ★★
28 mg Folic Acid ★

NUTRITIONAL ANALYSIS
amount per portion
401 kcals/1678 kJ
46.7 g Carbohydrate
7.9 g Protein ★★
21.8 g Fat ★
6.8 g Saturated Fat ★★
5.7 g Added Sugar ★★
7.2 g Fibre ★★
671 mg Salt ★★
94 mg Calcium ★★
2.5 mg Iron ★★
50 mg Folic Acid ★

Steamed Orange Pudding

Breadcrumbs replace some of the flour and help to keep the pudding light.

SERVES 4

2 oranges, peeled and thinly sliced

100 g (4 oz) self-raising wholemeal flour

50 g (2 oz) fresh wholemeal breadcrumbs

75 g (3 oz) polyunsaturated margarine

grated rind of 1 orange

75 g (3 oz) raisins, rinsed

25 g (1 oz) desiccated coconut

30 ml (2 tbsp) clear honey

1 egg, beaten

90 ml (6 tbsp) semi-skimmed milk

fruit purée or Greek strained yogurt, to serve

1 Lightly grease a 900 ml (1½ pint) pudding basin, then line with the orange slices.
2 Mix the flour and breadcrumbs in a bowl. Add the margarine, in small pieces, and rub in with the fingertips. Stir in the orange rind, raisins and coconut.
3 Add the honey, egg and milk to the dry ingredients. Mix to a soft consistency. Spoon into the basin and smooth the top.
4 Cover the basin with a double thickness of pleated greaseproof paper and tie securely with string. Steam for 1½ hours, or until well risen and firm to the touch. Turn out and serve hot with fruit purée or yogurt.

Fresh Peach Cobbler

This scone-topped pudding also works well with nectarines. Serve with creamy Greek yogurt or Fresh Peach Ice Cream (see page 150).

SERVES 6
4 ripe peaches, skinned, halved and sliced
45 ml (3 tbsp) unsweetened orange juice
30 ml (2 tbsp) clear honey
100 g (4 oz) plain wholemeal flour
7.5 ml (1½ tsp) baking powder
40 g (1½ oz) polyunsaturated margarine
25 g (1 oz) light muscovado sugar
about 75 ml (5 tbsp) semi-skimmed milk
15 g (½ oz) flaked almonds

1 Lightly grease a shallow 20 cm (8 inch) round dish. Put the peaches, orange juice and honey in the dish and mix gently so the peach slices are well coated. Set aside.

2 Sift the flour and baking powder into a bowl, adding all the bran left in the sieve, and rub in the margarine until the mixture resembles fine breadcrumbs. Stir in the sugar and mix to a soft dough with about 60 ml (4 tbsp) of the milk. Add more milk if necessary, to mix to a soft dough.

3 Roll out the scone dough on a lightly floured surface to a round about 18 cm (7 inches) in diameter. Cut into six equal wedges.

4 Arrange the wedges on top of the peaches. Brush with the remaining milk and sprinkle the almonds over the top.

5 Bake at 220°C (425°F) mark 7 for about 20 minutes, until the scone dough is well risen and golden brown. Serve at once.

NUTRITIONAL ANALYSIS
amount per portion
194 kcals/809 kJ
30.3 g Carbohydrate
3.8 g Protein ★
7.3 g Fat ★★★
1.2 g Saturated Fat ★★★★
8.0 g Added Sugar ★★
3.2 g Fibre ★★
162 mg Salt ★★★★
37 mg Calcium ★
1.2 mg Iron ★
19 mg Folic Acid

NUTRITIONAL ANALYSIS
amount per portion
139 kcals/583 kJ
29 g Carbohydrate
6.9 g Protein ★ ★
0.4 g Fat ★ ★ ★ ★
0.2 g Saturated Fat ★ ★ ★ ★
6.3 g Added Sugar ★ ★
3.5 g Fibre ★ ★
84 mg Salt ★ ★ ★ ★
103 mg Calcium ★ ★
0.9 mg Iron ★
34 mg Folic Acid ★

Blackberry and Apple Jellies

When fresh blackberries aren't in season, use frozen blackberries or fresh or frozen raspberries instead.

SERVES 4

20 ml (4 tsp) powdered gelatine

450 ml (¾ pint) unsweetened apple juice

175 g (6 oz) blackberries

25 g (1 oz) light muscovado sugar

150 ml (¼ pint) low-fat natural yogurt

½ eating apple, thinly sliced, to decorate

1 Mix 5 ml (1 tsp) gelatine and 150 ml (¼ pint) apple juice in a heatproof bowl and leave to soften for about 1 minute. Put the bowl over a saucepan of gently simmering water and stir until the gelatine dissolves. Remove from the heat and leave to cool.

2 Reserve 4 blackberries for decoration; arrange 50 g (2 oz) of the remaining berries in the base of 4 glasses. Pour the apple mixture into the glasses and chill for 30 minutes or until set.

3 Meanwhile, put the remaining berries in a saucepan with 200 ml (⅓ pint) of the remaining apple juice. Cover and simmer gently until the fruit is tender. Cool a little, then purée in a blender or food processor. If liked, rub through a fine nylon sieve to remove the seeds. Add sugar to taste.

4 Dissolve the remaining gelatine in the remaining apple juice as before. Add to the blackberry and apple purée and make up to 450 ml (¾ pint) with cold water if necessary. Chill for 30 minutes or until thick.

5 Lightly whisk the jelly, then fold in the yogurt. Pour into the glasses over the set apple jelly, cover and chill for 1 hour. Serve decorated with the reserved blackberries and apple slices.

Baked Fruit Cheesecake

This high-protein dessert will be enjoyed by all the members of the family.

NUTRITIONAL ANALYSIS
amount per portion
359 kcals/1501 kJ
42 g Carbohydrate
15 g Protein ★★★
15.6 g Fat ★★
6.5 g Saturated Fat ★★
23.8 g Added Sugar
1.8 g Fibre ★
500 mg Salt ★★
288 mg Calcium ★★★★
1.9 mg Iron ★★
18 mg Folic Acid

MAKES 8 SLICES

50 g (2 oz) polyunsaturated margarine

25 g (1 oz) medium oatmeal

75 g (3 oz) plain wholemeal flour

115 g (4½ oz) light muscovado sugar

7.5 ml (1½ tsp) ground ginger

700 g (1½ lb) ricotta cheese

3 eggs, size 3

finely grated rind of 1 lemon

60 ml (4 tbsp) Greek strained yogurt

2 kiwi fruit, peeled and sliced, and 225 g (8 oz) strawberries, hulled and sliced, to decorate

1 To make the base, melt the margarine in a saucepan and stir in the oatmeal, flour, 40 g (1½ oz) of the sugar and the ginger. Cook gently for 1-2 minutes, stirring, until well mixed. Press on to the base of an 18 cm (7 inch) loose-bottomed cake tin. Bake at 180°C (350°F) mark 4 for 5 minutes.
2 Meanwhile, beat the cheese until smooth, then add the eggs one at a time, blending in well. Add the lemon rind and remaining sugar and mix thoroughly.
3 Pour on to the baked base, smooth the surface and continue baking for 20 minutes. Carefully spoon the yogurt over the filling and bake for a further 20 minutes.
4 Cool for about 3 hours in the tin. When cold, carefully remove the cheesecake from the tin and decorate with the kiwi fruit and strawberries.

NUTRITIONAL ANALYSIS
amount per portion
409 kcals/1710 kJ
71.6 g Carbohydrate
6.6 g Protein ★★
12.8 g Fat ★★
2.1 g Saturated Fat ★★★
14.8 g Added Sugar ★
7.3 g Fibre ★★
305 mg Salt ★★★
82 mg Calcium ★★
3.4 mg Iron ★★★
31 mg Folic Acid ★

Spicy Apple Crumble

A crunchy, oaty crumble with a lot less fat than the conventional recipe.

SERVES 4

450 g (1 lb) cooking apples, peeled, cored and sliced
50 g (2 oz) sultanas
25 g (1 oz) light muscovado sugar
10 ml (2 tsp) ground cinnamon
50 g (2 oz) plain wholemeal flour
50 g (2 oz) plain white flour
50 g (2 oz) polyunsaturated margarine
100 g (4 oz) porridge oats
45 ml (3 tbsp) clear honey

1 Mix the apples, sultanas, sugar and cinnamon in an ovenproof dish. In a bowl, mix the flours and rub in the margarine, then add the oats and honey.
2 Sprinkle over the top of the apples. Bake at 180°C (350°F) mark 4 for about 45 minutes until golden.

NUTRITIONAL ANALYSIS
amount per portion
150 kcals/629 kJ
31.6 g Carbohydrate
5.3 g Protein ★
1.2 g Fat ★★★★
0.2 g Saturated Fat ★★★★
4.2 g Added Sugar ★★★
10.1 g Fibre ★★★
660 mg Salt ★★
65 mg Calcium ★★
2.5 mg Iron ★★
26 mg Folic Acid ★

Summer Pudding

Make this pudding in autumn with ripe plums and eating apples.

SERVES 6

8 slices day-old wholemeal bread, crusts removed
225 g (8 oz) strawberries, hulled, halved if large
450 g (1 lb) mixed soft fruits such as redcurrants, raspberries, loganberries and stoned cherries
75 ml (5 tbsp) apple juice
25 g (1 oz) light muscovado sugar

1 Place 1 slice of bread in the base of a 900 ml (1½ pint) pudding basin. Reserve 2 slices of bread and use the remainder to line the sides of the basin, cutting them to fit if necessary.
2 Put the fruit in a saucepan with the apple juice and sugar. Bring gently to the boil and cook for 2-3 minutes until the fruit is slightly softened.
3 Fill the basin with the fruit, pressing it down well. Place the reserved bread on the top, cutting it to fit. Place a saucer on top of the pudding and weigh it down. Chill for at least 6 hours or overnight.
4 Just before serving, invert the pudding on to a plate. Serve with Greek strained yogurt.

Crème Caramel

The addition of dried skimmed milk powder gives a thick set and a rich taste to this delicious dessert.

SERVES 4

100 g (4 oz) light muscovado sugar

568 ml (1 pint) semi-skimmed milk

1 vanilla pod or 1.25 ml (¼ tsp) vanilla essence

3 eggs

25 g (1 oz) dried skimmed milk powder

sliced strawberries, to decorate (optional)

1 Put half the sugar and 90 ml (6 tbsp) water into a saucepan. Stir over a low heat until the sugar dissolves, then boil rapidly without stirring until a deep golden brown. Pour into a 15 cm (6 inch) soufflé dish and cool.
2 Place the semi-skimmed milk and vanilla pod in a saucepan and slowly bring to the boil. Remove from the heat. Whisk together the eggs, remaining sugar and vanilla essence if used, and stir in the dried skimmed milk.
3 Remove the vanilla pod from the saucepan. (Rinse the pod and store for future use.) Pour the milk on to the egg mixture, whisking until the sugar and milk powder dissolve. Strain into the soufflé dish and cover. Place in a roasting tin half-filled with boiling water. Bake at 170°C (325°F) mark 3 for 1-1¼ hours until set. Cool and chill for at least 3 hours or overnight.
4 To turn out, place a serving dish over the top of the soufflé dish. Hold the 2 dishes firmly together and turn over. Give a sharp shake to release the suction, then set aside for a few minutes so the caramel drains over the custard. Decorate with strawberries, if liked.

NUTRITIONAL ANALYSIS
amount per portion
254 kcals/1060 kJ
36.9 g Carbohydrate
12.4 g Protein ★★
7.2 g Fat ★★★
3.3 g Saturated Fat ★★★
25 g Added Sugar
0.2 g Fibre
422 mg Salt ★★★
294 mg Calcium ★★★★
1.2 mg Iron ★
21 mg Folic Acid

Banana and Grape Brulée

This healthy version of the classic dessert uses less sugar and fat. So be careful not to overheat it when grilling or the cream and yogurt will curdle.

SERVES 4

2 bananas

225 g (8 oz) black grapes, seeded and halved

150 ml (¼ pint) soured cream

150 ml (¼ pint) Greek strained yogurt

25 g (1 oz) light muscovado sugar

1 Peel and slice the bananas, then mix with grapes; spoon into 4 ramekins. Mix the soured cream and yogurt and spoon over each. Cover and chill for 1 hour.
2 Sprinkle each with a little sugar and heat quickly under a hot grill until the sugar caramelises.

NUTRITIONAL ANALYSIS
amount per portion
222 kcals/929 kJ
26.5 g Carbohydrate
4.1 g Protein ★
11.9 g Fat ★★
7.5 g Saturated Fat ★★
6.3 g Added Sugar ★★
1.9 g Fibre ★
88 mg Salt ★★★★
84 mg Calcium ★★
0.5 mg Iron
18 mg Folic Acid

NUTRITIONAL ANALYSIS
amount per portion
262 kcals/1095 kJ
27.3 g Carbohydrate
5.0 g Protein ★
15.4 g Fat ★★
9.3 g Saturated Fat ★★
10 g Added Sugar ★★
2.1 g Fibre ★
157 mg Salt ★★★★
105 mg Calcium ★★
1.1 mg Iron ★
11 mg Folic Acid

Fresh Peach Ice Cream

Make use of plentiful ripe peaches when they are in season and prepare this ice cream. It can be kept in the freezer for up to 4 months.

SERVES 4

150 ml (¼ pint) semi-skimmed milk

1 egg, beaten

40 g (1½ oz) light muscovado sugar

150 ml (¼ pint) whipping cream

30 ml (2 tbsp) low-fat natural yogurt

4 very ripe peaches, skinned, stoned and chopped

1 Heat the milk to blood temperature in a saucepan. Pour on to the egg in a bowl, stirring. Add the sugar. Return to the pan and cook over gentle heat, stirring constantly, until the mixture thickens. Strain and set aside to cool for about 10 minutes.
2 Whip the cream until thick. Fold the cooled custard into the cream and stir in the yogurt. Pour into a shallow freezerproof container, cover and freeze for about 1 hour or until ice crystals begin to form around edges. Mash well.
3 Return to the freezer and freeze for about 2 hours or until mushy. Mash again.
4 Purée the peaches in a blender or food processer, then stir into the frozen mixture and mix well. Freeze for a further 2-3 hours or until firm. If frozen longer, transfer to the refrigerator 1-2 hours before serving, or leave at room temperature for ½-1 hour to soften.

NUTRITIONAL ANALYSIS
amount per portion
291 kcals/1217 kJ
35.6 g Carbohydrate
6.9 g Protein ★★
14.5 g Fat ★★
8.9 g Saturated Fat ★★
18.8 g Added Sugar
1.9 g Fibre ★
529 mg Salt ★★
182 mg Calcium ★★★
1.0 mg Iron ★
12 mg Folic Acid

Brown Bread Ice Cream

This is an old-fashioned favourite that has a delicious praline-like flavour.

SERVES 4

100 g (4 oz) fresh wholemeal breadcrumbs, including crusts

75 g (3 oz) light muscovado sugar

150 ml (¼ pint) whipping cream

300 ml (½ pint) low-fat natural yogurt

1 Mix the breadcrumbs with 50 g (2 oz) of the sugar and spread on a baking sheet. Bake at 200°C (400°F) mark 6 for 10-15 minutes, turning occasionally, until crisp and lightly browned. Alternatively, toast under the grill, turning frequently to prevent burning. Set aside to cool, then break up.
2 Whip the cream until thick, then stir in the yogurt and remaining sugar. Stir in the toasted breadcrumbs, reserving 25 g (1 oz) for the topping.
3 Pour into a freezerproof container and freeze for 4 hours until firm. Transfer to the refrigerator to soften 30 minutes before serving. To serve, scoop into serving dishes and sprinkle with the reserved crumbs.

Almond Fruit Salad

There is just a mild hint of almond seeping through the juices of the different fruits.

SERVES 6

1 small ripe melon
225 g (8 oz) seedless white grapes
2 kiwi fruits, peeled, halved and sliced
150 ml (¼ pint) orange juice
5 ml (1 tsp) almond flavouring
50 g (2 oz) whole almonds
450 g (1 lb) raspberries

1 Scoop out the melon flesh, discarding the skin and seeds. Mix the melon, grapes and kiwi fruit together in a bowl. Stir in the orange juice and almond flavouring, cover tightly and leave for at least 1 hour to allow the flavours to mingle.

2 Blanch the almonds in a bowl of boiling water for 2-3 minutes, then remove the skins. Toast the nuts under the grill until well browned; cool.

3 About 30 minutes before serving, stir the raspberries and nuts into the fruit salad. Serve at room temperature.

NUTRITIONAL ANALYSIS
amount per portion
130 kcals/544 kJ
20 g Carbohydrate
3.2 g Protein ★
4.6 g Fat ★★★
0.3 g Saturated Fat ★★★★
0.0 g Added Sugar ★★★★
8.1 g Fibre ★★★
55 mg Salt ★★★★
84 mg Calcium ★★
1.8 mg Iron ★★
45 mg Folic Acid ★

Kheer

These rice creams are a simple adaptation of a traditional Indian pudding. In the original recipe, full-cream milk and a great deal of sugar are used; this version is lighter and less sweet. If you like, whipping cream can be substituted for the Greek strained yogurt, although this will raise the fat content of the dessert.

SERVES 4

75 g (3 oz) pudding rice
seeds of 6 cardamoms, crushed
1.1 litres (2 pints) semi-skimmed milk
60 ml (4 tbsp) clear honey
2.5-5 ml (½-1 tsp) rose water
60 ml (4 tbsp) Greek strained yogurt
rose petals, to decorate (optional)

1 Put the rice and crushed cardamom seeds in a heavy-based non-stick saucepan. Pour in the milk, then add the honey and bring to the boil, stirring continuously.

2 Lower the heat and simmer for about 1¼ hours or until the rice is tender and the milk has reduced to a thick, creamy consistency. Stir frequently to prevent the milk and rice catching on the bottom of the pan.

3 Leave the kheer to cool, then cover the surface closely and chill overnight.

4 Stir in the rose water, then divide the kheer equally between 4 stemmed glasses. Very lightly spoon the yogurt on top of each serving, then place rose petals on top, if liked. Serve well chilled.

NUTRITIONAL ANALYSIS
amount per portion
265 kcals/1108 kJ
41.7 g Carbohydrate
11.6 g Protein ★★
6.8 g Fat ★★★
4.4 g Saturated Fat ★★
11.5 g Added Sugar ★★
0.4 g Fibre
381 mg Salt ★★★
373 mg Calcium ★★★★
0.3 mg Iron
19 mg Folic Acid

NUTRITIONAL ANALYSIS
amount per portion
158 kcals/661 kJ
36.9 g Carbohydrate
4.9 g Protein ★
0.1 g Fat ★★★★
0.0 g Saturated Fat ★★★★
0.0 g Added Sugar ★★★★
2.0 g Fibre ★
13 mg Salt ★★★★
12 mg Calcium
0.8 mg Iron ★
21 mg Folic Acid

Golden Fruit Jelly

The jelly can be made with any fresh fruit in season; no other sweetening is necessary.

SERVES 4

20 g (¾ oz) powdered gelatine

750 ml (1¼ pints) unsweetened apple juice

1 banana

1 dessert apple

1 ripe pear

1 Mix the gelatine and 75 ml (5 tbsp) water in a heatproof bowl and leave for about 5 minutes until softened. Put the bowl over a saucepan of gently simmering water until the gelatine dissolves. Remove from the heat and leave to cool slightly. Stir in the apple juice and mix well.

2 Meanwhile, prepare the fruit. Peel and slice the banana, core and dice the apple and core and dice the pear. Place the fruit in a 1.1 litre (2 pint) decorative jelly mould. Pour the liquid into the jelly mould and chill until set.

3 To unmould, lightly draw knife that has been dipped in hot water around the rim of the mould, then place the mould in hot water for 2-3 seconds. Put a damp serving plate over the mould and invert quickly, holding with both hands and shaking sharply.

11

Quick and Easy Baking

There is nothing quite like the delicious aroma of home baking coming from the kitchen. All these mouthwatering baking recipes contain wholesome ingredients, such as wholemeal flour, brown sugar, honey, fresh and dried fruit and yogurt. High in fibre, these tempting cakes and biscuits provide a healthy alternative to the shop-bought goods. Remember to eat them in moderation though.

NUTRITIONAL ANALYSIS
amount per portion
155 kcals/648 kJ
20.8 g Carbohydrate
3.5 g Protein ★
7.2 g Fat ★★★
1.3 g Saturated Fat ★★★★
1.5 g Added Sugar ★★★★
2.5 g Fibre ★
181 mg Salt ★★★★
15 mg Calcium
1.1 mg Iron ★
16 mg Folic Acid

Banana and Cinnamon Rock Cakes

The stripped bark of the cinnamon tree curls up as it dries until it becomes a stick. It is sold in this form or as ground cinnamon, used here to give a sweet spicy flavour to the cakes.

MAKES ABOUT 10
200 g (7 oz) plain wholemeal flour
7.5 ml (1½ tsp) baking powder
5 ml (1 tsp) ground cinnamon
75 g (3 oz) polyunsaturated margarine
15 ml (1 tbsp) light muscovado sugar
50 g (2 oz) sultanas
225 g (8 oz) ripe bananas, peeled
5 ml (1 tsp) lemon juice
1 egg, lightly beaten

1 Place the flour, baking powder and cinnamon into a bowl and rub in the margarine until the mixture resembles fine breadcrumbs. Stir in the sugar and sultanas.
2 Mash the bananas with the lemon juice, then stir in the egg. Pour this mixture into the dry ingredients and beat until well mixed.
3 Spoon the mixture into about 10 mounds on a baking sheet, allowing room for spreading.
4 Bake at 200°C (400°F) mark 6 for about 15 minutes or until the cakes are well risen and golden brown. Cool on a wire rack.

NUTRITIONAL ANALYSIS
amount per portion
275 kcals/1149 kJ
38.1 g Carbohydrate
5.7 g Protein ★
12.4 g Fat ★★
2.4 g Saturated Fat ★★★
12.5 g Added Sugar ★★
3.8 g Fibre ★★
310 mg Salt ★★★
46 mg Calcium ★
2.2 mg Iron ★★
26 mg Folic Acid ★

Banana Teabread

This teabread is quick and easy to make. The flavours will be even more pronounced if the bread is made a day in advance.

MAKES 8 SLICES
225 g (8 oz) plain wholemeal flour
10 ml (2 tsp) ground cinnamon
5 ml (1 tsp) ground mixed spice
100 g (4 oz) polyunsaturated margarine
100 g (4 oz) light muscovado sugar
2 eggs, size 2
2 large ripe bananas, peeled and mashed

1 Lightly grease and line a 450 g (1 lb) loaf tin. Place all the ingredients in a bowl. Beat well with a wooden spoon until evenly mixed. Spoon the mixture into the prepared tin and smooth the top.
2 Bake at 180°C (350°F) mark 4 for about 50 minutes or until well risen and firm to the touch. Turn out and cool on a wire rack. Serve sliced, spread with polyunsaturated margarine if liked.

Passion Cake

Topped with a mouthwatering sweetened soft cheese icing, grated carrots make this a moist cake.

NUTRITIONAL ANALYSIS
amount per portion
279 kcals/1166 kJ
26.6 g Carbohydrate
7.9 g Protein ★★
16.6 g Fat ★★
3.2 g Saturated Fat ★★★
10.5 g Added Sugar ★★
3.4 g Fibre ★★
504 mg Salt ★★
58 mg Calcium ★★
1.7 mg Iron ★★
30 mg Folic Acid ★

MAKES ABOUT 12 SLICES

100 g (4 oz) polyunsaturated margarine

100 g (4 oz) light muscovado sugar

3 eggs, beaten

225 g (8 oz) self-raising wholemeal flour

5 ml (1 tsp) baking powder

5 ml (1 tsp) ground mixed spice

450 g (1 lb) carrots, scrubbed and coarsely grated

finely grated rind of 1 lemon

30 ml (2 tbsp) lemon juice

100 g (4 oz) walnut pieces, chopped

200 g (7 oz) low-fat soft cheese

25 g (1 oz) icing sugar, sifted

chopped walnuts, to decorate

1 Grease and base line a 20.5 cm (8 inch) round springform cake tin. Cream the butter and sugar together in a bowl until pale and fluffy. Add the eggs, a little at a time, beating well after each addition.

2 Fold in the flour with the baking powder and spice. Stir in the carrots, lemon rind, 15 ml (1 tbsp) of the lemon juice and the walnuts. Spoon the mixture into the prepared tin and level the surface.

3 Bake at 180°C (350°F) mark 4 for about 1¼ hours or until well risen and golden brown. Turn out and cool on a wire rack. When completely cold, wrap the cake in greaseproof paper and foil, then store for 1 day before icing.

4 To make the icing, beat the cheese, icing sugar and remaining lemon juice together in a bowl until soft and creamy. Spread over the top of the cake using a palette knife. Decorate with walnuts.

NUTRITIONAL ANALYSIS
amount per portion
141 kcals/591 kJ
29.5 g Carbohydrate
4.5 g Protein ★
1.7 g Fat ★★★★
0.5 g Saturated Fat ★★★★
14.6 g Added Sugar ★
1.8 g Fibre ★
70 mg Salt ★★★★
55 mg Calcium ★★
1.1 mg Iron ★
13 mg Folic Acid

Yogurt Madeira Cake

Low-fat yogurt contains no more than 1.5 per cent milk fat. Here it adds moisture to this popular cake.

MAKES 12 SLICES
200 ml (7 fl oz) low-fat natural yogurt
finely grated rind of 1 lemon
175 g (6 oz) light muscovado sugar
2 eggs, size 2
225 g (8 oz) plain wholemeal flour
10 ml (2 tsp) baking powder
10 ml (2 tsp) ground mixed spice
thin strip of lemon peel

1 Line the base of a 15 cm (6 inch) deep round cake tin with greaseproof paper. Put the yogurt, lemon rind, sugar and eggs into a bowl and beat until mixed.
2 Sift in the flour, adding any bran left in the sieve, baking powder and spice, and mix to a batter. Pour the mixture into the prepared tin and lay the lemon peel on top.
3 Bake at 180°C (350°F) mark 4 for 50 minutes. Cover the top with a piece of greaseproof paper to prevent overbrowning and bake for a further 15-20 minutes or until the centre is firm.
4 Leave to cool in the tin for about 15 minutes. Run a knife around the edge of the tin, turn out and cool on a wire rack.

NUTRITIONAL ANALYSIS
amount per portion
190 kcals/794 kJ
23 g Carbohydrate
2.4 g Protein
10.5 g Fat ★★
1.5 g Saturated Fat ★★★★
10.7 g Added Sugar ★★
2.2 g Fibre ★
175 mg Salt ★★★★
23 mg Calcium
0.9 mg Iron ★
12 mg Folic Acid

Chewy Muesli Bars

A high-fibre alternative to biscuits, these fruit and nut muesli bars make a welcome addition to a lunch box.

MAKES 10
75 g (3 oz) polyunsaturated margarine
50 g (2 oz) light muscovado sugar
75 ml (3 fl oz) clear honey
100 g (4 oz) rolled oats
50 g (2 oz) sultanas
75 g (3 oz) mixed nuts, coarsely chopped
25 g (1 oz) ready-to-eat dried apricots, rinsed and chopped

1 Lightly grease a shallow 18 cm (7 inch) square baking tin. Melt the margarine in a saucepan, add the sugar and honey and stir over a low heat until the sugar is dissolved. Add the oats, sultanas, nuts and apricots, and mix well. Spoon the mixture into the prepared tin and level the surface.
2 Bake at 170°C (325°F) mark 3 for 30-35 minutes or until crisped and lightly browned.
3 Set aside to cool for 5 minutes in the tin, then cut into 10 fingers. Leave in the tin until completely cooled. Store in an airtight container.

Apricot and Almond Gingerbread

Dried apricots are full of concentrated goodness; they have a high mineral and fibre content and contain large amounts of carotene which is converted into vitamin A in the body.

NUTRITIONAL ANALYSIS
amount per portion
189 kcals/792 kJ
25.2 g Carbohydrate
3.8 g Protein ★
8.9 g Fat ★★★
1.6 g Saturated Fat ★★★★
7.7 g Added Sugar ★★
3.4 g Fibre ★★
237 mg Salt ★★★★
96 mg Calcium ★★
2.2 mg Iron ★★
12 mg Folic Acid

MAKES 12 SQUARES

100 g (4 oz) ready-to-eat dried apricots, rinsed and chopped

100 g (4 oz) plain wholemeal flour

100 g (4 oz) plain white flour

5 ml (1 tsp) ground cinnamon

15 ml (1 tbsp) ground ginger

25 g (1 oz) light muscovado sugar

100 g (4 oz) polyunsaturated margarine

100 g (4 oz) molasses

5 ml (1 tsp) bicarbonate of soda

150 ml (¼ pint) semi-skimmed milk, warmed

1 egg, size 2, beaten

25 g (1 oz) blanched almonds, split

1 Lightly grease and line a 27×18 cm (10¾×7 inch) baking tin with greased greaseproof paper. Pour boiling water over the apricots in a bowl and leave for 5 minutes, then drain.

2 Mix the flours and spices together in a bowl with the sugar and apricots. Melt the margarine and molasses in a small saucepan, then add to the dry ingredients and beat well.

3 Dissolve the bicarbonate of soda in the milk and gradually beat into the mixture. Add the egg and beat to form a smooth batter. Pour the batter into the prepared tin and sprinkle with the almonds.

4 Bake at 180°C (350°F) mark 4 for 40-45 minutes or until cooked through. Cool the gingerbread in the tin before turning out.

NUTRITIONAL ANALYSIS
amount per portion
201 kcals/841 kJ
47.8 g Carbohydrate
3.7 g Protein ★
0.9 g Fat ★★★★
0.2 g Saturated Fat ★★★★
10.9 g Added Sugar ★★
4.2 g Fibre ★★
79 mg Salt ★★★★
52 mg Calcium ★★
1.9 mg Iron ★★
13 mg Folic Acid

Malted Sultana Loaf

Malt extract is not as sweet as sugar and often used in drinks and baking. It can be bought in supermarkets or health food shops.

MAKES 12 SLICES
45 ml (3 tbsp) malt extract
450 g (1 lb) sultanas
100 g (4 oz) dark muscovado sugar
225 g (8 oz) self-raising wholemeal flour
1 egg, size 2, beaten

1 Grease and line a 900 g (2 lb) loaf tin with greased greaseproof paper. Put the malt extract, sultanas and sugar into a bowl with 450 ml (¾ pint) boiling water. Leave to soak overnight.

2 Sift the flour on to the malt and sultana mixture, adding any bran left in the sieve, then add the egg. Mix well. Pour the mixture into the prepared tin.

3 Bake at 170°C (325°F) mark 3 for about 1¾ hours or until risen and firm. Cover with greaseproof paper for the last 30 minutes to prevent overbrowning. Turn out and cool on a wire rack. Serve sliced and spread with a little polyunsaturated margarine.

NUTRITIONAL ANALYSIS
amount per portion
46 kcals/193 kJ
5.1 g Carbohydrate
0.8 g Protein
2.7 g Fat ★★★★
0.5 g Saturated Fat ★★★★
0.6 g Added Sugar ★★★★
0.6 g Fibre
67 mg Salt ★★★★
10 mg Calcium
0.4 mg Iron
4.0 mg Folic Acid

Molasses Cookies

Molasses is the residue left when cane sugar is refined. It contains some vitamins and minerals.

MAKES 16
100 g (4 oz) plain wholemeal flour
2.5 ml (½ tsp) bicarbonate of soda
2.5 ml (½ tsp) ground cinnamon
2.5 ml (½ tsp) ground ginger
2.5 ml (½ tsp) ground mixed spice
50 g (2 oz) polyunsaturated margarine
50 g (2 oz) light muscovado sugar
15 ml (1 tbsp) molasses

1 Lightly oil a baking sheet. Put the flour into a bowl and stir in the bicarbonate of soda and spices.

2 Place the margarine, sugar and molasses in a small saucepan and heat gently, stirring until melted. Pour over the flour and spice mixture and stir to a thick paste. Set aside to cool.

3 Roll into a sausage shape and slice into 16 pieces. Roll each piece into a ball. Place them well apart on the prepared baking sheet and flatten slightly with the palm of the hand.

4 Bake at 180°C (350°F) mark 4 for about 15 minutes. Leave on the baking sheet until firm, then cool on a wire rack. Store in an airtight container.

INDEX

alcohol, 7–8, 10–11

almonds: almond baked apples, 142

almond fruit salad, 151

apricot and almond gingerbread, 157

amino acids, 17–18

apples: almond baked 112

blackberry and apple jellies, 146

curried potato and apple soup, 45

plum and apple spread, 37

spicy apple crumble, 148

apricot and almond gingerbread, 157

aubergines: aubergine and bean gratin, 69

aubergine dip, 57

sesame aubergines, 135

spiced red lentils with aubergines and mushrooms, 118

avocado and peanut salad, 134

babies: congenital defects, 8, 11

development, 9

size, 14–15

baking, 153–8

balanced diet, 26–9

bananas: banana and cinnamon rock cakes, 154

banana and grape brulée, 149

banana teabread, 154

beans: aubergine and bean gratin, 69

pork and bean stew, 81

vegetable and bean soup, 48

beef: beef, walnut and orange casserole, 76

bobotie, 77

carpaccio with courgettes, 79

grilled marinated steak, 78

seekh kebabs, 80

beetroot with dill, 136

biscuits: molasses cookies, 158

blackberry and apple jellies, 146

blackcurrant sauce, duck breasts with, 98

bobotie, 77

broccoli, cauliflower and pepper salad, 135

brown bread ice cream, 150

buckwheat and lentil casserole, 117

burgers, spicy nut, 122

cabbage: pigeon and cabbage casserole, 100

cakes, 154–7

calcium, 23, 29

calories, 15–16

cannelloni, spinach and ricotta, 124

carbohydrates, 16, 18–19, 26

carpaccio with courgettes, 79

carrots: carrot soup, 44

vegetable vitality drink, 32

casseroles: beef, walnut and orange, 76

buckwheat and lentil, 117

casseroled chicken with figs, 95

chicken and tomato, 91

lamb and date, 82

Mediterranean fish stew, 110

pigeon and cabbage, 100

pork and bean, 81

tomato and veal, 87

cauliflower: cauliflower, broccoli and pepper salad, 135

cheesy cauliflower, 72

celeriac: celeriac and crab salad, 134

celeriac soup with dill, 41

celery: cream of celery soup, 41

cheese: cheese tarts, 65

cheesy cauliflower, 72

courgette and cheese scramble, 52

courgette pasticcio, 68

filo spinach pie, 120

fruit and cheese salad, 131

spinach and ricotta cannelloni, 124

vegetables baked with a feta cheese crust, 121

cheesecake, baked fruit, 147

chick-pea and parsnip soufflés, 126

chicken: casseroled chicken with figs, 95

chicken and sweetcorn chowder, 43

chicken and tomato casserole, 91

chicken dhansak, 93

chicken noodle soup, 44

chicken stir-fry salad, 74

chicken tacos, 59

devilled poussins, 92

nasi goreng, 94

shredded sesame chicken with peppers, 92

Chinese cabbage and prawn soup, 45

cigarettes, 25

citrus fruits, marinated sole and, 103

coconut sauce, tofu and vegetables in, 125

cod: fish pie, 107

marinated cod steaks, 106

Spanish cod with mussels, 103

West Country cod, 115

coffee, 24–5

courgettes: carpaccio with, 79

chilled courgette soup, 47

courgette and cheese scramble, 52

courgette pasticcio, 68

courgettes in orange sauce, 136

crab and celeriac salad, 134

cravings, 13

crème caramel, 149

crumble, spicy apple, 148

cucumber: iced tzaziki soup, 47

warm cucumber with herbs, 137

curried eggs, 63

curried potato and apple soup, 45

dates: date and yogurt scones, 35

lamb and date casserole, 82

desserts, 139–52

devilled poussins, 92

dip, aubergine, 57

drinks, 32–3

drugs, during pregnancy, 11, 12–13

duck: duck breasts with blackcurrant sauce, 98

stir-fried duck with pecan nuts, 98

eggs: baked tarragon eggs, 33

baked with smoked haddock, 60

courgette and cheese scramble, 52

curried eggs, 63

eggs in sauce verte, 62

shirred eggs and smoked salmon, 37

Spanish omelette, 54

energy, and food intake, 15–16

exercise, 26

fats, 17, 20–1, 26–7, 28

fennel, sliced potato baked with, 137

fibre, 28

figs, casseroled chicken with, 95

filo spinach pie, 120

fish and shellfish, 101–15

fish pie, 107

flans and tarts: cheese tarts, 65

French fruit tart, 141

haddock quiche, 69

pepper and onion flan, 64

pineapple tart, 140

folic acid, 22–3, 28, 29

food cravings, 13

French fruit tart, 141

fruit: almond fruit salad, 151

French fruit tart, 141

fruit and cheese salad, 131

golden fruit jelly, 152

summer pudding, 148

ginger: apricot and almond gingerbread, 157

turkey and ginger stir-fry, 97

grapes: banana and grape brulée, 149

guinea fowl with, 90

plaice with, 102

guinea fowl with grapes, 90

haddock: eggs baked with smoked haddock, 60

haddock quiche, 69

herrings: herrings in oatmeal, 34

Swedish herrings, 113

ice cream: brown bread, 150

fresh peach, 150

iron, 23–4, 28, 29

Italian-styule braised pork, 83

jellies: blackberry and apple, 146

golden fruit, 152

kebabs: chicken liver, 96

seekh kebabs, 80

kheer, 151

kilocalories, 15–16

lamb: lamb and date casserole, 82

lamb and olive pilaff, 85

lamb chops with mint, 82

lemon veal, 86

lentils: buckwheat and lentil casserole, 117

chicken dhansak, 93

spiced red lentils with aubergines and mushrooms, 118

lettuce and smoked mackerel dolmas, 111

liver: calf's liver with vermouth, 85

chicken liver kebabs, 96

mixed mushroom and chicken liver salad, 132

pan-fried liver and tomato, 84

mackerel: lettuce and smoked mackerel dolmas, 111

spiced grilled, 108

malted sultana loaf, 158

meat, 75–88

medicine, in pregnancy, 11–13